HarperCollins

# PORTUGAL

# LANGUAGE SURVIVAL GUIDE

**THE VISUAL PHRASE BOOK AND DICTIONARY**

HarperResource

*An Imprint of* HarperCollins*Publishers*

HarperCollins books may be purchased for educational, business, or
sales promotional use. For information please write: Special Markets
Department, HarperCollins Publishers Inc., 10 East 53rd Street,
New York, NY 10022.

First published 2003 by HarperCollins Publishers in the United Kingdom.

Consultants: Edite Vieira and Sue Tyson-Ward

Photography: Blackeye Photography
   *With additional photography* Edite Vieira: pp 76 (3), 78 (2), 79 (1),
   95 (1), 97 (2), 98 (1), 99 (2), 102 (1), 104 (1), 106 (1), 107 (2), 108 (1),
   110 (1)
   *and* Artville: pp 93 (2), 94 (1), 95 (1), 96 (1), 99 (1), 100 (1), 101 (1),
   104 (2), 105 (2), 106 (1), 109 (1), 110 (1), 112 (2)
   *Additional material from* Sue Tyson-Ward
   *Map:* Heather Moore
Layout: The Printer's Devil, Glasgow

Other titles in the HarperCollins Language Survival Guide series:
   France (0-06-053692-6)
   Spain (0-06-053740-X)
   Italy (0-06-053693-4)
   Greece (0-06-057975-7)

ISBN 0-06-057977-3

04 05 06 07 08              10 9 8 7 6 5 4 3 2 1

Printed in Italy by Amadeus SpA

# CONTENTS

# USEFUL WEBSITES

**Currency Converters**
www.x-rates.com

**Foreign Office Advice**
www.fco.gov.uk/travel/
countryadvice.asp

**Passport Office**
www.ukpa.gov.uk

**Health Advice**
www.thetraveldoctor.com
www.doh.gov.uk/traveladvice

**Driving Abroad**
www.drivingabroad.co.uk/
driving_tips_countries/
portugal/driving_in_portugal.htm

**Pets**
www.defra.gov.uk/animalh/
quarantine/qindex.shtml

**Weather**
www.bbc.co.uk/weather

**Facts**
www.cia.gov/cia/publications/fact-
book/geos/po.html

**Internet cafes**
www.cybercafes.com

**Transport**
www.cp.pt *(Portuguese Railways)*
www.metrolisboa.pt *(Lisbon
Metro)*

**Tourism**
www.portugalinsite.com
*(Portuguese Tourist Office)*
www.portugal.org *(Welcome to
Portugal)*
www.portugal-live.net *(Portugal
live)*

**Accommodation**
www.turihab.pt *(Rural properties
to rent)*
www.pousadas.com *(Luxury
properties to rent, often former
convents, etc)*
www.roteiro-campista.pt *(Guide to
campsites of Portugal)*

**Food & Wine**
www.gastronomias.com *(in
Portuguese only)*
www.restaurantes.netopia.pt
*(Restaurant guide in Portuguese)*
www.ivv.pt *(Guide to Portuguese
wine and wine-growing areas)*

# INTRODUCTION

As technology sweeps across the world, travellers aren't just faced with the prospect of speaking a foreign language – they also have foreign machines to contend with. Machines for parking, for dispensing cash, for buying tickets and food. Often there is nobody about to ask how they work. *Collins Language Survival Guides* address this problem by showing photographically signs and situations you might come across.

The things that throw you are often the ones that look familiar – such as buses, trains or phones – but which operate slightly differently.

There are usually codes to how things operate and though you might not think you are aware of them, you are probably using them everyday: the colour-coding for roads (blue for motorways, green for major roads, yellow for temporary signs) or when buying milk (generally blue for whole milk, green for semi-skimmed and red for skimmed). It's when these familiar codes don't work in the same way, that you feel slightly at a loss and probably more unsure than you need be. By making a note of how these types of things work and knowing a few keywords, you will feel much more confident.

The unique combination of practical information, photos and phrases found in this book provides the key to hassle-free travel and the colour-coding below shows how information is presented and how to access it as quickly as possible.

 *General, practical information which will provide useful tips on getting the best out of your trip*

**keywords** ◀

| | |
|---|---|
| **direita** | these are words that are useful to know both |
| *dee-***ray***-tuh* | when you see them written down or when |
| right | you hear them spoken |
| **esquerda** | |
| ***shkehr***-duh* | |
| left | |

keywords

**key talk** ▶

short, simple phrases that you can change and adapt to suit your own situation

| | |
|---|---|
| **excuse me!** | **can you help me ?** |
| faz favor! | pode-me ajudar ? |
| *fash fav-**or*** | ***pod**-muh a-zhoo-**dar*** |
| **do you know where ...?** | |
| sabe onde é...? | |
| *sab **oñ**-duh e...* | |

talking

The **Food Section** allows you to choose more easily from what is on offer both for snacks and at restaurants.

The practical 5000-word English–Portuguese, Portuguese–English **Dictionary** means that you will never be stuck for words.

# SPEAKING PORTUGUESE

Portuguese is much easier to read than to speak. However, the pronunciation guide used in this book is as near as possible to the real sound. The syllable to be stressed is marked in **heavy italics**. Note that in conversation, words tend to slide into each other with unstressed syllables being slurred and some sounds being almost swallowed up.

## VOWELS (a, e, i, o, u)

| open (long) sound | closed (short) sound |
|---|---|
| a e.g. **saco** sah-koo | e.g. **fama** fam-uh |
| e e.g. **ver** vehr | e.g. **de** duh |
| o e.g. **cobra** koh-bruh | e.g. **voltar** vol-tar |

**NOTE:** *The article a sounds like uh (as in English **the**), unless stressed, e.g. à*

*e can sound like ay, e.g. **fecho** fay-shoo, but tends to be silent at the end of words, e.g. **pode** (pod) unless stressed, e.g. **bebé** (bay-**bay**).*

*The word e (meaning **and**) always sounds like ee (as in **police**)*

*o can sound like oo, e.g. **vaso** vah-zoo, and the article o always sounds like oo*

*i sounds like ee, e.g. **fica** fee-kuh*

*u usually sounds like oo, e.g. **luvas** loo-vush*

## VOWEL COMBINATIONS

**ai** = y, e.g. **mais** = mysh     **oi** = oy, e.g. **coisa** = **koy**-zuh

**ei** = ay, e.g. **peixe** = paysh **ou** = oh, e.g. **outro** = **oh**-troo

## NASAL VOWELS

*Vowels with a tilde ~, or followed by m (**um**) or n (**in**) should be pronounced nasally (let air out through nose as well as mouth), similar to French. We have represented this sound in the pronunciation by ñ, e.g.*

| **tem** = tayñ | **com** = koñ | **um** = ooñ |
|---|---|---|
| **pão** = powñ | **manhã** = man-**yañ** | **põe** = poyñ |

## OTHER LETTERS

*Try to recognize the sounds of the following:*

- **ç serviço** ser-**vee**-soo
- **nh tenho** **ten**-yoo
- **ch chá** sha
- **r/rr** at the start or middle of word rolled
- **g gelo** **zhay**-loo (soft like s in pleasure)
- **s** (between vowels) **coisa** **koy**-zuh
  (after vowel and at end of word) **está** shta, **lápis** **lah**-peesh
- **h** always silent
- **j loja** **loh**-zhuh (soft like s in pleasure)
- **x caixa** **ky**-shuh
- **lh mulher** mool-**yehr**
- **z** (at end of word) **faz** fash

# EVERYDAY TALK

*There are three forms of address in Portuguese, formal (**Senhor/a**), semi-formal (**você**) and informal (**tu**). You should always stick to the formal with older people until you are invited to use the informal **tu**.*

**yes**
sim
*seeñ*

**no**
não
*nowñ*

**ok/that's fine**
está bem
*shta bayñ*

**please**
por favor/faz favor
*poor fa-**vor**/fash fa-**vor***

**thank you** (said by man)
obrigado
*oh-bree-**gah**-doo*

**thank you** (said by woman)
obrigada
*oh-bree-**gah**-duh*

**thanks very much**
muito obrigado(a)
***mweeñ**-too oh-bree-**gah**-doo(-duh)*

**don't mention it**
de nada
*de **nah**-duh*

**hello/hi**
olá
*oh-**la***

**goodbye**
adeus
*a-**day**-oosh*

**good morning/day**
bom dia
*boñ **dee**-uh*

**good afternoon/evening**
boa tarde
***boh**-uh tard*

**good night**
boa noite
***boh**-uh noyt*

**see you later**
até logo
*a-**te** log-oo*

**excuse me!**
por favor/faz favor!
*poor fa-**vor**/fash fa-**vor***

**sorry!**
desculpe!
*dush-**koolp***

**I am sorry**
lamento
*la-**meñ**-too*

**I don't understand**
não compreendo
*nowñ kom-pree-**en**-doo*

**I don't know**
nao sei
*nowñ say*

## Addressing people

If you have been introduced to someone, you would greet them with *bom dia, Senhor Lopes* or *bom dia, minha Senhora*. In a shop a simple *olá* and *adeus* is fine. You may hear the expression *não faça cerimónia* (*nowñ **fah**-suh suh-ree-**mon**-yuh*). It means 'please don't stand on ceremony' i.e. if you are offered a second helping of food, don't refuse it out of politeness!

**how are you?**
como está?
*koh-moo shta*

**fine thanks**
bem, obrigado(a)
*bayñ oh-bree-**gah**-doo(-duh)*

**and you?**
e você?
*ee **voh**-suh*

**hi, Paula!**
olá, Paula!
*oh-**la** paoo-luh*

**bye, Carlos!**
adeus, Carlos!
*a-**day**-oosh **car**-loosh*

**see you tomorrow**
até amanhã
*a-**te** a-man-**yañ***

*Asking for something in a shop or bar, you would ask for what you want, adding **por favor**.*

| | keyword | |
|---|---|---|
| **1** | **um** | *ooñ* |
| **2** | **dois** | *doysh* |
| **3** | **três** | *tresh* |
| **4** | **quatro** | *kwa-troo* |
| **5** | **cinco** | *seeñ-koo* |
| **6** | **seis** | *saysh* |
| **7** | **sete** | *set* |
| **8** | **oito** | *oy-too* |
| **9** | **nove** | *nov* |
| **10** | **dez** | *desh* |

**a ... please**
um/uma ... por favor
*ooñ/**oo**-muh ... poor fa-**vor***

**a milky coffee**
um galão
*ooñ ga-**lowñ***

**a beer**
uma cerveja
***oo**-muh suhr-**vay**-zhuh*

**a tea and 2 beers, please**
um chá e duas cervejas, por favor
*ooñ sha ee **doo**-ush suhr-**vay**-zhush poor fa-**vor***

**the ... please**
o/a ... por favor
*oo/uh ... poor fa-**vor***

**the menu, please**
a ementa, por favor
*uh ee-**men**-tuh poor fa-**vor***

**the bill, please**
a conta, por favor
*uh **koñ**-tuh poor fa-**vor***

**another...**
outro/outra...
*oh-troo/oh-truh...*

**is that everything?**
é tudo?
*e **too**-doo*

**another beer**
outra cerveja
*oh-truh suhr-**vay**-juh*

**another milky coffee**
outro galão
*oh-troo ga-**lowñ***

**2 more beers**
mais duas cervejas
*mysh **doo**-ush suhr-**vay**-zhush*

**2 more milky coffees**
mais dois galões
*mysh doysh ga-**lowñsh***

## To catch someone's attention

The easiest way to catch someone's attention is with *faz favor* or *desculpe*. Many Portuguese do speak English. If you are trying to get past someone, perhaps in a busy market or street, you can say *com licença* (*koñ lee-**sen**-suh*). You would also use this phrase when entering someone's home.

**excuse me!**
desculpe!
*deesh-**koolp***

**can you help me?**
pode-me ajudar?
***pod**-muh a-zhoo-**dar***

**do you know where ... is?**
sabe onde é...
*sab **oñ**-duh e...*

**how do I get to...?**
como se vai a...?
***koh**-moo suh vy uh...*

*By combining key words and phrases you can build up your language and adapt the phrases to suit your own situation.*

| | | |
|---|---|---|
| **tem...?**<br>**do you have...?** | **do you have a map?**<br>tem um mapa?<br>*tayñ ooñ **ma**-puh* | **do you have a room?**<br>tem um quarto?<br>*tayñ ooñ **kwar**-too* |
| **quanto?**<br>**how much?** | **how much is the cheese?**<br>quanto é o queijo?<br>*kwañ-too e oo **kay**-zhoo* | **how much is the ticket?**<br>quanto é o bilhete?<br>*kwañ-too e oo beel-**yet*** |
| **queria...**<br>**I'd like...** | **I'd like a cake**<br>queria um bolo<br>*kree-uh ooñ **bol**-oo* | **I'd like an ice-cream**<br>queria um gelado<br>*kree-uh ooñ zhuh-**lah**-doo* |
| **preciso de...**<br>**I need...** | **I need a taxi**<br>preciso dum táxi<br>*pruh-**see**-zoo dooñ **tak**-see* | **I need a receipt**<br>preciso dum recibo<br>*pruh-**see**-zoo dooñ ruh-**see**-boo* |
| **quando?**<br>**when?** | **when does it open?**<br>quando abre?<br>*kwañ-doo a-bruh* | **when does it close?**<br>quando fecha?<br>*kwañ-doo **fay**-shuh* |
| **a que horas?**<br>**when?** | **when does it leave?**<br>a que horas parte?<br>*uh kee **o**-rush part* | **when does it arrive?**<br>a que horas chega?<br>*uh kee **o**-rush **sheh**-guh* |
| **onde?**<br>**where?** | **where is the bank?**<br>onde é o banco?<br>*oñ-duh e oo **bañ**-koo* | **where is the hotel?**<br>onde é o hotel?<br>*oñ-duh e oo oh-**tel*** |
| **há...?**<br>**is there...?** | **is there a market?**<br>há um mercado?<br>*a ooñ mer-**kah**-doo* | **where is there a market?**<br>onde há um mercado?<br>*oñ-duh ha ooñ mer-**kah**-doo* |
| **não há...**<br>**there is no...** | **there is no bread**<br>não há pão<br>*nowñ a powñ* | **is there no train?**<br>não há comboio?<br>*nowñ a koñ-**boy**-yoo* |
| **posso...?**<br>**can I...?** | **can I smoke?**<br>posso fumar?<br>*pos-soo foo-**mar*** | **can I hire a car?**<br>posso alugar um carro?<br>*pos-soo a-loo-**gar** ooñ **kar**-roo* |
| | **where can I buy milk?**<br>onde posso comprar leite?<br>*oñ-duh **pos**-soo koñ-**prar** layt* | |
| **está...?**<br>**is it...?** | **is it open?**<br>está aberto?<br>*shta a-**ber**-too* | **is it closed?**<br>está fechado?<br>*shta fuh-**sha**-doo* |
| **gosto de...**<br>**I like...** | **I like dancing**<br>gosto de dançar<br>*gosh-too duh dan-**sar*** | **I don't like coffee**<br>não gosto de café<br>*nowñ **gosh**-too duh kuh-**fe*** |

*These are a selection of small but very useful words to know.*

**keywords keywords keywords keywords keywords**

**grande**
*graňd*
large

**pequeno**
*puh-kay-noo*
small

**um pouco**
*ooň poh-koo*
a little

**chega**
*sheh-guh*
that's enough

**mais perto**
*mysh pehr-too*
nearest

**quente/frio**
*kent/free-oo*
hot/cold

**caro demais**
*kah-roo duh-mysh*
too expensive

**e**
*ee*
and

**com/sem**
*koň/sayň*
with/without

**para**
*pa-ruh*
for

**o meu/a minha**
*oo may-oo/uh meen-yuh*
my

**este/esse**
*esht/esh*
this one/that one

**imediatamente**
*ee-med-yat-a ment*
straightaway

**mais tarde**
*mysh tard*
later

**a large car**
um carro grande
*ooň kar-roo graňd*

**a small car**
um carro pequeno
*ooň kar-roo puh-kay-noo*

**a little, please**
um pouco, por favor
*ooň poh-koo poor fa-vor*

**that's enough**
chega
*sheh-guh*

**where is the nearest bank?**
onde é o banco mais perto?
*oň-duh e oo baň-koo mysh pehr-too*

**it is too expensive**
é caro demais
*e kah-roo duh-mysh*

**it is too big**
é grande demais
*e graňd duh-mysh*

**is it full?**
está cheio?
*shtuh shay-oo*

**is it free?**
está livre?
*shtuh leev-ruh*

**a hot chocolate and a cake**
um chocolate quente e um bolo
*ooň shoo-koo-laht kayňt ee ooň boh-loo*

**with cold milk**
com leite frio
*koň layt free-oo*

**with lemon**
com limão
*koň lee-mowň*

**without ice**
sem gelo
*sayň zhay-loo*

**without sugar**
sem açúcar
*sayň a-zoo-kar*

**for me**
para mim
*pa-ruh meeň*

**for her/him**
para ele/ela
*pa-ruh el/el-uh*

**my passport**
o meu passaporte
*oo may-oo pas-suh-port*

**my keys**
as minhas chaves
*ush meen-yush sha-vush*

**I'd like this one**
queria este
*kree-uh esht*

**I'd like that**
queria esse
*kree-uh esh*

**I need a taxi straightaway**
preciso dum táxi imediatamente
*pruh-see-zoo dooň tak-see ee-med-yat-a ment*

**is it far?**
é longe?
*e lonzh*

**I'll call back later**
chamo mais tarde
*sha-moo mysh tard*

*It is always good to be able to say a few words about yourself to break the ice, even if you won't be able to tell your life story.*

**my name is...**
chamo-me...
*sha-moo-muh...*

**I am from...**
sou de...
*soh duh...*

**I am on holiday**
estou de férias
*shtoh duh fehr-yush*

**I am here on business**
estou aqui a negócios
*shtoh a-kee uh nuh-gos-yoosh*

**I am single**
sou solteiro(a)
*soh sol-tay-roo(-ruh)*

**I am married**
sou casado(a)
*soh ka-zah-doo(-duh)*

**I have a boyfriend**
tenho namorado
*teñ-yoo na-moo-rah-doo*

**I have a girlfriend**
tenho namorada
*teñ-yoo na-moo-rah-duh*

**I am a widow**
sou viúva
*soh vee-oo-vuh*

**I am a widower**
sou viúvo
*soh vee-oo-voo*

**I am divorced**
sou divorciado(a)
*soh dee-voors-yah-doo(-duh)*

**I am separated**
sou separado(a)
*soh suh-pa-rah-doo(-duh)*

**I have a son/a daughter**
tenho um filho/uma filha
*ten-yoo ooñ feel-yoo/oo-muh feel-yuh*

**I have three children**
tenho três filhos
*ten-yoo tresh feel-yoosh*

**I work**
trabalho
*tra-bal-yoo*

**I am retired**
sou reformado(a)
*soh ruh-foor-mah-doo(-duh)*

**I am a student**
sou estudante
*soh shtoo-dant*

**you have a beautiful home**
tem uma linda casa
*tayñ oo-muh leeñ-duh kah-zuh*

**the meal was delicious**
a refeição estava deliciosa
*uh ruh-fay-sowñ shta-vuh duh-lees-yoh-zuh*

**thanks for your hospitality**
gratos pelo convite
*grah-toosh peh-loo koñ-veet*

**I've enjoyed myself very much**
diverti-me muito
*dee-ver-tee-muh mweeñ-too*

**we'd like to come back**
gostaríamos de voltar
*goosh-tuh-ree-a-moosh duh vol-tar*

**we must stay in touch**
devemos ficar em contacto
*duh-veh-moosh fee-kar ayñ koñ-tak-too*

**what is your address?**
qual é a sua morada?
*kwal e uh soo-uh moo-rah-duh*

*Although problems are not something anyone wants, you might come across the odd difficulty, and it is best to be armed with a few phrases to cope with the situation.*

**excuse me!**
faz favor!
*fash fa-vor*

**can you help me?**
pode-me ajudar?
*pod-muh a-zhoo-dar*

**I don't speak Portuguese**
não falo português
*nowñ fa-loo poor-too-gezh*

**do you speak English?**
fala inglês?
*fa-luh eeñ-glezh*

**I am lost**
estou perdido(a)
*shtoh puhr-dee(-duh)*

**we are lost**
estamos perdidos(as)
*shta-moosh pur-dee-doosh(-dush)*

**I have lost...**
perdi...
*puhr-dee...*

**my purse**
o meu porta-moedas
*oo may-oo por-ta-mwed-ush*

**my passport**
o meu passaporte
*oo may-oo pa-sa-port*

**I have left...**
deixei...
*day-shay...*

**in the restaurant**
no restaurante
*noo rush-toh-rant*

**on the train**
no comboio
*noo koñ-boy-yoo*

**I have missed...**
perdi...
*puhr-dee...*

**the flight**
o voo
*voh-oo*

**my connection**
a minha ligação
*uh meen-yuh lee-guh-sowñ*

**I need to get to...**
preciso de ir a...
*pruh-see-zoo duh eer a...*

**how can I get there today?**
como posso ir para lá hoje
*koh-moo pos-soo eer pa-ruh la ozh*

**my luggage hasn't arrived**
a minha bagagem não chegou
*uh meen-yuh ba-gah-zhayñ nowñ shuh-goh*

**the case is damaged**
a mala está partida
*uh mah-luh shta par-tee-duh*

**I have no money**
não tenho dinheiro
*nowñ ten-yoo deen-yay-roo*

**this is my address**
esta é a minha morada
*esht e uh meen-yuh moo-rah-duh*

**someone's stolen my...**
roubaram-me...
*roh-bah-rowñ-muh...*

**handbag**
a mala
*uh mah-luh*

**mobile phone**
o telemóvel
*oo tuh-luh-moh-vel*

**money**
o dinheiro
*oo deen-yay-roo*

**that man is following me**
aquele homem está-me a seguir
*a-kel o-mayñ shta-muh uh suh-geer*

**go away!**
vá-se embora!
*vah-suh ayñ-boh-ruh*

**leave me alone!**
deixe-me em paz!
*day-shuh-muh ayñ pash*

**I am sorry, I did not know**
lamento muito, não sabia
*la-men-too mweeñ-too nowñ sa-bee-uh*

*The Portuguese expect to receive good service and quality. They will complain when things are not to their liking.*

**there is no...**
não há...
*nowñ a...*

**there is no toilet paper**
não há papel higiénico
*nowñ a pa-**pel** eezh-**yen**-ee-koo*

**it is dirty**
está sujo(a)
*shta **soo**-zhoo(-zhuh)*

**the bath is dirty**
a banheira está suja
*uh ban-**yay**-ruh shta **soo**-zhuh*

**it is broken**
está partido(a)
*shta par-**tee**-doo(-duh)*

**can you mend it?**
pode arranjá-lo?
*pod ar-ran-**zha**-loo*

**the ... does not work**
o/a ... não funciona
*oo/uh ... nowñ foons-**yoh**-nuh*

**the ... do not work**
os/as ... não funcionam
*oosh/ush ... nowñ foons-**yoh**-nawñ*

**it is very noisy**
há muito barulho
*a **mweeñ**-too ba-**rool**-oo*

**the room is too small**
o quarto é muito pequeno
*oo **kwar**-too e **mweeñ**-too puh-**kay**-noo*

**it is very hot** (room)
é muito quente
*e **mween**-too kent*

**it is very cold** (room)
é muito frio
*e **mween**-too **free**-oo*

**it is very expensive**
é muito caro(a)
*e **mween**-too **kah**-roo(-ruh)*

**why are you charging me so much?**
porque está a pedir tanto?
***poor**-kuh shta uh puh-**deer** tan-too*

**I want to complain**
quero apresentar uma queixa
***keh**-roo a-pruh-sen-**tar oo**-muh **kay**-shuh*

**where is the manager?**
onde está o gerente?
***on**-duh shta oo zhuh-**rent***

**we want to order**
queremos pedir
*kuh-**reh**-moosh puh-**deer***

**the service is not good**
o serviço não é bom
*oo suhr-**vee**-soo nowñ e boñ*

**it is cold** (food, drink)
está frio(a)
*shta **free**-oo(-uh)*

**this coffee is cold**
o café está frio
*oo kuh-**fe** shta **free**-oo*

**this isn't what I ordered**
isto não é o que eu pedi
***eesh**-too nowñ e oo **kay**-oo puh-**dee***

**please take this off the bill**
por favor, tire isto da conta
*poor fa-**vor** tee-**reesh**-too duh **koñ**-tuh*

**there is a mistake**
há um engano
*a ooñ ayñ-**ga**-noo*

**please check the bill**
por favor, verifique a conta
*poor fa-**vor** vuh-**ree**-fee-kee uh **koñ**-tuh*

**I want a refund**
quero um reembolso
***keh**-roo ooñ ree-ayñ-**bol**-soo*

**I want to return this**
quero devolver isto
***keh**-roo duh-vol-**vehr eesh**-too*

# EVERYDAY PORTUGAL

*The next four pages should give you an idea of the type of things you will come across in Portugal.*

**Aberto** ◄ OPEN

**Encerrada**

CLOSED ▲

OPENING HOURS ►

*from 08.30 to 15.00*

*Mon to Fri*

**Horário de Abertura**

das 8,30h às 15,00h

de Segunda a Sexta Feira

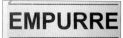

**Informações**

INFORMATION ▲

Smaller shops open from 8.30/9 am to 12.30/1pm, and again from 2/2.30 to 6 or 7 pm, Mon–Fri. Most close Sat afternoon and all day Sun. Large shopping centres stay open late every day.

**EMPURRE**

PUSH ▲

◄ *Casa da Sorte*, or House of Luck, sells lottery tickets.

**PUXE**

PULL ▲

Lottery tickets are also sold at shops displaying these signs ▼

*Lotaria Clássica* 26.ª Ord. **3** €5

Lotaria Comemorativa do 50º Aniversário da Força Aérea Portuguesa

DÉCIMO

16194

**16194**

:: totobola
:: totoloto

◄ A typical lottery ticket

| | | |
|---|---|---|
| **do you have...?** | **stamps** | **postcards** |
| tem...? | selos | postais |
| *tayñ...* | *sel-oosh* | *poosh-tysh* |
| **where can I buy...?** | **film** | **batteries** |
| onde posso comprar...? | rolos | pilhas |
| *oñ-duh pos-soo koñ-prar...* | *roh-loosh* | *peel-yush* |

Monedas *coins*

Notas *notes*

The euro symbol

Ticket and paying machines are now more widespread.

Normal post boxes are red.

Blue post boxes are for *Correio Azul*, priority mail.

▲ CASH DESK/PAY HERE

**Entrada**

▲ ENTRANCE

▼ EXIT

**Saída**

▲ EMERGENCY EXIT

**excuse me!**
desculpe!
*deesh-koolp*

**what does this mean?**
que quer dizer isto?
*kuh kayr dee-zehr eesh-too*

**how does this work?**
como funciona?
*koh-moo foonss-yoh-nuh*

**can you explain?**
pode-me explicar?
*pod-muh eks-plee-kar*

talking

◀ Service is usually included in a restaurant bill so tipping is discretionary.

**Vende-se**

▲ FOR SALE

▼ NO SMOKING

## NÃO FUMAR

▲ AIR-CONDITIONED

Smoking is widespread in Portugal, especially in eating and drinking establishments. It is forbidden to smoke on public transport, although not everyone adheres to the rules.

ENTRY PROHIBITED ▼

Proibida a passagem

▲ You can usually also buy stamps and postcards at a *tabacaria*.

**Perigo!**

▲ DANGER!

**can I smoke?**
posso fumar?
*pos-soo foo-mar*

**I don't smoke**
não fumo
*nowñ foo-moo*

**an ashtray, please**
un cinzeiro, por favor
*ooñ seeñ-zay-roo poor fa-vor*

**do you mind if I smoke?**
importa-se que eu fume?
*eeñ-por-tuh-suh kuh ay-oo foom*

**please don't smoke**
por favor não fume
*poor fa-vor nowñ foom*

**in a non-smoking area**
em zona de não-fumador
*ayñ zoh-na duh nowñ foo-ma-dor*

talking

*Public toilets in Portugal are hard to find. The best option is to use those at public attractions (museums, etc) where there may be an attendant doling out rations of loo paper. You are expected to tip them out of courtesy. Clean toilets are found in larger stores (not commonplace outside Lisbon or Oporto) or in modern hotels. Most people use the toilets in small bars and cafés, where you may have to ask at the bar for a key. Cleanliness can vary greatly.*

### Serviços
▲ TOILETS

◀ *Sanitários* (superloos) are beginning to appear in some towns and cities.

**HOMENS**
▲ GENTS

**SENHORAS**
▲ LADIES

Superloos carry easy-to-follow instructions in Portuguese, French and English. ▶

### Ocupado
▲ OCCUPIED

▼ FREE

### Livre

 **frio** ◀ COLD

HOT ▶ **quente**

---

**excuse me! where is the toilet?**
por favor! onde é a casa de banho?
*poor fa-**vor** oñ-duh e uh **kah**-zuh duh **ban**-yoo*

**do you have a key for the toilet?**
tem a chave para a casa de banho por favor?
*tayñ uh shav **pa**-ruh uh **kah**-zuh duh **ban**-yoo poor fa-**vor***

**is there a disabled toilet?**
há casa de banho para deficientes?
*a **kah**-zuh duh **ban**-yoo **pa**-ruh duh-feess-**yentsh***

**where can I change the baby?**
onde posso mudar o bébé?
*oñ-duh **pos**-soo moo-**dar** oo bay-**bay***

talking talking talking

*Portuguese people are very polite and helpful and many speak English. Unlike some other Mediterranean countries, the Portuguese are quite happy to queue and wait their turn, which adds to the impression that they are very happy to stop and help you.*

Most town centres have street maps.

*To find where you are, look for this symbol*

PARA SE SITUAR NA PLANTA
PROCURE ESTA MARCA

VOCÊ ESTÁ AQUI

**Você está aqui**
**YOU ARE HERE**

▲ TOURIST INFORMATION OFFICE

ask me Lisboa

◀ Ask Me Lisboa is Lisbon's tourist information service.

**excuse me!**
desculpe!
*dush-koolp*

**do you know where... is?**
sabe onde é...?
*sab oñ-duh e...*

**how do I get to...?**
como se vai para...?
*koh-moo suh vy pa-ruh...*

**is this the right way to...?**
a/o ... é por aqui?
*oo/uh ... e poor a-kee*

**do you have a map of the town?**
tem um mapa de cidade?
*tayñ ooñ mah-puh duh see-dad*

**can you show me on the map?**
pode-me indicar no mapa?
*pod-muh eeñ-dee-kar noo mah-puh*

**I'm looking for...**
procuro...
*proh-koo-roo...*

**where are...?**
onde são...?
*oñ-duh sowñ...*

**is it far?**
é longe?
*e lonzh*

**is this the right way to the station?**
a estação é por aqui?
*uh shta-sowñ e poor a-kee*

**a street directory**
um guia da cidade
*ooñ gee-uh duh see-dad*

*pictogram indicating town centre (**centro**)* — centro

*town hall* — Camara Municipal

*fire station* — Bombeiros

*youth hostel* — CENTRO DE JUVENTUDE

Hotel

Normal signs are white; hotels are usually blue; places of interest are brown; and sports venues orange.

*Chiado museum*

museu do Chiado

estádio — *football stadium*
z. comercial — *shopping area*

*Church & Convent of St Francis*

Igreja e Convento de São Francisco

LARGO DA MADALENA

◄ *Largo* **SQUARE**

*Rua* ► **ROAD/STREET**

RVA D.FRANCISCO GOMES NOTABILISSIMO PRELADO 1739–1815

TRAVESSA DO BOVZELA

▲ *Travessa* SIDE STREET

◄ Esquerda
**LEFT**

**RIGHT**
Direita ►

**à direita**
a dee-*ray*-tuh
to/on the right

**à esquerda**
ash-*kehr*-duh
to/on the left

**sempre en frente**
sayñpr ayñ freñt
straight ahead

**siga**
*see*-guh
keep going

**vire**
veer
turn

**rua**
*roo*-uh
road

**largo/praça**
*lar*-goo/*prah*-suh
square

**semáforo**
suh-*maf*-oo-roo
traffic lights

**igreja**
ee-*gray*-zhuh
church

**primeira**
pree-*may*-ruh
first

**segunda**
suh-*gooñ*-duh
second

**longe**
lonzh
far

**perto de**
*pehr*-too duh
near to

**ao lado de**
ow *lah*-doo duh
next to

**em frente**
ayñ frent
opposite

**até**
a-*te*
until

Banks are easy to find in Portugal, and many bank staff speak good English. To exchange money you may have to go first to the **Câmbio** counter, then pick up your money at the **Caixa**. In some banks you take a ticket or disc with a number on it to await your turn at the **Caixa**; your number will then be called out. Modern banks have automatic doors allowing access to cash machines after hours. Airports, some stations and large banks also have automatic currency-exchange machines with instructions in a choice of languages. The most widely accepted credit cards are Visa, Mastercard and American Express. When you use your credit card you may be asked to key your pin number into a countertop keypad, so make sure you've memorised it. The keypad carries instructions in both English and Portuguese.

▲ Banks' names usually include the words *banco* or *caixa*. The main ones are Banco Espírito Santo, BNU and Caixa Geral de Depósitos. ▼

▲ *Multibanco* is the term for ATM.

Banks in tourist areas may open later than the normal 3pm closing.

### Horário de Abertura
### das 8,30h às 15,00h
### de Segunda a Sexta Feira

*Multibanco* machines are common and offer a range of services. Screen instructions are often in English and Portuguese. To withdraw cash you can key in the exact amount or a combination of pre-set amounts using the keys on the left of the panel. ▼

▲ **OPENING TIMES**
*8am to 3pm
Mon to Fri*

balance — SALDOS
check transactions — CONSULTA MOVIMENTOS
payment services — PAGAMENTO SERVIÇOS
other amounts — OUTROS LEVANTAM.

EUR 20 · EUR 100 · EUR 40 · EUR 150 · EUR 60 · EUR 200 · EUR 80 · CARREGAM. PMB

1 2 3 · 4 5 6 · 7 8 9 · 0 00

**anular** cancel
**corrigir** correct / error
**continuar** continue

Indoor *Multibancos* often carry a sign like this (*all hours*). ▶

Portugal's currency is the euro, which breaks down into 100 euro cents. Euro notes are the same across Europe. The coins are officially cents, but Portuguese people call them *cêntimos* (*sen-tee-moosh*). The reverse of the coins carry different designs in each European member country.

Notes: 5, 10, 20, ◀ 50, 100, 200, 500

▲ Coins: 2 euro, 1 euro, 50 cent, 20 cent, 10 cent, 5 cent, 2 cent, 1 cent

*Portugal operates on the same time as the UK.*

## keywords kewords kewords

**manhã**
*man-yañ*
morning

**tarde**
*tard*
afternoon

**esta tarde**
*esh-tuh tard*
this afternoon

**esta noite**
*esh-tuh noyt*
this evening

**hoje**
*ohzh*
today

**amanhã**
*a-man-yañ*
tomorrow

**ontem**
*oñ-tayñ*
yesterday

**agora**
*a-goh-ruh*
now

**mais tarde**
*mysh tard*
later

**às ... menos um quarto**
*ash ... may-nooz ooñ kwar-too*
at a quarter to ...

**às vinte e cuatro horas**
*ash veent ee kwa-troo o-rush*

**às vinte e três horas**
*ash veent ee tresh o-rush*

**às onze**
*ash oñz*

**às vinte e duas horas**
*ash veent ee doo-ush o-rush*

**às dez**
*ash desh*

**às vinte e uma horas**
*ash veent ee oo-muh o-rush*

**às nove**
*ash nov*

**às vinte horas**
*ash veent o-rush*

**às oito**
*ash oy-too*

**às dezanove horas**
*ash dez-uh-nov o-rush*

**às sete**
*ash set*

**às vinte para as ...**
*ash veent pa-ruh ush ...*
at twenty to ...

**às dezoito horas**
*ash dez-oy-too o-rush*

**às ... menos vinte**
*ash ... may-noosh veent*
at twenty to ...

## talking

**when is the next...?**
quando parte o próximo...?
*kwañ-doo part oo pross-ee-moo...*

**train**
comboio
*koñ-boy-yoo*

**bus**
autocarro
*ow-too-kar-roo*

**boat**
barco
*bar-koo*

**when is...?**
a que horas é...?
*uh kee o-rush e...*

**breakfast**
o pequeno-almoço
*oo puh-kay-noo al-moh-soo*

**dinner**
o jantar
*oo zhan-tar*

**when does it leave?**
quando parte?
*kwañ-doo part*

**when does it arrive?**
quando chega?
*kwañ-doo sheh-guh*

**when does it open?**
quando abre?
*kwañ-doo ah-bruh*

**when does it close?**
quando fecha?
*kwañ-doo fay-shuh*

*Days of the week are often abbreviated to 2ª feira (Mon), 3ª feira (Tue), 4ª feira (Wed), 5ª feira (Thurs) and 6ª feira (Fri).*

**à meia-noite**
*a may-uh-noyt*
at midnight

**às ... e um quarto**
*ash ... ee ooñ kwar-too*
at quarter past ...

**às doze**
*ash dohz*

**à uma**
*a oo-muh*

**às treze horas**
*ash trez o-rush*

**às duas**
*ash doo-ush*

**às catorze horas**
*ash ka-torz o-rush*

**às três**
*ash tresh*

**às quinze horas**
*ash keenz o-rush*

**às quatro**
*ash kwa-troo*

**às dezasseis horas**
*ash dez-uh-saysh o-rush*

**às cinco**
*ash seeñ-koo*

**às dezassete horas**
*ash dez-uh-set o-rush*

**às seis**
*ash saysh*

**às ... e meia**
*ash ... ee may-uh*
at half past ...

**às dezanove e trinta**
*ash desh-uh-nov ee treeñ-tuh*
at 19.30

**segunda-feira**
*suh-goon-duh-fay-ruh*
Monday

**terça-feira**
*ter-suh-fay-ruh*
Tuesday

**quarta-feira**
*kwar-tuh-fay-ruh*
Wednesday

**quinta-feira**
*keen-tuh-fay-ruh*
Thursday

**sexta-feira**
*saysh-tuh-fay-ruh*
Friday

**sábado**
*sa-ba-doo*
Saturday

**domingo**
*doo-meen-goo*
Sunday

**what time is it, please?**
que horas são, por favor?
*kee o-rush sowñ poor fa-vor*

**it's...**
são...
*sowñ...*

**it's 9 o'clock**
são nove horas
*sowñ nov o-rush*

**what is the date?**
qual é a data?
*kwal e uh dah-tuh*

**it is the 8th of May**
é o (dia) oito de Maio
*e oo (dee-uh) oy-too duh my-oo*

**it is the 16 of July 2003**
é o dezasseis de Julho de dois mil e três
*e oo dez-uh-saysh du zhool-yoo duh doysh meel ee tresh*

**which day?**
que dia?
*kuh dee-uh*

**which month?**
que mês?
*kuh mesh*

*All timetables use the 24-hour clock. You can buy excellent rail timetables for the whole network, and bus and rail stations also have printed timetables for local and regional travel. You can look up rail timetables on **www.cp.pt**, the Portuguese Railways' website.*

**Categoria**
type of train (including boat transfer for Lisbon)

**Número**
number

**Classe**
class

| Categoria | | R | R | R | R | 🚢 | IR | R | R | 🚢 | IC |
|---|---|---|---|---|---|---|---|---|---|---|---|
| Número | | 4701 | 5903 | 5709 | 5004 | 17829 | 871 | 5715 | 5902 | 17857 | 581 |
| Classe | | 2 | 2 | 1-2 | 2 | 2 | 1-2 | 1-2 | 2 | 2 | 1-2 |
| Serviços Disponibilizados | | | | | | ♒ | ♒ | | | ♒ | ♒ |
| Observações | | | | | | | | | | | 🍴 |
| Lisboa (T. do Paço) | P | | | | | 8.10 | | | | 13.20 | |
| Barreiro 🚢 | C | | | | | 8.40 | | | | 13.50 | |
| Barreiro | P | | | | | | 8.55 | | | | 14.25 |
| Barreiro-A | | | | | | | | | | | |
| Lavradio | | | | | | | | | | | |
| Baixa da Banheira | | | | | | | | | | | |
| Alhos Vedros | | | | | | | | | | | |
| Moita | | | | | | | | | | | |
| Penteado | | | | | | | | | | | |
| Pinhal Novo | C | | | | | | 9.06 | | | | |
| Pinhal Novo | P | | | | | | 9.08 | | | | |
| Venda do Alcaide | | | | | | | | | | | |
| Palmela | | | | | | | | | | | |
| Setúbal | C | | | | | | 9.23 | | | | |
| Setúbal | P | | | | | | 9.25 | | | | |

**Serviços disponibilizados**
Services available

**Observações**
Information

▲ Train timetables like this can be obtained from regional or national railway stations.

▼ Key to timetable symbols

| | SIMBOLOGIA: | |
|---|---|---|
| Intercity trains | **IC** | Comboio Intercidades |
| Inter-regional trains | **IR** | Comboio Interregional |
| Regional trains | **R** | Comboio Regional |
| River ferry connection | 🚢 | Ligação Fluvial |
| Seat reservation obligatory | 🅁 | Reserva obrigatória de lugar |
| Bar service | ♒ | Serviço de Bar |
| Meal service in 1st class | 🍴 | Serviço de refeição no lugar em 1ª Classe |
| Restaurant and bar service | ✕ | Serviço de Restaurante e Bar |
| Not a daily service | ⌇ | Comboio não diário |

talk

**do you have a timetable?**
tem um horário?
*tayñ ooñ oo-rar-yoo*

**can you explain the timetable, please?**
pode-me explicar o horário, por favour?
***pod**-muh eks-plee-**kar** oo o-**rar**-yoo poor fa-**vor***

Timetables, especially in tourist areas, will often have English translations alongside the Portuguese. ▼

| PARTIDA / CHEGADA DEPARTURE / ARRIVALS | | | | | 12:05 |
|---|---|---|---|---|---|
| SERVICE / PISTA SERVICE / TRACK | PROCEDÊNCIA ORIGIN | DESTINO DESTINATION | CHEGADA ARRIVAL | PARTIDA DEPARTURE | ATRASO DELAY |
| NO2 | | | | 18:00 | |
| NO2 | | ALBUFEIRA | | 13:00 | |
| NO6 | | OLHAO | | 13:10 | |
| NO2 | | LOULE | | 13:20 | |
| EX | EVORA | | 13:20 | | |
| EX | ELVAS | | 13:20 | | |
| NO7 | | V.R.S.ANTÓ | | 13:25 | |
| NO4 | | S.B.ALPORT | | 13:35 | |
| NO8 | | QUARTEIRA | | 13:35 | |
| NO8 | | ALBUFEIRA | | 13:35 | |

Yellow line bus timetable ▶

Paragem
*stop number*

Designação
*name of stop*

Um ▬STUB▬ à sua porta

STUB
LINHA AMARELA

STUB:
- LINHA AMARELA -
URBANA 2

| PARAGEM | DESIGNAÇÃO | HORÁRIO |
|---|---|---|
| 2.1 | Rotunda Abade de Bagal | H.00 |
| 2.2 | Av. Abade de Bagal | H.02 |
| 2.3 | Av. Abade de Bagal – S. Tiago | H.03 |
| 2.4 | Escola do Campo Redondo | H.04 |
| 2.5 | Eixo Atlântico | H.04 |
| 2.6 | Hospital | H.05 |
| 2.7 | Rua Padre António Vieira | H.06 |
| 2.8 | I. P. B. – Cantina | H.08 |
| 2.9 | I. P. B. – Residência | H.08 |
| 2.10 | Av. Sá Carneiro – Viaduto | H.09 |
| 2.11 | Av. Sá Carneiro | H.10 |
| 2.12 | Rua 5 de Outubro | H.12 |
| 2.13 | Rua Alexandre Herculano | H.13 |
| 2.14 | Praça da Sé | H.14 |
| 2.15 | Principal | H.15 |
| 2.16 | Governo Civil | |
| 2.17 | Escola Primária de S. Sebastião | H.20 |
| 2.18 | Escola Secundária Miguel Torga | H.20 |
| 2.19 | Rua Norberto Lopes | H.21 |
| 2.20 | Av. Cidade de Zamora | |
| 2.21 | Rotunda da Av. Cidade de Zamora | H.22 |
| 2.22 | Av. do Sabor | |
| 2.23 | Seminário de S. José | H.24 |
| 2.24 | Rua Dr. Abílio Vaz das Neves | H.25 |
| 2.25 | Av. João de Cruz | H.27 |
| 2.26 | Escola Secundária Abade de Bagal | |
| 2.27 | Escola Secundária Emídio Garcia | H.30 |
| 2.28 | Centro de Saúde | |
| 2.29 | Câmara Municipal | H.32 |
| 2.30 | Av. Aguedo de Oliveira I | |
| 2.31 | Av. Aguedo de Oliveira II | H.34 |
| 2.32 | Rua de Nogueira | |
| 2.33 | Rua de Terra Fria | H.36 |
| 2.34 | Bairro da Mãe D'Água | |
| 2.35 | I.S.L.A. | H.38 |
| 2.36 | Zona Desportiva | |
| 2.37 | Hospital Distrital | H.40 |
| 2.38 | Av. Abade de Bagal | |
| 2.39 | Escola Campo Redondo | H.42 |
| 2.40 | Largo S. Tiago | H.44 |

Nota: As linhas funcionam de 2ª e 6ª feira de hora a hora, entre as 08H (inclusive) e as 20H (exclusive), aos minutos indicados

U2

Janeiro (zhuh-*nay*-roo) Jan
Fevereiro (fuh-*vray*-oo) Feb
Março (*mahr*-soo) March
Abril (a-*breel*) April
Maio (*my*-oo) May
Junho (zhoon-yoo) June
Julho (*zhool*-yoo) July
Agosto (a-*gosh*-too) Aug
Setembro (suh-*tem*-broo) Sep
Outubro (oh-*too*-broo) Oct
Novembro (nov-*ayñ*-broo) Nov
Dezembro (duh-*zayñ*-broo) Dec

| | |
|---|---|
| 2ªf | Mon |
| 3ªf | Tues |
| 4ªf | Wed |
| 5ªf | Thur |
| 6ªf | Fri |
| Sáb | Sat |
| Dom | Sun |

**Nota: As linhas funcionam de 2ª a 6ª feira de hora a hora, entre as 08H (inclusive) e as 20H (exclusive), aos minutos indicados**
Note: The routes operate from Mon to Fri hourly, between 8am (inclusive) and 8pm (exclusive) at the minutes indicated.

*Tickets for transport are **bilhetes**. Tickets for cinema, theatre, museums and other forms of entertainment are also known as **entradas** (admission charges).*

◀ 1-day Lisbon travel card for unlimited travel on buses, trams and funiculars. As with all public transport tickets, you must validate it on the first journey you make. Insert the ticket into the validating machine so the blue square at the top right corner is punched.

*valid only on the day stamped for an unlimited number of journeys*

▶ You have to validate any ticket you buy for public transport in a validating machine. These are found at the entrance of buses, train platforms and metro stations. Simply insert your ticket in the slot for punching.

Local train ticket from Lisbon to Cascais.

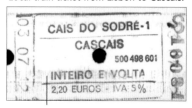

**FULL RETURN**

◀ A 1-trip ticket for one of Lisbon's funicular or lift journeys up the city's steep-sided hills. The top right corner is clipped off by the validating machine.

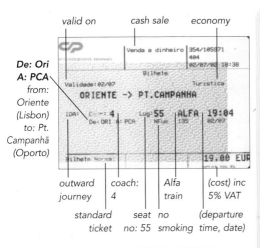

valid on
cash sale
economy

De: Ori
A: PCA
from:
Oriente
(Lisbon)
to: Pt.
Campanhã
(Oporto)

outward journey
coach: 4
Alfa train
(cost) inc 5% VAT

standard ticket
seat no: 55
no smoking
(departure time, date)

validate your ticket at the entrance and exit to the metro

A single (*simples*) ticket for the Lisbon Underground ▶

There is a range of Metro tickets on offer, including return (*ida e volta*), 10 journey (*10 viagens*), one day (*diário*) and 7-day (*7 dias*).

Saver tickets for unlimited local train and bus travel are available.

◀

*trains for tomorrow and following days*

▼ Advance booking

**COMBOIOS DE AMANHÃ E DIAS SEGUINTES**

---

### keywords

**um bilhete**
ooñ beel-*yet*
a ticket

**uma caderneta de 10 viagens**
oo-muh kad-er-nay-tuh duh desh vee-ah-zhayñ
a book of 10 tickets

**um passe**
ooñ pas
a travel card

**simples/de ida**
seeñ-pluhsh/ duh ee-duh
single

**de ida e volta**
duh ee-duh ee vol-tuh
return

**hoje/amanhã**
ohzh/a-man-yañ
today/ tomorrow

**adulto**
ah-dool-too
adult

**criança**
kree-añ-suh
child(ren)

**estudante**
shtoo-dañt
student

**de terceira idade**
duh ter-say-ruh ee-dad
over-60

**deficiente**
duh-feess-yent
disabled

# PUBLIC TRANSPORT 28

*Local and longer-distance bus services are cheap and reliable. You can buy single tickets from the driver as you enter, or buy books of multi-tickets (**módulos**) which work out slightly cheaper. As you enter the bus, validate the ticket in the yellow machine behind the driver. On some buses you enter at the front and get off at the middle or back. The tourist card, **Lisboa card**, includes access to public transport.*

◀ **BUS STATION**
As well as **terminal rodoviário**, you may also see **terminal de camionagem**.

stop — platform —

start of queue at point marked on pavement

destinations and route numbers

◀ Destination and route numbers are on the front

**VENDA E INFORMAÇÃO** (CARRIS)

▲ Ticket Sales and Information desk for bus carrier Carris

**TICKET OFFICE/ INFORMATION** ▼

▶ A modern ticket office (**bilheteira**)

There are route maps at most bus ◀ stops. ▼

▲ The ticket validating machine is behind the driver's seat. You must validate your ticket when you get on board.

▲ Old (above) and new trams (right) in Lisbon.

*push the button on the new tram to open the doors*

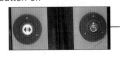

*For wheel-chair access*

**where do I catch a bus to...?**
onde apanho um autocarro para...?
*oñ-**duh** a-**pan**-yoo ooñ ow-too-**kar**-roo **pa**-ruh...*

**which bus goes to...?**
que autocarro vai para...?
*kuh ow-too-**kar**-roo vy **pa**-ruh...*

**is there a bus to...?**
há autocarro para...?
*a ow-too-**kar**-roo **pa**-ruh...*

**which bus goes to the centre?**
que autocarro vai ao centro?
*kuh ow-too-**kar**-roo vy ow **señ**-troo*

**does this bus go to...?**
este autocarro vai a...?
*esht ow-too-**kar**-roo vy uh...*

**can you tell me when to get off?**
pode-me dizer quando devo sair?
*pod-**muh** dee-**zehr** kwan-doo **deh**-voo suh-**eer***

**excuse me!**     **this is my stop**
com licença!     esta é a minha paragem
*koñ lee-**sen**-suh*     *esh-tuh e uh **meen**-yuh pa-**rah**-zhayñ*

talking talking talking

*Lisbon has a metro system which was expanded for the Expo 98 exhibition, with modern, tiled stations and new trains. The network is compact, with four different branch lines. You can buy a range of tickets ranging from singles to multi-journey passes. Oporto is gradually constructing and expanding its own system.*

Three styles of sign for ▶
Lisbon's Metropolitano
underground system

◀
Metro maps, with details of stops for transport connections, shopping and parking, are available from Metro stations and Tourist Information Offices.

Colégio Militar

Alameda

Marquês de Pombal

Oriente

▲ Stops on each of the four Metro lines are colour-coded

Colour coding for the lines ▼

linha **Azul**    linha **Amarela**    linha **Verde**    linha **Vermelha**

**BLUE LINE**    **YELLOW LINE**    **GREEN LINE**    **RED LINE**

KEY ── Legenda

*you are here* ── Está aqui

🚊 Interface com caminho de ferro — *train connections*

🚌 Interface com autocarros suburbanos — *suburban bus connections*

⛴ Interface com barcos — *boat connections*

Metro map key ▶

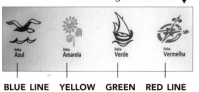

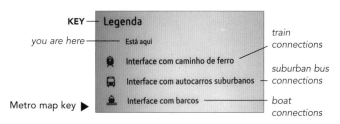

Ticket machines are ▶
simple to operate.

Automatic ticket machines
are common. Choose your
ticket using a touch screen
(above) in English,
Portuguese, Spanish or
French. You can pay by coins
(*moedas*), notes (*notas*) or
card (shown by the *MB* sign,
for *Multibanco*).

▲ Ticket barrier

**a single ticket**
um bilhete simples
*ooñ beel-yet seeñ-plush*

**a book of 10 journeys**
uma caderneta de dez viagens
*oo-muh kad-er-nay-tuh duh desh vee-ah-zhayñ*

**where is the nearest metro station?**
onde é a estação de metro mais próxima?
*oñ-duh e uh shta-sowñ duh met-roo mysh pross-ee-muh*

**have you a map of the metro?**
tem um guia do metro?
*tayñ ooñ gee-uh doo met-roo*

**I'm going to...**
vou a...
*voh uh...*

**I want to go to...**
quero ir para...
*kehr-oo eer pa-ruh...*

**do I have to change?**
tenho que mudar?
*ten-yoo kuh moo-dar*

**where?**
onde?
*oñ-duh*

**which line is it for...?**
qual é a linha para...?
*kwal e uh leen-yuh pa-ruh...*

**in which direction?**
em que direcção?
*ayñ kuh dee-reh-sowñ*

**which station is it for...?**
qual é a estação de metro para...?
*kwal e uh shta-sowñ duh met-roo pa-ruh...*

**excuse me!**
com licença!
*koñ lee-señ-suh*

**I'm getting off here**
desço aqui
*desh-oo a-kee*

talking talking talking talking

The national rail network is called CP (**Caminhos de Ferro Portugueses**). Tickets can be bought at all stations, and reservations for the **Alfa** and **Rápido** trains may be booked at travel agents. High-speed trains link the Algarve with Lisbon, and from there to Oporto and the north. There is also a high-class 'sleeper' from Lisbon to Madrid. Although the total network does not cover all areas, train travel is one of the best ways to see Portugal. Most people travel in second class, which is more than adequate. First class is around 40% more expensive. There is a variety of discounts for children, students and older people, and a range of travel cards and passes. It is difficult to transport bicycles on Portuguese trains.

**TICKET OFFICES ▶**

## BILHETEIRAS

Logo of Portugal's state railway

**◀ AUTOMATIC MACHINE**

**where is the station?**
onde é a estação?
*oñ-duh e uh shta-sowñ*

**to the station, please**
para a estação, por favor
*pa-ruh uh shta-sowñ poor fa-vor*

**a ticket to...**
um bilhete para...
*ooñ beel-yet pa-ruh...*

**a single ticket to...**
um bilhete simples para...
*ooñ beel-yet seeñ-plush pa-ruh...*

**a return ticket**
um bilhete de ida e volta
*ooñ beel-yet duh ee-duh ee vol-tuh*

**2 returns to...**
dois de ida e volta para...
*doysh duh ee-duh ee vol-tuh pa-ruh...*

**a child's ticket to...**
meio bilhete para...
*may-oo beel-yet pa-ruh...*

**lst/2nd class**
primeira/segunda classe
*pree-may-ruh/suh-gooñ-duh klas*

**smoking**
fumador
*foo-ma-dor*

**non smoking**
não-fumador
*nowñ foo-ma-dor*

**is there a supplement to pay?**
paga-se suplemento?
*pah-ga-suh soo-pluh-meñ-too*

**do I need to book?**
tenho que reservar?
*ten-yoo kuh ruh-ser-var*

**I want to book...**
queria reservar...
*kree-uh ruh-ser-var...*

**a seat**
um lugar
*ooñ loo-gar*

**two seats**
dois lugares
*doysh loo-gah-rush*

talking talking talking talking

**Destino**
destination

**Comboio**
train type

**Hora**
time

**Linha**
platform

**Observações**
information

**Partidas**
departures

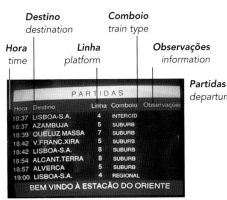

| Hora | Destino | Linha | Comboio | Observações |
|------|---------|-------|---------|-------------|
| 18:37 | LISBOA-S.A. | 4 | INTERCID | |
| 18:37 | AZAMBUJA | 5 | SUBURB | |
| 18:39 | QUELUZ MASSA | 7 | SUBURB | |
| 18:42 | V.FRANC.XIRA | 5 | SUBURB | |
| 18:42 | LISBOA-S.A. | 8 | SUBURB | |
| 18:54 | ALCANT.TERRA | 8 | SUBURB | |
| 18:57 | ALVERCA | 5 | SUBURB | |
| 19:00 | LISBOA-S.A. | 4 | REGIONAL | |

BEM VINDO À ESTAÇÃO DO ORIENTE

▲ welcome (**bem vindo**) to the Eastern Station

◀
Modern ticket validating machine in railway station.
As on other forms of public transport, train tickets must be validated before you travel.

◀ **Linha** and **Gare** both mean 'platform' ▶

**de ida**
duh **ee**-duh
single

**de ida e volta**
duh **ee**-duh ee **vol**-tuh
return

**reserva**
ruh-**ser**-vuh
reservation

**suplemento**
soop-luh-**meñ**-too
supplement

**ligação**
lee-guh-**sowñ**
connection

**lugar**
loo-**gar**
seat

**à janela**
a zhuh-**nel**-uh
by the window

**voltado**
vool-**tah**-doo
facing

**de costas**
duh **kosh**-tush
backwards

**fumador**
foo-ma-**dor**
smoking

**não-fumador**
nowñ-foo-ma-**dor**
non-smoking

the train to...
o combio para...
oo koñ-**boy**-yoo pa-ruh...

is this the train for ...?
é este o comboio para...?
e esht oo koñ-**boy**-yoo pa-ruh...

which platform does it leave from?
de que linha parte?
duh kuh **leen**-yuh part

this is my seat
este é o meu lugar
esht e oo **may**-oo loo-**gar**

talking

# TAXI

*Taxis – generally Mercedes – are widely available. You can hire one from a taxi stand or **praça**, hail them in the street or ring for them. They are cheap, but charges rise after 10pm, at weekends and on holidays. Luggage is charged at a flat rate. Meters don't operate outside city limits, so check the fare before you travel.*

◀ Taxi sign in airport

◀ Taxi lights on roof. If the green lights are on, the taxi is occupied. 1 light means it is operating at the cheaper rate, 2 lights at the higher rate.

▲ Taxi-stand sign (**2 filas** = 2 queues)

◀ Older taxis are black and green; more modern taxis are beige.

**talking talking talking**

**where can I get a taxi?**
onde se pode arranjar um táxi?
*oñ-duh suh pod ar-ran-**zhar** ooñ **tak**-see*

**to the airport, please**
ao aeroporto, por favor
*ow uh-er-roo-**por**-too poor fa**vor***

**to this address, please**
a esta morada, por favor
*uh **esh**-tuh moo-**rah**-duh poor fa**vor***

**please order me a taxi**
chame-me um táxi, por favor
***shah**-muh-muh ooñ **tak**-see poor fa-**vor***

**for now**
para agora
*pa-ruh a-**goh**-ruh*

**for ... o'clock**
para as...
*pa-ruh ash...*

**can I have a receipt**
pode-me dar um recibo
***pod**-muh dar ooñ ruh-**see**-boo*

**keep the change**
guarde o troco
*gward oo **troh**-koo*

**how much will it cost?**
quanto vai a custar?
***kwan**-too vy a koosh-**tar***

**how much is it to the centre?**
quanto custa ao centro?
***kwan**-too **koosh**-tuh ow **señ**-troo*

# CAR HIRE

*Car-hire firms are abundant in the Algarve, and there are desks in the airport and main holiday complexes and hotels. Lisbon and Oporto airports also have car-hire desks. In other areas check in yellow pages (**páginas amarelas**). To hire a car you must be 23 or over and have held a driving licence for a year. Check the policy carefully, what to do in case of problems, and whether you can take the car over the border or on ferries.*

**Automóveis Rent a Car**

**air auto RENT·A·CAR**
*TARIFA / SPECIAL RATES*
Rua dos Bombeiros, Ed. Horizonte, Loja Sul
Tel.: 289 30 02 00 · Fax: 289 30 02 02 · 8125 Quarteira

| G R P | MARCA/MODELO TYPE OF CAR | KMS. ILIMITADOS INLIMITED KMS. 3 - DIAS / 3 - DAYS | KMS. ILIMITADOS INLIMITED KMS. 7 - DIAS / 7 - DAYS |
|---|---|---|---|

**I'd like to hire a car**
queria alugar um carro
*kree-uh a-loo-gar ooñ kar-roo*

**for one day**
para um dia
*pa-ruh ooñ dee-uh*

**for ... days**
para ... dias
*pa-ruh ... dee-ush*

**I'd like...**
queria...
*kree-uh...*

**a small car**
um carro pequeno
*ooñ kar-roo puh-kay-noo*

**a large car**
um carro grande
*ooñ kar-roo grañd*

**a people carrier**
um monovolume
*ooñ moh-noo-voh-loom*

**an automatic**
um carro automático
*ooñ kar-roo ow-too-mah-tee-koo*

**how much is it?**
quanto é?
*kwan-too e*

**is there a kilometre charge?**
paga-se quilometragem?
*pah-guh-suh kee-loh-may-trah-zhayñ*

**I am ... old**
tenho ... anos
*ten-yoo ... ah-noosh*

**here is my driving licence**
aqui está a minha carta de condução
*a-kee esh-tuh uh meen-yuh kar-tuh duh koñ-doo-sowñ*

**what is included in the insurance?**
que inclui o seguro?
*kuh eeñ-klwee oo suh-goo-roo*

**could you show me how the controls work?**
podia mostrar-me os comandos?
*po-dee-uh moosh-trar-muh oosh koo-mañ-doosh*

**what do I do if the car breaks down?**
que devo fazer se o carro avariar?
*kuh deh-voo fa-zehr soo kar-roo a-va-ree-ar*

**can I hire a child-seat?**
posso alugar um assento para crianças?
*pos-soo a-loo-gar ooñ uh-sayñ-too pa-ruh kree-añ-sush*

**how is it fitted?**
como se monta?
*koh-moo suh moñ-tuh*

talking talking talking talking talking talking

# BOATS

*In Lisbon there is an extensive system of ferry boats crossing the Tagus, transporting people (and vehicles) to and from the southern banks of the river. Some companies run leisure cruises up and down the river; these are also particularly common and well worth the trip in Oporto, on the river Douro. In the Algarve you will also find day trips exploring the rocky coast, and a good number of fishing trips from resorts such as Portimão and Lagos.*

▲ **BELÉM FERRY TERMINAL**

**TIMETABLES** ▼

▼ **RIVER QUAY**

◀River Tagus ferry

---

**how do I get to the river ferry terminal?**
como se vai para a estação fluvial?
*koh-moo suh vy pa-ruh uh shta-sowñ floo-vee-al*

**when is the next...**
quando parte o próximo...?
*kwan-doo part oo pros-see-moo...*

**ferry**
ferry-boat
*ferry-boat*

**boat**
barco
*bar-koo*

**a ticket**
um bilhete
*ooñ beel-yet*

**a car and two people**
um carro e duas pessoas
*ooñ kar-roo ee doo-ush puh-so-ush*

**where does the boat leave from?**
de onde parte o barco?
*duh oñ-duh part oo bar-koo*

**how long is the trip?**
quanto dura a viagem?
*kwan-too doo-ruh uh vee-ah-jayñ*

**when do we arrive in...?**
a que horas chegamos a...?
*uh kee o-rush sheh-gah-moosh uh...*

# DRIVING

*If you are taking your own car into Portugal you will need your driving licence, registration documents, insurance, breakdown cover and ID (passport). Driving in Portugal can be a harrowing experience, with overtaking on bends, tailgating and drink-driving all common. As in many southern European countries, impatience is rife, with over-use of the horn, although road-rage is quite rare.*

| A2 | IP4 | IC2 | N224 | M536 |
|:--:|:--:|:--:|:--:|:--:|
| **12** | **12** | **8** | **15** | **9** |

▲ Blue *auto-estrada* sign with km markers

▲ Red main highway sign

▲ Ordinary main-road sign

▲ Original main road

▲ Urban highway

### Speed restrictions

| built up area | 50 km/h |
|---|---|
| normal roads | 100 km/h |
| motorway | 120 km/h |

▲ Portuguese number plate P on the blue panel is for Portugal, and the last 2 letters indicate the district of registration.

▼ Direction indicators

**NORTH**

**norte**

**EAST**

**oeste**

**leste**

**WEST**

**sul**

**SOUTH**

Pictogram ▶ on road signs indicating the town centre

**we are going to...**
vamos a...
*vah-moosh uh...*

**how many kilometres is it?**
quantos quilómetros são?
*kwan-toosh kee-loh-muh-troosh sowñ*

**how do I get to the motorway?**
como se vai para a auto-estrada?
*koh-moo suh vy pa-ruh uh ow-too-shtrah-duh*

**which is the best route?**
qual é o melhor caminho?
*kwa-le oo mel-yor ka-meen-yoo*

**can you show me on the map?**
pode-me indicar no mapa?
*pod-muh een-dee-kar noo mah-puh*

Cartaxo

**SERVICES AREA (GRÂNDOLA)** ▶

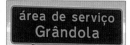
área de serviço Grândola

▲ Signs you will see on entering (above) and leaving (below) villages. ▼

Cartaxo

◀ 30 km/h limit

End of ▶ 30 km/h limit

DAS 9 AS 19H. EXCEPTO CARGAS E DESCARGAS

*no parking 9am to 7pm except loading and unloading*

Tolls are payable on motorways and Lisbon bridges. ▼

PORTAGEM PÉAGE

**SAÍDA**
▲ EXIT

**TODAS AS DIRECÇÕES**
▲ ALL ROUTES

**DEVAGAR**
▲ SLOW DOWN

◀ Toll machine. Press the red button and take your ticket.

▲ Signs show what vehicles can use each lane on particular days

**is this the road to ... ?**
esta é a estrada para...?
*esht e uh **shtrah**-duh **pa**-ruh...*

**I am sorry, I did not know that...**
desculpe, não sabia que...
*dush-**koolp** nowñ suh-**bee**-uh kuh...*

**I could not park here**
não é permitido estacionar aqui
*nowñ e pur-mee-**tee**-doo shtas-yoo-**nar** a-**kee***

**how do I get to... ?**
como se vai para...?
*koh-moo suh vy **pa**-ruh...*

**it is a one-way street**
é sentido único
*e sayñ-**tee**-doo **oo**-nee-koo*

**there is a ... speed limit**
tem um limite de...
*tayñ ooñ **lee**-mee-tay duh...*

*There are a number of motorways (**auto-estradas**) in Portugal. They are toll roads, as are the two bridges into Lisbon from the south. You pay at the toll booth. **Via Verde** is for drivers who subscribe to the automatic express electronic toll service. SOS phones are available for emergency breakdown assistance on motorways.*

▲ Blue motorway (*auto-estrada*) signs indicate road numbers and destinations. E indicates this is also a European route.

2 marks = **SAFETY**

1 mark = **DANGER**

▲ Chevron-shaped distance warnings are painted on some motorways. Drivers are meant to keep 2 markers behind the car in front.

◀ Motorway sign

**AUTO-ESTRADA**

▶ Overhead *Via Verde* indicator. Do not drive in these lanes.

## If you break down on the motorway

If you break down on the motorway, you should put on your hazard warning lights and place your warning triangle about 100m behind the car. Then make your way to the emergency phone. An arrow on the distance indicator will show you which way the nearest phone is. It is never more than 1km away. The police will arrange for a recovery vehicle to come to you.

**my car's broken down**
tenho o carro avariado
*ten-yoo oo **kar**-roo a-vuhr-**yah**-doo*

**what should I do?**
que devo fazer?
*kuh **dev**-oo fa-**zehr***

**I am on my own**
estou só
*shtoh soh*

**it is a blue Fiat**
é um Fiat azul
*e ooñ **fee**-at a-**zool***

**the registration number is…**
a matricula é…
*uh mah-**tree**-koo-luh e…*

**the car is…**
o carro está…
*oo **kar**-roo shta…*

**after exit…**
depois da saída…
*duh-**poysh** duh sah-**ee**-duh…*

**before exit…**
antes da saída…
*an-tesh duh sah-**ee**-duh*

*Parking can be a real problem in Portuguese towns. You may commonly come across cars parked in strange places, as Portuguese drivers often pull in regardless of conditions. It is safer to look for signs to parking areas and pay a small fee, than end up with a **multa** (fine) or be towed away. Disabled parking spaces are scarce. In busy areas you may see young men and boys finding spaces for drivers. They may look scruffy, but they are also quick to spot gaps and guide you in. Just remember, they expect a tip.*

**RETIRE AQUI O SEU BILHETE** — *get your ticket here*

▲ Pay and Display sign

On-street parking meter sign

▶ **PAY HERE**

**zona P pago**

dias úteis: 08 às 20h
sábados: 08 às 13h

In larger towns, parking may be underground.

◀ **PAYMENT ZONE**
*dias úteis* = weekdays
*sábados* = Saturdays

*Premir para abrir*
*Press to open*
Here, the driver presses the red button for a ticket to open the barrier to the car park.

**NO PARKING ENTRANCE AND EXIT OF ▼ WORKS VEHICLES**

NÃO ESTACIONAR
ENTRADA E SAÍDA DE
VIATURAS DA OBRA

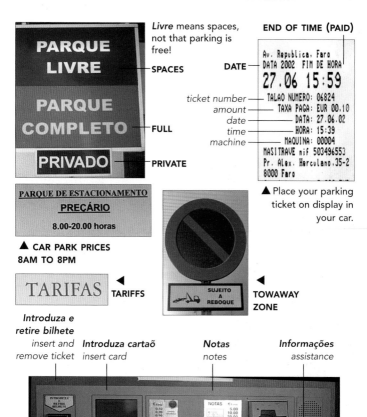

**PARQUE LIVRE** — SPACES

*Livre* means spaces, not that parking is free!

**PARQUE COMPLETO** — FULL

**PRIVADO** — PRIVATE

END OF TIME (PAID)

DATE

Av. Republica, Faro
DATA 2002 FIM DE HORA
**27.06 15:59**
ticket number — TALAO NUMERO: 06824
amount — TAXA PAGA: EUR 00.10
date — DATA: 27.06.02
time — HORA: 15:39
machine — MAQUINA: 00004
MASITRAVE nif 503496553
Pr. Alex. Herculano,35-2
8000 Faro

▲ Place your parking ticket on display in your car.

**PARQUE DE ESTACIONAMENTO**
**PREÇÁRIO**
8.00-20.00 horas

▲ CAR PARK PRICES
8AM TO 8PM

TARIFAS ◀ TARIFFS

SUJEITO A REBOQUE ◀ TOWAWAY ZONE

*Introduza e retire bilhete*
insert and remove ticket

*Introduza cartaõ*
insert card

*Notas*
notes

*Informações*
assistance

▲ Many automatic machines in Portugal have an English language option.

**where's the best place to park?**
onde é o melhor sitio para estacionar?
*oñ-duh e oo mel-**yor** **seet**-yoo **pa**-ruh shtass-yoo-**nar***

**can I park here?**
posso estacionar aqui?
***pos**-soo shtass-yoo-**nar** a-**kee***

**how long for?**
por quanto tempo?
*poor **kwan**-too **teñ**-poo*

**do I need to pay?**
tenho que pagar?
***ten**-yoo kuh puh-**gar***

**the ticket machine doesn't work**
o paquímetro não funciona
*oo pa-**kee**-may-troo nowñ foonss-**yoh**-nuh*

talking

*Most filling stations operate in the same way as in the UK, with self-service pumps, although in smaller areas you will still find one- or two-pump garages which are attended. Filling stations are scarce in rural areas. Note when you are filling up your car that diesel is **gasóleo** and petrol is **gasolina**.*

**Super**
*LRP*

**Sem Chumbo**
*unleaded*

**Gasóleo**
*diesel*

Larger stations have pre-pay machines. You key in before you begin how much you want to pay.

▶

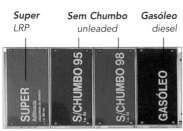

▲ Pumps are colour coded as at home.

▲ You can pay with major credit cards (listed on the side of the machine) and instructions are in Portuguese and English.

AIR
AND
WATER
◀

▶

**PRÉ-FIXAÇÃO**
**(em EUROS)**

1 NÃO RETIRE A PISTOLA
2 PRESSIONE AS TECLAS AS VEZES NECESSÁRIAS
3 CONFIRME NO MOSTRADOR O VALOR PRETENDIDO
4 RETIRE A PISTOLA, ABASTEÇA E ...
... PAGUE NA CAIXA

**PRE-FIXED AMOUNT**
1 Don't remove nozzle
2 Press buttons as required
3 Confirm on the keypad the amount required
4 Remove nozzle, fill up, and pay at the cash desk

SWITCH OFF
ENGINE

**where is the nearest petrol station?**
onde é a estação de serviço mais perto?
*oñ-duh e uh shta-sowñ duh sehr-vee-soo mysh pehr-too*

**... worth of unleaded petrol**
... euros de gasolina sem chumbo
*... eur-oosh duh ga-zoo-lee-nuh sayñ shoom-boo*

**number...**
número...
*noo-muh-roo...*

**fill it up, please**
encha, por favor
*eñ-shuh poor fa-vor*

**please check the oil**
pode verificar o óleo, por favor
*pod vuh-ree-fee-kar oo ol-yoo poor fa-vor*

*talking*

If you belong to a driving organisation and have European cover, you will be able to use **ACP**, the Portuguese breakdown service. Otherwise, you will have to rely on local garages.

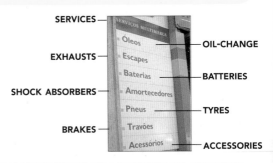

SERVICES — Óleos — OIL-CHANGE
EXHAUSTS — Escapes
— Baterias — BATTERIES
— Amortecedores
SHOCK ABSORBERS — 
— Pneus — TYRES
— Travões
BRAKES — 
— Acessórios — ACCESSORIES

**my car has broken down**
o meu carro está avariado
*oo may-oo kar-roo shta a-va-ree-ah-doo*

**it won't start**
não pega
*nowñ peg-uh*

**the battery is flat**
a bateria está descarregada
*uh ba-tuh-ree-uh shta dush-kar-ruh-ga-duh*

**it won't go**
não anda
*nowñ añ-duh*

**I have a flat tyre**
tenho um furo
*ten-yoo ooñ foo-roo*

**I've run out of petrol**
não tenho gasolina
*nowñ ten-yoo gaz-oo-lee-nuh*

**where is the nearest garage?**
onde é a oficina mais perto?
*oñ-duh e uh o-fee-see-nuh mysh pehr-too*

**the ... is not working**
o/a ... não funciona
*oo/uh ... nowñ foons-yoh-nuh*

**the ... are not working**
os/as ... não funcionam
*oosh/ush ... nowñ foons-yoh-nowñ*

**can you repair it?**
pode arranjá-lo?
*pod ar-rañ-zha-loo*

**how long will it take?**
quanto tempo leva?
*kwañ-too teñ-poo leh-vuh*

**when will it be ready?**
quando estará pronto?
*kwañ-doo shta-ra proñ-too*

**how much will it cost?**
quanto vai custar?
*kwañ-too vy koosh-tar*

**can you replace the windscreen?**
pode substituir o pára-brisas?
*pod sub-shteet-weer oo pa-ruh-bree-zush*

**do you have the parts?**
tem as peças?
*tayñ ush pes-ush*

**is it serious?**
é grave?
*e grav*

# SHOPPING

*i* Shopping is an everyday activity in Portugal, with busy town-centre morning markets. Small supermarkets, called **mini-mercados**, can also be found in many towns. Small shops tend to close for lunch from 1–3pm but are open later in the evening. Normal shops are usually closed on Saturday afternoons and Sundays. Non-EU residents can claim back VAT (**IVA**) on a number of goods – shops display 'Tax Free' signs. Tourists in Lisbon can claim a range of discounts by using the **Lisboa Card**, sold at Tourist Offices.

**keywords**

**padaria**
*pa-duh-**ree**-uh*
baker's

**talho**
*tal-yoo*
butcher's

**charcutaria**
*shar-koot-uh-**ree**-uh*
delicatessen

**mercearia**
*muhr-see-uh-**ree**-uh*
grocer's

**pastelaria**
*pash-tuh-luh-**ree**-uh*
cake shop

**supermercado**
*soo-per-mer-**ka**-doo*
supermarket

**peixaria**
*pay-shuh-**ree**-uh*
fishmonger's

**tabacaria**
*ta-buh-kuh-**ree**-uh*
tobacconist's

◀ On-street kiosks sell newspapers, magazines, postcards, stamps, cigarettes and novelties.

▼ Crafts shop

▲ BUTCHER'S

▲ Older style of tobacconist/newsagent with a small bar

▲ Stationer's with photocopy service

▼ BOOKSHOP

◀ SALE

*Supermercados* and *hipermercados* are usually found on the outskirts of towns. They offer free parking and are open late. Popular chains include **Pão de Açúcar**, **Continente**, **Jumbo** and **Carrefour**. They have extensive ranges of items, from food and drink to clothes, books and household goods. In the fruit and veg sections you may have to weigh the items on an electronic scale and press a button to print off a price label.

▲ Popular supermarket chains

**CHECK THE PRICE** Signs flag up wall-mounted bar-code scanners

**HYPERMARKET – SHOPS ▶**

Hipermercado - Lojas

**TO TAKE A TROLLEY**

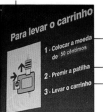

— 1 insert a 50 cêntimos coin

— 2 remove the key

— 3 take the trolley

*this* receipt is needed for guarantee, exchange and refunds (**PVP inclui IVA** = sale price inc. VAT)

Este talão é indispensável para efeitos de garantia trocas e devoluções P.V.P. inclui IVA

---

**where can I buy...?**
onde posso comprar...?
*oñ-duh **pos**-soo koñ-**prar**...*

**do you have...?**
tem...?
*tayñ...*

**I am looking for...**
estou à procura de...
*shtoh a pro-**koo**-ruh duh...*

**where is there a market?**
onde há um mercado?
***oñ**-duh a ooñ mer-**kah**-doo*

**can I pay with this card?**
posso pagar com este cartão?
***pos**-soo pa-**gar** koñ esht kar-**towñ***

**matches**
fósforos
*fosh-foo-roosh*

**how much does it cost?**
quanto custa?
*kwan-too **koosh**-tuh*

**a present**
um presente
*ooñ pruh-**sent***

**a tin-opener**
um abre-latas
*ooñ a-bruh-**la**-tush*

**a good wine**
um bom vinho
*ooñ boñ **veen**-yoo*

**which day?**
em que dia?
*ayñ kuh **dee**-uh*

talking talking talking

*Portugal uses all metric weights and measures, so fruit and veg, meat, fish, hams and cheeses are measured in kilos and grams. Some cheeses are also sold in slices (**fatias**) or in small caskets or boxes, such as ricotta-style fresh cheese. Liquids are sold by can, carton, bottle or litre, and wine can be bought in a large demi-john called a **garrafão**.*

▲ Fruit and vegetables are generally sold by the kilo, although larger items, such as cauliflowers, are sold individually.

Pre-packed shellfish, here ▶ **mexilhão** (mussels) and **ameïjoa** (clams), are sold by the kilo.

semi-skimmed (**meio gordo** = half fat)

◀ Milk is sold in colour-coded cartons.

full fat

skimmed (**magro** = low-fat)

The general word for bread ▶ is **pão**, although there are many variations depending on type, shape and size. This baguette is organically produced (**biológico**).

▲ FREE-RANGE EGGS

▼ 6 FRESH EGGS

**CONSUMIR DE PREFERÉNCIA ANTES DE:**

▲ BEST BEFORE:

▲ WITHOUT ADDED SUGAR

▼ 33% LESS FAT

**INGREDIENTES:**
Batatas, gordura vegetal e sal.

▲ INGREDIENTS: *potatoes, vegetable fat and salt*

▼ NUTRITIONAL INFORMATION

| INFORMAÇÃO NUTRICIONAL | |
|---|---|
| per 100 g — Conteúdo Médio Por 100g | |
| calories — Valor Energético | 470 kcal |
| | 1970 kJ |
| protein — Proteínas | 8,0 g |
| carbohydrate — Glícidos | 58 g |
| fat — Lípidos | 23 g |

**a bit of that cheese**
um pouco desse queijo
*ooñ poh-koo des-suh kay-zhoo*

**a little more**
um pouco mais
*ooñ poh-koo mysh*

**a little less**
um pouco menos
*ooñ poh-koo men-oosh*

**that's enough, thanks**
chega, obrigado(a)
*sheh-guh oh-bree-gah-doo(-duh)*

**10 slices of cooked ham**
dez fatias de fiambre
*desh fa-tee-ush duh fee-añ-bruh*

**200 grams of cured ham**
duzentos gramas de presunto
*doo-zayñ-toosh gra-mush duh pruh-zoon-too*

**a litre of milk**
um litro de leite
*ooñ lee-troo duh layt*

**a bottle of mineral water**
uma garrafa de água mineral
*oo-muh gar-raf-uh duh ag-wuh mee-nuh-ral*

| **still** | **fizzy** |
|---|---|
| sem gás | com gás |
| *sayñ gazh* | *koñ gazh* |

**a tin of...**
uma lata de...
*oo-muh la-tuh duh...*

| **a jar** | **a packet** |
|---|---|
| um frasco | um pacote |
| *ooñ frash-koo* | *ooñ pa-kot* |

**half a dozen eggs**
meia dúzia de ovos
*may-uh doo-zee-uh dov-oosh*

**that's everything**
mais nada
*mysh nah-duh*

## Everyday Foods

| | |
|---|---|
| **beef** | a carne de vaca *karn duh **vah**-kuh* |
| **biscuits** | as bolachas *boo-**lah**-shush* |
| **bread** | o pão *powñ* |
| **bread** (brown) | o pão integral *powñ een-tuh-**gral*** |
| **bread roll** | o papo-seco *pah-poo-**seh**-koo* |
| **butter** | a manteiga *man-**tay**-guh* |
| **cakes** | os bolos *boh-loosh* |
| **cheese** | o queijo *kay-zhoo* |
| **chicken** | a galinha *ga-**leen**-yuh* |
| **chocolate** | o chocolate *shoo-koo-**laht*** |
| **coffee** | o café *kuh-**fe*** |
| **cream** | a nata *nah-tuh* |
| **crisps** | as batatas fritas *ba-**tah**-tush **free**-tush* |
| **eggs** | os ovos *oh-voosh* |
| **fish** | o peixe *paysh* |
| **flour** | a farinha *fa-**reen**-yuh* |
| **ham** (cooked) | o fiambre *fee-**am**-bruh* |
| **ham** (cured) | o presunto *pruh-**zoon**-too* |
| **herbal tea** | a tisana *tee-**za**-nuh* |
| **honey** | o mel *mel* |
| **jam** | a compota *kom-**pot**-uh* |
| **juice** | o sumo *soo-moo* |
| **lamb** | o carneiro *kar-**nay**-roo* |
| **margarine** | a margarina *mar-guh-**ree**-nuh* |
| **marmalade** | a doce de laranja *dohss duh la-**ran**-zhuh* |
| **milk** | o leite *layt* |
| **olive oil** | o azeite *a-**zayt*** |
| **orange juice** | o sumo de laranja *soo-moo duh la-**ran**-zhuh* |
| **pasta** | as massas *mas-sush* |
| **pepper** | a pimenta *pee-**men**-tuh* |
| **pork** | a carne de porco *karn duh **por**-koo* |
| **quince jam** | a marmelada *mar-mel-**ah**-duh* |
| **rice** | o arroz *a-**rosh*** |
| **salt** | o sal *sal* |
| **salt cod** | o bacalhau *ba-kal-**yow*** |
| **sardines** | as sardinhas *sar-**dee**-nush* |
| **stock cube** | o cubo concentrado *koo-boo kon-sayñ-**trah**-doo* |
| **sugar** | o açúcar *a-**soo**-kar* |
| **tea** | o chá *sha* |
| **tomatoes** (tin) | a lata de tomates *lah-tuh duh to-**matsh*** |
| **tuna** | o atum *a-**tooñ*** |
| **vinegar** | o vinagre *vee**nah**-gruh* |
| **yoghurt** | o iogurte *yoh-**goort*** |

## Fruit

| | |
|---|---|
| apples | as maçãs ma-*sañsh* |
| apricots | os damascos da-*mash*-koosh |
| bananas | as bananas ba-*nah*-nush |
| cherries | as cerejas suh-*ray*-jush |
| grapefruit | a toranja too-*ran*-juh |
| grapes | as uvas *oo*-vush |
| lemon | o limão lee-*mowñ* |
| melon | o melão me-*lowñ* |
| nectarines | as nectarinas nek-tuh-*ree*-nush |
| oranges | as laranjas la-*ran*-zhush |
| peaches | os pêssegos *peh*-suh-goosh |
| pears | as pêras *peh*-rush |
| pineapple | o ananás a-nuh-*nash* |
| plums | as ameixas a-*may*-shush |
| raspberries | as framboesas frañ-*bway*-zush |
| strawberries | os morangos moo-*rañ*-goosh |
| watermelon | a melancia mel-añ-*see*-uh |

## Vegetables

| | |
|---|---|
| asparagus | os espargos *shpar*-goosh |
| aubergine | a beringela ber-een-*zhe*-luh |
| broccoli | os brócolos *broh*-koo-loosh |
| cabbage | a couve *kohv* |
| carrots | as cenouras suh-*noh*-rush |
| cauliflower | a couve-flor kohv-*flor* |
| coriander | os coentros koo-*eñ*-troosh |
| courgettes | as courgettes koor-*zhetsh* |
| french beans | o feijão verde fay-zhowñ-*vehrd* |
| garlic | o alho *al*-yoo |
| kale | a couve galega kohv ga-*leh*-guh |
| leeks | os alhos-porros al-yoosh-*por*-rosh |
| lettuce | a alface al-*fass* |
| mushrooms | os cogumelos koo-goo-*mel*oosh |
| onions | as cebolas suh-*bol*ush |
| olives | as azeitonas a-zay-*toh*-nush |
| parsley | a salsa *sal*-suh |
| peas | as ervilhas ehr-*veel*-yush |
| peppers | os pimentos pee-*men*-toosh |
| potatoes | as batatas ba-*tah*-tush |
| pumpkin | a abóbora a-*bob*-oo-ruh |
| spinach | os espinafres shpee-*na*-frush |
| sweet potatoes | as batatas doces buh-*ta*-tush *doh*-sush |
| tomatoes | os tomates too-*matsh* |
| turnip tops | as nabiças na-*bee*-sush |

*The cheapest places to buy clothes and shoes are at weekly and monthly markets, or **feiras**, with bargains in jeans, jackets and footwear. In towns, shoe shops are plentiful. Portuguese shoes are elegant and great value for money. The Portuguese are very well-dressed, and Lisbon especially has become a fashion mecca, with names such as Ana Salazar and the popuar Spanish store, **Zara**.*

## keywords

**aberto até às...**
a-**ber**-too a-**te** ash...
open until...

**cave**
kav
basement

**rés-do-chão**
res-doo-**showñ**
ground floor

**andar/piso**
an-**dar**/**pee**-soo
floor

**caixa**
ky-shuh
cash desk

**desconto**
dush-**koñ**-too
discount

**saldo**
sal-doo
sale

**senhoras**
sun-**yor**-suh
ladies'

**homem**
o-**mayñ**
men's

**crianças**
kree-**añ**-sush
children

**R/C**
*Ground Floor*

**Senhora**
*Ladieswear*

**Comple-mentos**
*Accessories*

**1º Piso**
*First Floor*

**Homem**
*Menswear*

▼ Store Guide

▲ CASH DESK

▲ A Lisboa card entitles you to discounts in many shops around the city.

◀ SHOE SHOP

## talking

**which floor is/are...?**
em que andar está/estão...?
*ayñ kuh an-**dar** shta/shtowñ...*

**toys**
os brinquedos
*oosh breeñ-**kay**-doosh*

**shoes**
os sapatos
*oosh sa-**pah**-toosh*

**household goods**
artigos de ménage
*ar-**tee**-goosh duh-may-**nazh***

### Women's clothes sizes

| UK/Australia | 8 | 10 | 12 | 14 | 16 | 18 | 20 | 22 |
|---|---|---|---|---|---|---|---|---|
| Europe | 36 | 38 | 40 | 42 | 44 | 46 | 48 | 50 |
| US/Canada | 6 | 8 | 10 | 12 | 14 | 16 | 18 | 20 |

### Men's clothes sizes (suits)

| UK/US/Canada | 36 | 38 | 40 | 42 | 44 | 46 |
|---|---|---|---|---|---|---|
| Europe | 46 | 48 | 50 | 52 | 54 | 56 |
| Australia | 92 | 97 | 102 | 107 | 112 | 117 |

### Shoes

| UK/Australia | 2 | 3 | 4 | 5 | 6 | 7 | 8 | 9 | 10 | 11 |
|---|---|---|---|---|---|---|---|---|---|---|
| Europe | 35 | 36 | 37 | 38 | 39 | 41 | 42 | 43 | 45 | 46 |
| US/Canada women | 4 | 5 | 6 | 7 | 8 | 9 | 10 | 11 | 12 | - |
| US/Canada men | 3 | 4 | 5 | 6 | 7 | 8 | 9 | 10 | 11 | 12 |

### Children's Shoes

| UK/US/Canada | 0 | 1 | 2 | 3 | 4 | 5 | 6 | 7 | 8 | 9 | 10 | 11 |
|---|---|---|---|---|---|---|---|---|---|---|---|---|
| Europe | 15 | 17 | 18 | 19 | 20 | 22 | 23 | 24 | 26 | 27 | 28 | 29 |

**can I try this on?**
posso provar isto?
*pos*-soo pro-*var* eesh-too

**do you have size ...?**
tem medida...?
*tayñ* muh-*dee*-duh...

**do you have this in my size?**
tem isto na minha medida?
*tayñ* eesh-too nuh *meen*-yuh muh-*dee*-duh

**it's too big**
é muito grande
e *mweeñ*-too grañd

**I need a size...**
preciso duma medida...
pruh-*see*-zoo *doo*-muh muh-*dee*-duh...

**where are the changing rooms?**
onde é o gabinete de provas?
*oñ*-duh e oo ga-bee-*net* duh *prov*-ush

**I'm just looking**
só estou a ver
so shtoh uh vehr

**shoe size 40, please**
número quarenta, por favor
*noo*-muh-roo kwa-*reñ*-tuh poor fa*vor*

**I take shoe size...**
calço número...
*kal*-soo *noo*-muh-roo...

**it's too small**
é muito pequeno
e *mweeñ*-too puh-*ke*-noo

**smaller**
mais pequeno
*mysh* puh-*ke*-noo

**bigger**
maior
mah-*yor*

talking talking talking

*You can buy stamps from tobacconists, kiosks and some hotels, as well as from the Post Office. There are also automatic stamp machines in or near town squares and at airports and railway stations.*

▲ CTT ( post office) sign

◀ Next-collection times may be shown by a dial on the post box.

Modern stamp machines have instructions in English ▼

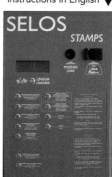

◀ Blue post boxes are for priority, or first-class post; ordinary post boxes are red.

**where is the post office?**
onde é o correio?
*oñ-duh e oo koor-ray-oo*

**do you have stamps?**
tem selos?
*tayñ sel-oosh*

**10 stamps, please**
dez selos, por favor
*desh sel-oosh poor fa-vor*

| **for postcards** | **for letters** |
|---|---|
| para postais | para cartas |
| *pa-ruh poosh-tysh* | *pa-ruh kar-tush* |

**to Britain**
para a Grã-Bretanha
*pa-ruh uh grañ-bruh-tahn-yuh*

**to the US**
para os Estados Unidos
*pa-ruh oosh shtah-doosh oo-nee-doosh*

**I'd like to send this...**
queria mandar isto...
*kree-uh man-dar eesh-too...*

**registered**
registado
*ruh-zhees-tah-doo*

**by priority post**
por correio azul
*poor koor-ray-oo a-zool*

**how much is it to send this parcel?**
quanto custa mandar este embrulho?
*kwan-too koosh-tuh man-dar aysht ayñ-brool-yoo*

**where can I post these cards?**
onde posso por estes postais no correio?
*oñ-duh pos-soo por esh-tesh poosh-tysh noo koor-ray-oo*

talking talking talking

◀ In the post office, you sometimes take a ticket and wait for your number.

30-minute photo-developing service ▶

**rolo**
*roh-loo*
film

**pilhas**
*peel-yush*
battery

**em mate**
*ayñ mat*
mat

**com brilho**
*koñ breel-yoo*
glossy

**diapositivos**
*dee-a-poh-zee-tee-voosh*
slides

**máquina digital**
*mah-kee-nuh dee-zhee-tal*
digital camera

**tirar fotos**
*tee-rar fo-toosh*
to take pictures

◀ Photo booths can be found in airports, some railway stations and larger shopping centres.

**where can I buy film?**
onde posso comprar rolos?
*oñ-duh pos-soo koñ-prar roh-loosh*

**tapes for this camcorder**
cassettes para esta video
*ka-setsh pa-ruh esht veed-yoo*

**a colour film**
um rolo a cores
*ooñ roh-loo uh koh-rush*

**24**
vinte e quatro
*veen-tee-kwa-troo*

**36**
trinta e seis
*treen-tuh saysh*

**can you develop this film?**
pode revelar este rolo?
*pod ruh-vuh-lar aysht roh-loo*

**when will the photos be ready?**
quando estão prontas as fotos?
*kwan-doo shtowñ pron-tush ush foh-toosh*

**can you take a picture of us, please?**
pode-nos tirar uma foto, por favor?
*pod-noosh tee-rar oo-muh foh-too poor fa-vor*

**can I take pictures here?**
posso tirar fotos aqui?
*pos-soo tee-rar foh-toosh a-kee*

# PHONES

*Call boxes are easy to find. The older type are silver kiosks with tricky-to-open folding doors; more modern ones are beige or blue, and more open. You can also call internationally from some post offices and telecom shops. Most have instructions in several languages, including English. You can buy phone cards from post offices, telecom shops and newsagents.*

◀ You can usually use coins or a phone card. Older phones take coins only. Emergency numbers are displayed in most phone booths. ▼

**do you have phonecards?**
tem cartões telefónicos?
*tayñ kar-**towñsh** tuh-luh-**fo**-nee-koosh*

**a phonecard**
um cartão telefónico
*ooñ kar-**towñ** tuh-luh-**fo**-nee-koo*

**for 50/100 units**
de cinquenta/cem impulsos
*duh seeñ-**kweñ**-tuh/sayñ eeñ-**pool**-soosh*

**Mr Lopes, please**
o Senhor Lopes, por favor
*oo sun-**yor** lopsh poor fa-**vor***

**Mrs Lopes, please**
a Senhora Lopes, por favor
*uh sun-**yor**-uh lopsh poor fa-**vor***

**can I speak to...?**
posso falar com...?
***pos**-soo fa-**lar** koñ...*

**this is Caroline**
daqui fala Caroline
*da-**kee** fa-luh caroline*

**can you give me an outside line, please**
pode dar-me uma linha, por favor
*pod **dar**-muh **oo**-muh **leen**-yuh poor fa-**vor***

**I want to make a reverse charge call**
quero fazer uma chamada a cobrar no destinatário
***keh**-roo fa-**zehr oo**-muh sha-**mah**-duh uh koo-**brar** noo dush-tee-na-**tar**-yoo*

**what is you phone number?**
qual é o seu número de telefone?
*kwal e oo **say**-oo **noo**-muh-roo duh tuh-luh-**fon***

**my number is...**
o meu número é...
*oo **may**-oo **noo**-muh-roo e...*

# Comunicações

▲ Logo of PT, the Portuguese telecoms company

CTT CORREIOS

Comunicar
é um impulso natural.

**50**
Telecom Card PT

▲ Phone cards are very popular, with a range from different companies such as *CTT*, *PT*, *Marconi* and *Onicard*.

| International dialling codes | |
|---|---|
| UK 00 44 | Australia 00 61 |
| USA 00 1 | Portugal 00 351 |

Páginas
Amarelas
paginasamarelas.pt

◀ YELLOW PAGES

| Portuguese phone numbers are given in single digits | | | |
|---|---|---|---|
| **21** | **882** | **03** | **48** |
| dois, um | oito, oito, dois | zero, três | quatro, oito |

**keywords**

**cartão telefónico**
kar-**towñ** tuh-luh-**fo**-nee-koo
phonecard

**telemóvel**
tuh-luh-**mo**-vel
mobile

**indicativo**
een-dee-kuh-**tee**-voo
dialling code

**moedas**
**mwed**-ush
coins

**marcar**
mar-**kar**
to dial

**chamada**
sha-**mah**-duh
phone call

**TELEMÓVEL PROIBIDO**
▼ *mobiles prohibited*

**talking**

**I'll call back...**
chamarei...
sha-muh-**ray**...

**later**
mais tarde
mysh tard

**tomorrow**
amanhã
a-man-**yañ**

**have you a mobile?**
tem telemóvel?
tayñ tuh-luh-**mo**-vel

**what's your mobile number?**
qual é o seu número de telemóvel?
kwal e oo **say**-oo **noo**-muh-roo duh tuh-luh-**mo**-vel

**my mobile number is...**
o meu número de telemóvel é...
oo **may**-oo **noo**-muh-roo duh tuh-luh-**mo**-vel e...

*As yet there are few internet cafés outside the Algarve, Oporto and Lisbon. Likewise, there are few places you can fax, but hotels, telecom offices and tourist offices may be able to send one for you. The suffix for Portuguese websites is **.pt***

The Portuguese word for 'at' is **arroba** (ar-**roh**-buh).

**sapo.pt** is a popular Portuguese search engine.
▼

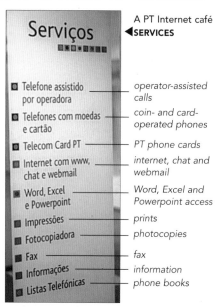

A PT Internet café
◄SERVICES

| Serviços | |
|---|---|
| Telefone assistido por operadora | operator-assisted calls |
| Telefones com moedas e cartão | coin- and card-operated phones |
| Telecom Card PT | PT phone cards |
| Internet com www, chat e webmail | internet, chat and webmail |
| Word, Excel e Powerpoint | Word, Excel and Powerpoint access |
| Impressões | prints |
| Fotocopiadora | photocopies |
| Fax | fax |
| Informações | information |
| Listas Telefónicas | phone books |

**do you have e-mail?**
tem e-mail?
*tayñ e-mail*

**my e-mail address is...**
o meu endereço de e-mail é...
*oo **may**-oo eñ-duh-ruh-**sowñ** duh e-mail e...*

**what is your e-mail address?**
qual é o seu endereço de e-mail?
*kwal e oo **say**-oo eñ-duh-ruh-**sowñ** duh e-mail*

**caroline.smith@anycompany.co.uk**
caroline ponto smith@collins ponto co ponto uk
*caroline **pon**-too smith ar-**roh**-buh **pon**-too co **pon**-too uk*

**can I send an e-mail?**
posso mandar um e-mail?
*pos-soo man-**dar** ooñ e-mail*

**did you get my e-mail?**
recebeu o meu e-mail?
*ruh-suh-**bay**-oo oo **may**-oo e-mail*

**can you send it by e-mail?**
pode mandá-lo por e-mail?-
*pod man-**da**-loo poor e-mail*

**can I book by e-mail?**
posso fazer a reserva por e-mail?
*pos-soo fa-**zehr** uh ruh-**zer**-vuh poor e-mail*

talking talking

◀ A public internet phone, usually found at airports. Choose from several options along the top of the touch screen (below).

**188 net**
(national info)

**informações**
information

**telefone**
phone

**e-mail**

**internet**

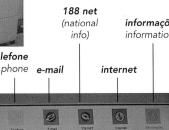

*Números Úteis*
Useful Numbers

**ajuda**
azh-**oo**-duh
help

**notícias**
noh-**teess**-yush
news

**pesquisa**
pesh-**kee**-zuh
search

**caixa de correio**
**ky**-shuh duh koo-**ray**-oo
mailbox

**procurar**
proh-koo-**rar**
find

**corpo/título**
**kor**-poo/**tee**-too-lo
text/title

**ambos**
am-**boosh**
both

---

**I want to send a fax**
quero mandar um fax
**keh**-roo man-**dar** ooñ faks

**can I send a fax from here?**
posso mandar um fax daqui?
**pos**-soo man-**dar** ooñ faks da-**kee**

**how much is it to send a fax?**
quanto custa mandar um fax?
**kwan**-too **kush**-tuh man-**dar** ooñ faks

**what is your fax number?**
qual é o seu número de fax?
kwal e oo **say**-oo **noo**-muh-roo duh faks

**my fax number is...**
o meu número de fax é...
oo **may**-oo **noo**-muh-roo duh faks e...

**do you have a fax?**
tem fax?
tayñ faks

**can I receive a fax here?**
posso receber um fax aqui?
**pos**-soo ruh-suh-**beer** ooñ faks a-**kee**

**it has ... pages**
tem ... páginas
tayñ ... **pah**-zhee-nush

**can you confirm the number?**
pode confirmar o número?
pod koñ-feer-**mar** oo **noo**-muh-roo

**did you get my fax?**
recebeu o meu fax?
ruh-suh-**bay**-oo oo **may**-oo faks

# OUT & ABOUT

*Most museums are closed on Mondays. For the most part, museums, castles and art galleries charge small admission fees, although younger people and pensioners can usually get in at a discount or for free.*

▲ **TOURIST INFORMATION OFFICE**

▲ Museum street sign. Street signs to places of interest are normally brown.

**HISTORICAL TOWN CENTRE** ▲

▲ Blue *rua* (street/road) plaque. This one commemorates a Portuguese governor of India.

Ticket for the football museum in Lisbon ▼

**NON-MEMBER**

▶

Lisbon's 'artshuttle' bus ferries visitors around the city to places of cultural interest. The Lisboa Card, available from tourist offices, lets you travel on the bus for free.

▲ Town maps and what's on guides are available free from all tourist offices.

◀ Museum ticket showing payment details

**espectáculo**
*shpek-ta-koo-loo*
show

**exposição**
*eks-pos-ee-sowñ*
exhibition

**visitas guiadas**
*vee-zee-tush*
*gee-a-dush*
guided tours

**jardim botânico**
*zhar-deeñ*
*boot-a-nee-koo*
botanic gardens

**diário**
*dee-a-ree-oo*
daily

**igreja**
*ee-gray-zhuh*
church

**jovens**
*zho-vayñ*
young people (5–15)

**crianças**
*kree-an-sush*
children

**excuse me, where is the tourist office?**
desculpe, onde é o turismo?
*dush-koolp oñ-duh e oo too-reezh-moo*

**do you have...?**
tem...?
*tayñ...*

**a map of the town**
um mapa da cidade
*ooñ ma-puh duh see-dad*

**leaflets**
folhetos
*fool-yet-oosh*

**we'd like to visit ...**
queríamos visitar...
*kree-a-moosh vee-zee-tar...*

**how do we get there?**
come se vai para lá?
*koh-moo suh vy pa-ruh la*

**when can we visit...?**
quando podemos visitar...?
*kwañ-doo poo-de-moosh vee-zee-tar...*

**when does it close?**
a que horas fecha?
*uh kee o-rush fay-shuh*

**are there any excursions?**
há algumas excursões?
*a al-goo-mush shkoor-soyñsh*

**where does it leave from?**
de onde parte?
*duh oñ-duh part*

*Most sports are based on outdoor activities: e.g. surfing, fishing and golf, with many world-class courses. In national parks and reserves you can walk, ride and cycle. Football is the most popular spectator sport. Large hotels in tourist areas often have a swimming pool, tennis court and/or gym. Many towns have a public indoor pool where you are expected to wear a swimming cap (**touca**).*

**▲ SPORTS CENTRE**

Portugal's beautiful National Stadium still hosts the cup final every year. ▼

▶ Horse-riding is popular in Portugal. The lovely Lusitano breed is seen at its best at the colourful annual *Golegã* (Ribatejo) Horse Fair in Nov.

**▼ BEACHES**

talking talking talking

| **where can we...?** | **play tennis** | **play golf** |
|---|---|---|
| onde podemos...? | jogar ténis | jogar golfe |
| *oñ-duh poo-**de**-moosh...* | *zhoo-**gar** tennis* | *zhoo-**gar** golf* |

**where can we go horse-riding?**
onde podemos andar a cavalo?
*oñ-duh poo-**de**-moosh an-**dar** uh ka-**va**-loo*

| **how much is it...?** | **per hour** | **per day** |
|---|---|---|
| quanto é...? | por hora | por dia |
| *kwañ-too e...* | *poor **o**-ruh* | *poor **dee**-uh* |

| **is there a swimming pool?** | **is it dangerous?** | **are there currents?** |
|---|---|---|
| há piscina? | é perigoso? | há correntes? |
| *a peesh-**zee**-nuh* | *e pree-**goh**-zoh* | *a koor-**reñ**-tush* |

| **where can one...?** | **go windsurfing** | **go waterskiing** |
|---|---|---|
| onde se pode... | fazer windsurf | fazer esqui aquático |
| *oñ-duh suh pod...* | *fa-**zer** windsurf* | *fa-**zer** shkee ak-**wa**-tee-koo* |

**can I hire a beach umbrella?**
posso alugar uma sombrinha?
*pos-soo a-loo-**gar** oo-muh som-**breen**-yuh*

Signs explain beach flag colour-codings.
Red: danger; Green: clear; Yellow: caution;
Blue check: safe. ◀

▶ Some beaches are arranged by activity zone.

▶ Flyer for a club

Fado poster
**jantar e espectáculo = 20 euros por pessoa (vinho incluído)** dinner & show = 20 euros per person (wine included)
**só espectáculo = 10 euros por pessoa (2 bebidas incluídas)** show only = 10 ◀ euros per person (2 drinks included)

---

**we'd like to go to a football match**
queríamos assistir a um jogo de futebol
*kree*-uh-moosh a-sees-*teer* uh ooñ **zhoh**-goo duh foot-**bol**

**where can we get tickets?**
onde podemos comprar bilhetes?
*oñ*-duh poo-**de**-moosh koñ-**prar** beel-**yetsh**

**how do we get to the stadium?**
como se vai para o estádio?
**koh**-moo suh vy **pa**-ruh oo **shtad**-yoo

**what time is the match?**
quando começa o jogo?
**kwañ**-doo koo-**mes**-suh oo **zhoh**-goo

talking

# ACCOMMODATION

*There are many types of accommodation: **hotel**, **pensão** or **residência/residencial** (guest houses, offering breakfast only), **albergaria** or **estalagem** (inns), or **pousadas** (state-run luxury hotels, often in sites of historical interest). You can also stay on farms, booked through **Turismo Rural and Agroturismo**, or in private homes, with **Turismo de Habitação**, as well as the normal range of tourist options. Most can be arranged with the help of Tourist Offices.*

▲ Larger hotels are signposted in blue.

◀ Hotels and guest houses are starred 1–5. R means *Residencial*, so this is a guest house.

*Residencials* are reasonably cheap guest houses. They offer no meals apart from breakfast.

## Booking in advance

The Portuguese tourist office (**www.portugalinsite.com**) can help with booking rooms and often get better rates than you could yourself.

| | | |
|---|---|---|
| **I'd like to book a room...** | **single** | **double** |
| queria reservar um quarto... | individual | de casal |
| *kree-uh ruh-zer-var ooñ kwar-too...* | *eeñ-dee-veed-wal* | *duh ka-zal* |

**we'd like to stay ... nights**
queríamos ficar ... noites
*kree-uh-moosh fee-kar ... noytsh*

**from ... till...**
do dia ... ao dia...
*doo dee-uh ... ow dee-uh...*

| | | |
|---|---|---|
| **I will confirm...** | **by e-mail** | **by fax** |
| confirmarei... | por e-mail | por fax |
| *koñ-feer-ma-ray...* | *poor e-mail* | *poor fax* |

**my name is...**  **my credit card number is...**
o meu nome é... o número de meu cartão de crédito é...
*oo may-oo nom e...oo noo-muh-roo duh may-oo kar-towñ duh kre-dee-too e...*

**valid until**
válido até...
*val-ee-doo a-tay...*

**RECEPTION ▶**

Logo of the
state-run
Pousadas
chain ▶

Hotels have to post information about rooms

and
meals
on the
back of
bed-
room
doors.

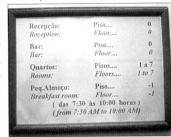

▲ Room slip. Keep it to
get your key and, in larger
hotels, to get your meals.

---

**do you have a room for tonight?**
tem um quarto para esta noite?
*tayñ ooñ **kwar**-too **pa**-ruh **esh**-tuh noyt*

**a single room**
um quarto individual
*ooñ **kwar**-too een-dee-veed-**wal***

**a double room**
um quarto de casal
*ooñ **kwar**-too duh ka-**zal***

**with twin beds**
com duas camas
*koñ **doo**-ush **kah**-mush*

**with a double bed**
com cama de casal
*koñ **kah**-muh duh ka-**zal***

**with bath**
com casa de banho
*koñ **kah**-zuh duh **bahn**-yoo*

**with shower**
com chuveiro
*koñ shoo-**vay**-roo*

**with an extra bed for a child**
com uma cama extra para uma criança
*koñ **oom**-uh **kah**-muh **aysh**-truh **par**-uh **oo**-muh kree-**añ**-suh*

**how much is it...?**
qual é o preço...?
*kwal e oo **pray**-soo...*

**per night**
por noite
*poor noyt*

**per week**
por semana
*poor suh-**mah**-nuh*

**can you suggest somewhere else?**
pode aconselhar outro sítio?
*pod a-kon-sel-**yuhr** oh-troo **seet**-yoo*

talking talking talking talking

*If you are staying in self-catering accommodation, your gas supply for cooking and water-heating may be bottled. Check you understand how the bottle connects and what you need to do if it runs out (there may be extra bottles supplied). Plugs are 2-pin (20 v), so you will need an adapter for your UK appliances. You can buy these at airports or in travel shops.*

▲ Apartments for rent

Recycling bins are becoming fairly common; even litter bins in the street are often divided according to the type of rubbish you are throwing away. ▼

**PAPER / CARDBOARD**

▲ **ROOMS AVAILABLE**

You may also see *Vagas*, Vacancies.

▶ **GLASS**

# Esgotado

▲ **FULL**

You may also see *lotado*

▶ **PACKAGING**

### ▲ YOUTH HOSTEL

Youth hostels vary in the range of facilities they offer; some of them cater for the disabled.

▲ Logo of Portugal's youth hostel association

**detergente para a louça**
*duh-ter-**zheñt** pa-ruh uh loh-suh*
washing-up liquid

**detergente para a roupa**
*duh-ter-**zheñt** pa-ruh uh **roh**-puh*
washing powder

**sabão**
*suh-**bowñ***
soap

**abre-latas**
*a-bruh-**la**-tush*
tin-opener

**velas**
***veh**-lush*
candles

**fósforos**
***fosh**-foo-roosh*
matches

**os sacos do lixo**
*oosh **sa**-koosh doo **lee**-shoo*
bin liners

**there is no...**
não há...
*nowñ a...*

**how does this work?**
como é que isto funciona?
*koh-moo e kuh **eesh**-too fooñss-**yoh**-nuh*

**how does ... work?**
como funciona...?
*koh-moo fooñss-**yoh**-nuh*

**the cooker**
o fogão
*oo foh-**gowñ***

**the washing machine**
a máquina de lavar roupa
*uh **mah**-kee-nuh duh la-**var** roh-puh*

**is there always hot water?**
há sempre água quente?
*a **sem**-pruh **ahg**-wuh kent*

**what are the neighbours called?**
qual é o nome dos vizinhos?
*kwal e oo nom doosh vee-**zeen**-yoosh*

**whom do I contact if there are problems?**
quem posso contactar em caso de problemas?
*kayñ **pos**-soo koñ-tak-**tar** ayñ **kah**-zoo duh proo-**bleh**-moosh*

**when is the rubbish collected?**
quando levam o lixo?
***kwañ**-doo **leh**-vowñ oo **lee**-shoo*

**where do we leave the rubbish?**
onde pomos o lixo?
***oñ**-duh **poh**-moosh oo **lee**-shoo*

**can you give us an extra set of keys?**
pode-nos dar um duplicado das chaves?
***pod**-noosh dar ooñ doo-plee-**kah**-doo dush **sha**-vush*

# CAMPING

*To camp on sites, get an International Card from the UK Camping and Caravanning club. Overnight stops at non-designated sites are possible in restricted areas, but not the Algarve. Prices are very reasonable, but some sites can be pretty basic. The definitive campsite guide is the **Roteiro Campista**, available from bookshops. Tourist Offices also have lists of sites.*

▲ Road sign for a campsite

▲ NO PLACES

▲ Drivers are warned not to camp on the beach. Offsite camping is not allowed in the Algarve.

**we're looking for a campsite**
procuramos um parque de campismo
*pro-koo-**ra**-moosh ooñ park duh kam-**peezh**-moo*

**have you any places?**
tem lugares?
*tayñ loo-**ga**-rush*

**we'd like to stay for ... nights**
queríamos ficar ... noites
*kree-**a**-moosh fee-**kar** ... noytsh*

**how much is it a night?**
quanto é por noite?
*kwañ-too e poor noyt*

**per tent**
por tenda
*poor **teñ**-duh*

**per caravan**
por caravana
*poor ka-ruh-**va**-nuh*

**can we park the caravan here for tonight?**
podemos estacionar a caravana aqui para esta noite?
*poo-**deh**-moosh shtas-yoo-**nar** uh ka-ruh-**va**-nuh a-**kee** pa-ruh esht noyt*

**is there a restaurant on the campsite?**
há um restaurante no parque?
*a ooñ rush-toh-**rant** noo park*

**do you have a more sheltered site?**
tem um lugar mais abrigado?
*tayñ ooñ loo-**gar** mysh a-bree-**gah**-doo*

**can we camp here for tonight?**
podemos acampar aqui para esta noite?
*poo-**deh**-moosh a-kam-**par** a-kee **pa**-ruh esht noyt*

talking talking talking talking

- disabled WCs — WC DEFICIENTES
- tennis - pool — TÉNIS - PISCINA
- washing machines — MÁQUINAS LAVAR
- communal area — POLIVALENTE
- café, restaurant — CAFÉ RESTAURANTE
- playpark — PARQUES INFANTIS
- lounge — SALA CONVÍVIO
- ice-cream shop — GELADARIA
- car wash — LAVAGEM CARROS

▲ **DRINKING FOUNTAIN**

▲ **RECEPTION**

▲ **SINKS FOR HAND-WASHING**

▲ **DISHWASHERS**

▲ **TOILETS**

Typical campsite tariff
*Preços, por dia*
▼ Prices per day

- adults
- children (5-12)
- small tent
- large tent
- caravan
- car
- bus
- motorhome
- use of kitchen
- extra awning
- motorbikes
- trailers
- boats/trailer
- hot baths

**is there a launderette near here?**
há uma lavandaria automática perto daqui?
*a **oo**-muh la-van-duh-**ree**-uh ow-too-**ma**-tee-kuh **pehr**-too da-**kee***

**where can I wash some clothes?**
onde posso lavar a roupa?
***oñ**-duh **pos**-soo la-**var** uh **roh**-puh*

**do you have a laundry service?**
tem serviço de lavandaria?
*tayñ suhr-**vee**-soo duh la-van-duh-**ree**-uh*

**when will my clothes be ready?**
quando está pronta a minha roupa?
***kwañ**-doo shta **proñ**-tuh uh **meen**-yuh **roh**-puh*

**is there an iron?**
há um ferro de engomar?
*a ooñ **fer**-roo duh ayñ-goo-**mar***

**where is the dry-cleaner's?**
onde é a tinturaria?
***oñ**-duh e uh teen-too-ruh-**ree**-uh*

talking

*Access and facilities for the disabled are quite scant, with few toilets, buses with access or buildings with ramps. Lisbon and Oporto have a special dial-a-ride bus for the disabled, and a limited taxi service operates in some larger cities. The organisation **Secretariado Nacional de Reabilitação** publishes a guide to disabled facilities throughout Portugal.*

Disabled parking sign

Disabled access sign

▲ **PRIORITY CHECKOUT FOR PREGNANT AND DISABLED PEOPLE**

Priority is also given on seats by the door on public transport.

◄

*Para aceder ao Piso -1, dirija-se por favor, ao Balcão de Informações*
To get to the first floor, please go to the information desk

**are there any disabled toilets?**
há casas de banho para deficientes?
*a **kah**-zuh duh **ban**-yoo pa-ruh duh-fees-**yeñtsh***

**is there a wheelchair accessible entrance?**
há uma entrada para cadeiras de rodas?
*a **oo**-muh en-**tra**-duh pa-ruh ka-**day**-rush duh **roh**-dush*

**is it possible to visit ... in a wheelchair?**
pode-se visitar ... numa cadeira de rodas?
*pod-suh vee-zee-tar ... **noo**-muh ka-**day**-ruh duh **roh**-dush*

**is there a reduction for the disabled?**
há desconto para deficientes?
*a dush-**koñ**-too **pa**-ruh duh-fees-**yeñtsh***

**I need a bedroom on the ground floor**
preciso dum quarto no rés-do-chão
*pruh-**see**-zoo dooñ **kwar**-too noo rezh-doo-**showñ***

**I use a wheelchair**
uso cadeira de rodas
***oo**-soo ka-**day**-ruh duh **roh**-dush*

**where is the lift?**
onde é o elevador?
***oñ**-duh e oo ee-luh-va-**dor***

*talking talking talking*

# WITH KIDS

*Portugal is a very family-orientated country and children are a focal point of activities. It is not unusual to see children out until quite late in town squares, at café-bars and in restaurants with their families, and they are very well behaved. There are child discounts for train travel, at many attractions and at most hotels.*

**PRIORITY FOR:**
**DISABLED**
**PREGNANT**
**THOSE**
**CARRYING**
**BABIES**

**CHILDREN'S PLAYGROUND ▼**

▼ *Piso rebaixado* Floor lowers (to help those with prams)

**a child ticket, please**
um bilhete de criança, por favor
*ooñ beel-yet duh kree-an-suh poor fa-vor*

**he/she is ... years old**
ele/ela tem ... anos
*el/el-uh tayñ ... a-noosh*

**is there a reduction for children?**
fazem descontos para crianças?
*fa-zayñ dush-kon-toosh pa-ruh kree-an-sush*

**do you have ...?**
tem...?
*tayñ...*

**a high chair**
uma cadeira alta
*oo-muh ka-day-ruh*

**a cot**
um berço
*ooñ behr-soo*

**do you sell...?**
vende...
*vend...*

**nappies**
fraldas
*fral-dush*

**baby wipes**
toalhitas
*twal-yee-tush*

**dummies**
chupetas
*shoo-pet-ush*

**is it ok to give to children?**
pode-se dar às crianças?
*pod-suh dar ash kree-añ-sush*

**a small portion**
uma porção pequena
*oo-muh por-sowñ puh-kay-nuh*

**is there a play park near here?**
há um parque infantil perto daqui?
*a ooñ park een-fan-teel pehr-too dah-kee*

talking

# HEALTH

You should fill in an E111 form before you leave the UK.
They are available from post offices and should be stamped
by them. This form entitles you to free care from a doctor and
dentist in an emergency. If you are charged for treatment, including
consultations, get a receipt to claim back your costs once in the
UK. (See p. 72 for more information on hospitals.) For minor
ailments, try the **Farmácia** (Pharmacy) in the first instance.

▲ **HEALTH CENTRE**

Duty chemist rotas are available from
Tourist offices and in free English-
language newspapers in tourist areas. ▼

▲ Duty chemist notices
for Saturday (*Sábado*)
and Sunday (*Domingo*)

Green cross
pharmacy sign ▼

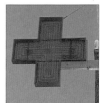

**where is the nearest chemist?**
onde é a farmácia mais perto?
*oñ-duh e uh far-**ma**-see-uh mysh **pehr**-too*

**have you something for...?**
tem alguma coisa para...
*tayñ al-**goo**-muh **koy**-zuh pa-ruh...*

**heartburn**
a azia
*uh a-**zee**-uh*

**mosquito bites**
picadas de mosquitos
*pee-**ka**-dush duh moosh-**kee**-toosh*

**diarrhoea**
a diarreia
*uh dee-uh-**ray**-uh*

**I need...**
preciso de...
*pruh-**see**-zoo duh...*

**antihistamine**
antihistamínico
*an-tee-ees-ta-**mee**-nee-koo*

**antibiotics**
antibióticos
*an-tee-bee-**ot**-ee-koosh*

**◀ DENTAL CLINIC**

CLÍNICA DENTÁRIA
BENTO FERREIRA
BOCA e DENTES — *mouth & teeth*

▶ You can call an ambulance using the emergency number 112.

**I don't feel well**
não me sinto bem
*nowñ muh **seeñ**-too bayñ*

**he/she is ill**
ele/ela está doente
*el/**el**-uh shta doo-**ent***

**I need a doctor**
preciso dum médico
*pruh-**see**-zoo dooñ **med**-ee-koo*

**can the doctor come here?**
o médico pode vir aqui?
*oo **med**-ee-koo pod veer a-**kee***

**my son/my daughter has a very high temperature**
o meu filho/a minha filha tem febre muito alta
*oo **may**-oo **feel**-yoo/uh **meen**-yuh **feel**-yuh tayñ **feb**-ruh **al**-tuh*

**he/she has a rash**
ele/ela tem uma irritação de pele
*el/**el**-uh tayñ **oo**-muh ee-ree-tuh-sowñ duh pel*

**he/she has been sick**
ele/ela vomitou
*el/**el**-uh voh-**mee**-toh*

**I have a pain here**
doi-me aqui
***doy**-muh a-**kee***

**I am on this medication**
estou a tomar este remédio
*shtoh a too-**mar** esht ruh-**med**-yoo*

**I'm pregnant**
estou grávida
*shtoh **gra**-vee-duh*

**I am on the pill**
tomo a pílula
***toh**-moo uh **pee**-loo-luh*

**I'm breastfeeding**
estou a amamentar
*shtoh uh a-ma-men-**tar***

**I have cystitis**
tenho cistite
*ten-yoo seesh-**teet***

**I'm diabetic**
sou diabético(a)
*soh dee-uh-**bet**-ee-koo(-kuh)*

**I am allergic to...**
sou alérgico(a) a...
*soh a-**ler**-zhee-koo(-kuh) a...*

**I have high blood pressure**
tenho a tensão alta
***ten**-yoo uh ten-**sowñ** al-tuh*

**are there any contra-indications?**
tem contra-indicações?
*tayñ **koñ**-truh-een-dee-kuh-**soyñsh***

**I need a receipt for my insurance**
preciso dum recibo para o seguro
*pruh-**see**-zoo dooñ ruh-**see**-boo **pa**-ruh oo suh-**goo**-roo*

**I need a dentist**
preciso dum dentista
*pruh-**see**-zoo dooñ den-**tees**-tuh*

**I have toothache**
tenho uma dor de dentes
***ten**-yoo **oo**-muh dor duh dentsh*

**my filling has come out**
caiu-me o chumbo
*ka-**yoo**-muh oo **shooñ**-boo*

**can your repair the dentures?**
pode reparar a dentadura?
*pod ruh-pa-**rar** uh den-tuh-**doo**-ruh*

talking talking talking talking talking

*The Accident and Emergency department (**Serviço de Urgência**) in Portugal works in a similar way to the UK. Be prepared to complete a number of forms in reception – take your passport and other documents, and your E111 with you.*

visitors —
blood unit —
chapel —

▲ Hospital departments directory board

**ACCIDENT AND EMERGENCY ▼**

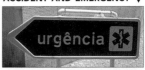

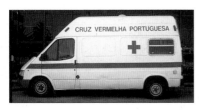

◀ Red Cross ambulance

---

## If you need to go to hospital

**will he/she have to go to hospital?**
tem que ir para o hospital?
*tayñ kuh eer **pa**-ruh oo osh-pee-**tal***

**where is the hospital?**
onde é o hospital?
***oñ**-duh e oo osh-pee-**tal***

**where is the nearest A&E department?**
onde é o serviço de urgência mais perto?
***oñ**-duh e oo suhr-**vee**-soo duh oor-**zhen**-see-uh mysh **pehr**-too*

**please take me to the hospital**
leve-me ao hospital, por favor
***lev**-muh ow osh-pee-**tal** poor fa-**vor***

**I need to go to A&E**
preciso de ir ao serviço de urgência
*pruh-**see**-zoo deer ow suhr-**vee**-soo duh oor-**zhen**-see-uh*

**when are visiting hours?**
quais são as horas de visita?
*kwysh sowñ ush **o**-rush duh **vee**-zee-tuh*

**which ward?**
qual é a enfermaria?
*kwal e uh en-fuhr-**ma**-ree-uh*

**can you explain what the problem is?**
pode explicar qual é o problema?
*pod eks-plee-**kar** kwal e oo proo-**bleh**-muh*

# EMERGENCY

The emergency number 112 connects you to any of the emergency services (**Polícia, Bombeiros, Ambulância**). It is operated in Portuguese, French and English. There are several branches of the police: **GNR** (National Guard, military); **PSP** (Public Security Police), **Brigâda de Trânsito** (Traffic Police), the **PJ** (Crimefighters) and **Guarda Fiscal** (Customs & Excise).

◀ PSP and (far left) GNR stations

*Bombeiros* fire brigade ▶

| | | |
|---|---|---|
| **help!** | **can you help me!** | |
| socorro! | pode-me ajudar? | |
| *soo-**kor**-roo* | ***pod**-muh a-joo-**dar*** | |
| **call...** | **the police** | **an ambulance** |
| chame... | a polícia | uma ambulância |
| *shahm...* | *uh poo-**lees**-yuh* | *oo-muh am-boo-**lans**-yuh* |
| **there's a fire!** | **call the fire brigade!** | |
| há fogo! | chame os bombeiros! | |
| *a **foh**-goo* | *sham oosh bom-**bay**-roosh* | |
| **someone has stolen my...** | **my money** | **my passport** |
| roubaram-me... | o dinheiro | o passaporte |
| *roh-**ba**-rowñ-muh...* | *oo deen-**yay**-roo* | *oo pas-sa-**port*** |

**here are my insurance details**
aqui está o meu seguro
*a-**kee** shta oo **may**-oo suh-**goo**-roo*

**how much is the fine?**
quanto é a multa?
***kwañ**-too e uh **mool**-tuh*

**I'm lost**
estou perdido(a)
*shtoh puhr-**dee**-doo(-duh)*

**I've been raped**
fui violado(a)
*fwee vee-oh-**lah**-doo(-duh)*

**where is the police station?**
onde é a esquadra?
*oñ-duh e uh **shkwa**-druh*

**I want to report a theft**
quero participar um roubo
***keh**-roo par-tee-see-**par** ooñ **roh**-boo*

**my car has been broken into**
assaltaram-me o carro
*sa-sal-**ta**-rown-muh oo **kar**-roo*

**I need a report for my insurance**
preciso dum relatório para o meu seguro
*pruh-**see**-zoo dooñ ruh-la-**tor**-yoo **pa**-ruh oo **may**-oo suh-**goo**-roo*

*talking talking talking talking talking*

# FOOD
## AND
# DRINK

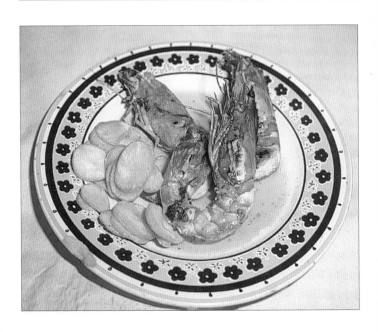

# PORTUGUESE FOOD

In Portugal you can expect to find excellent meals at reasonable prices. The Portuguese are very fond of their food, and good places to eat, whether at the higher or lower end of the price range, will always be well patronised by locals – a good indication for visitors.

Breakfast (**pequeno-almoço**) is mostly milky coffee, a roll with butter and perhaps some ham or cheese. It may be taken at a cafeteria on the way to work, to save time.

A mid-morning break might call for another coffee with a cake.

Lunch (**almoço**) is served from 1pm and may be simply bean or vegetable soup with a roll, eaten standing in a café, cafeteria or patisserie (**pastelaria**) if time is short. Many people prefer a proper lunch, usually of soup, a meat or fish dish with vegetables and salad, and dessert (fruit, ice-cream or pudding), with wine, beer or fruit juice and followed by strong coffee.

Dinner (**jantar**), served after 7 or 7.30pm, follows the same pattern as lunch. Portions are large, so don't order too much to begin with. Some restaurants will serve half-portions or allow two people to share.

◀ Salt cod is found everywhere in Portugal. It needs soaking before cooking, when it can be served in innumerable ways. If you are uncertain of the taste, try the dishes below.

▲ **Bacalhau com natas** Salt-cod with cream

▲ **Pastéis de bacalhau** Salt-cod cakes

**Bacalhau com batatas**
▼ Salt-cod with potatoes

▲ **Sapateira** Dressed crab

*Portuguese food is generally uncomplicated yet very flavour-some and distinctive. Fish dominates some menus (grilled, fried, poached and sometimes baked) but there is also ample choice of meat dishes, including steak, lamb or kid (stewed and roasted), pork (a favourite meat), game and poultry. Freshly mixed salad laced with the local olive oil is a favourite accompaniment to almost anything in addition to the potatoes, rice or vegetables that may form part of the dish. Every dish (fish, meat or eggs) will always be served with some kind of accompaniment.*

▼ **Porco Assado** Roast Pork

Bread is served at every meal in Portugal, along with butter ▲ and other spreads. You will generally be charged for these items only if you eat them. There are many kinds of bread and larger loaves; look out also for maize (polenta) loaves, called **broa**.

**where can I/we have a snack?**
onde se pode comer alguma coisa?
*on-duh suh pod koo-**mehr** al-**goo**-muh **koy**-zuh*

**can you recommend a good local restaurant?**
pode recomendar um bom restaurante local?
*pod ruh-koo-men-**dar** ooñ boñ rush-toh-**rant** loo-**kal***

**how do we get to the restaurant?**
como se vai para o restaurante?
*koh-moo suh vy **pa**-ruh oo rush-toh-**rant***

**are there any vegetarian restaurants here?**
há algum restaurante vegetariano aqui?
*a al-**gooñ** rush-toh-**rant** vuh-zhuh-tuhr-**yah**-noo a-**kee***

**do I need to book?**
preciso de reservar?
*pruh-**see**-zoo duh ruh-ser-**var***

**what do you recommend?**
o que recomenda?
*oo kuh ruh-koo-men-**men**-duh*

talking talking talking

*It is common to be served small cheeses (fresh or dried) as a starter to go with the wonderful Portuguese bread and rolls. Cheeses are made from ewes' milk, goats' milk or a mixture of the two. Desserts can be either fresh fruit in season, ice cream or pudding – usually sweet and rich, made with lots of eggs.*

**pudim flan**
poo-**deeñ** flan
crème
caramel

**queijo fresco**
**kay**-zhoo
**fresh**-koo
fresh cheese

**fruta**
**froo**-tuh
fruit

**bolo**
**boh**-loo
cake

**mais nada**
mysh **nah**-duh
nothing else

◀ *Torta de laranja* orange roll (left)
*Pastéis de nata* custard cakes

*Bolos de amêndoa*
▼ *Almond cakes*

◀ *Bolo de arroz* Rice cake

**I'd like a drink**
queria uma bebida
**kree**-uh **oo**-muh buh-**bee**-duh

**I'd like a ... please**
queria um/uma ... por favor
**kree**-uh ooñ/**oo**-muh ... poor fa-**vor**

**what would you like?**
que quer tomar?
kuh kehr too-**mar**

**a white coffee**
um café com leite
ooñ kuh-**fe** koñ layt

**an espresso**
um café
ooñ kuh-**fe**

**a decaff coffee**
um café descafeinado
ooñ kuh-**fe** dush-ka-fay-**nah**-doo

**a hot chocolate**
um chocolate quente
ooñ shoo-koo-**laht** keñt

**a tea with milk**
um chá com leite
ooñ sha koñ layt

**with toast**
com torradas
koñ toor-**rah**-dush

**an orange juice**
um sumo de laranja
ooñ **soo**-moo duh luh-**rañ**-zhuh

**a strawberry milkshake**
um batido de morangos
ooñ ba-**tee**-doo duh moo-**rañ**-goosh

**a half bottle of white wine**
meia garrafa de vinho branco
**may**-uh gar-**rah**-fuh duh **veen**-yoo **brañ**-koo

**a lager**
uma cerveja
**oo**-muh suhr-**vay**-zhuh

**a bottle of mineral water**
uma garrafa de água mineral
**oo**-muh gar-**rah**-fuh **dahg**-wuh mee-nuh-**ral**

**sparkling**
com gás
koñ gas

**still**
sem gás
sayñ gas

▲ In the tourist towns of the Algarve it can be difficult to find a great variety in ice-creams (*gelados*).

◀ Popular *Bolo Podre* (rotten cake – the name coming from the cake's dark colour) is made with honey, olive oil and aniseed. It comes from the Ribatejo and Alentejo provinces where olive oil is produced.

▲ *Sandes e sumo* Sandwiches and juice
Served at cafés and snack bars

**talking**

**can we eat?**
podemos comer?
*poo-day-mosh koo-mehr*

**do you have a dish of the day?**
tem prato do dia?
*tayñ prah-too doo dee-uh*

**what sandwiches do you have?**
que sandes tem?
*kuh santsh tayñ*

**I'd like an ice cream**
queria um gelado
*kree-yuh ooñ zhuh-lah-doo*

**a table for two**
uma mesa para dois
*oo-muh may-zuh pa-ruh doysh*

**what is the dish of the day?**
qual é o prato do dia?
*kwal e oo prah-too doo dee-uh*

**what cakes do you have?**
que bolos tem?
*kuh boh-loosh tayñ*

**what flavours do you have?**
que sabores tem?
*kuh suh-boh-rush tayñ*

*In Portugal, many restaurants close on Sunday or Monday, so check beforehand if there is a place you particularly want to eat. As usual, popular restaurants are best booked in advance. All establishments are required by law to display their prices outside, so you will be prepared for the cost before going in.*

▲ 1a on the sign outside denotes a first-class restaurant.

There are specialist shellfish restaurants (*marisqueira*) in both seaside and inland towns, but ordinary restaurants will also have a range of shellfish dishes. ▼

RESTAURANTE ESPLANADA BAR — *open-air*

A *Casa de Pasto* is a modest restaurant serving homely food.
▶

CASA DE PASTO

**I'd like to book a table**
queria reservar uma mesa
*kree-uh ruh-zer-var oo-muh may-zuh*

**for tonight**
para esta noite
*pa-ruh esh-tuh noyt*

**for lunch**
para o almoço
*pa-ruh oo al-moh-soo*

**for dinner**
para o jantar
*pa-ruh oo zhun-tar*

**in a non-smoking area**
em zona de não-fumador
*ayñ zoh-nuh duh nowñ-foo-muh-dor*

**for ... people**
para ... pessoas
*pa-ruh ... puh-so-ush*

**for tomorrow night**
para amanhã à noite
*pa-ruh a-man-yañ a noyt*

**at mid-day**
ao meio-dia
*ow may-oo-dee-uh*

**at 8 o'clock**
às oito
*ash oy-too*

**in the name of Smith**
em nome de Smith
*ayñ nom duh smith*

*Especialidades Tostas Mistas*
— *Cheese and ham toasted sandwiches are a speciality!*

◀ A *Casa das Tostas* is a snack-bar selling toasted sandwiches, a very popular snack.

*Churrascarias* (also spelt *churrasqueira*) are popular take-away establishments which sell *frango à Piri-piri*, or *frango de churrasco*
▼ (barbecued chicken with chilli sauce), a legacy from the ex-colony of Mozambique and now adapted to European tastes.

**where should we sit?**
onde podemos sentar-nos?
*oñ-duh poo-**day**-moosh señ-**tar**-noosh*

**the menu, please**
a ementa, por favor
*uh ee-**men**-tuh poor fa-**vor***

**the wine list, please**
a lista de vinhos, por favor
*uh **leesh**-tuh duh **veen**-yoosh poor fa-**vor***

**can you recommend a local dish?**
pode recomendar uma especialidade local?
*pod ruh-koo-men-**dar** **oo**-muh shpuss-yalee-**dahd** loo-**kal***

**what is this?**
o que é isto?
*oo kuh e **eesh**-too*

**I'll have this**
quero isto
***keh**-roo **eesh**-too*

**is it good?**
é bom?
*e boñ*

**do you have any vegetarian dishes?**
tem algum prato vegetariano?
*tayñ al-**gooñ** **prah**-too vay-zhuh-tuhr-**yah**-noo*

**more bread, please**
mais pão, por favor
*mysh powñ poor fa-**vor***

**more butter, please**
mais manteiga, por favor
*mysh muhn-**tay**-guh poor fa-**vor***

**the bill, please**
a conta, por favor
*uh **koñ**-tuh poor favor*

**we would like to pay separately**
queremos pagar separadamente
*kuh-**reh**-moosh puh-**gar** suh-pa-rah-duh-**ment***

talking talking talking talking

*Many restaurants offer an **Ementa Turística**, a set menu with a few choices, usually including traditional cuisine, offering an excellent way of eating well and cheaply. Check if wine is included. **Pratos do Dia**, or Dish of the Day, is another menu heading to look out for. This type of menu uses fresh ingredients daily, and meals are served speedily.*

## ADEGA NORTENHA
### PRATOS DO DIA

Dishes of the Day

**Conquilhas/Amêijoas** Cockles/Clams
**Dobrada feijão branco**
Tripe with beans (stew)
**Massinha corvina** Sea bream pasta
**Iscas à Portuguesa**
Liver Portuguese style
**Bifes Atum Cebolada**
Tuna steaks in onion and tomato sauce
**Pescada c/ (= com) feijão verde**
Poached hake with green beans
**Sardinhas p/ (= para) assar** Grilled sardines
**Carapau p/ assar**
Grilled horse mackerel
**Sargo p/ grelhar** Grilled sea bream
**Eirós p/ grelhar** Grilled large eel
**Bacalhau p/ assar** Baked salt-cod
**Carapau (arr.) conquilhas (arroz de)**
Horse mackerel with cockles risotto
**Eirós c/ arroz de conquilhas** Large eel with cockles risotto

◀ You will often be given fairly substantial appetisers before the meal you have ordered arrives.

*Look out for **açordas** in Portuguese restaurants. These are homely dishes which are very popular in family-run restaurants. They consist of bread cooked with herbs (such as coriander and garlic), sometimes served with fried or grilled fish. They can also be main dishes in their own right. It is worth trying these local specialities as they are extremely tasty, although not necessarily elegant to look at. This is comfort food at its best.*

**Açorda de gambas**
*Large prawns in thick bread soup*
**Atum cebolada**
*Tuna in onion and tomato sauce*
**Picanha fatiada**
*Sliced beef*
**Bifes do lombo:** *Fillet steak*
**A Porto fino:** *with fine Port sauce*
**Tropical:** *with a spicy sauce*
**Ao pimenta:** *with a pepper sauce*
**Cogumelos e natas:** *with a mushroom and cream sauce*

A traditional set menu
As it does not mention bread, butter, wine or water, these items may be charged for separately, along with taxes.

▶

Menu

## ementa

Traditional kale, potato and **chouriço** soup ———— caldo verde

\*

Baked salt-cod with potatoes ———— bacalhau assado no forno com batatas
and    e
Special dish for children ———— prato especial p/a criança

\*

Fruit salad ———— salada de fruta

\*

Coffee ———— café

# TEA & COFFEE

*Coffee in Portugal is generally good, although the quality can be mixed in hotels. If you want a small, strong, espresso-like coffee, ask for **um café** or **uma bica**. A small, white coffee, is called **um garoto** (or **um pingo**, in the Oporto area). A regular-size milky cup will be **uma chávena de café com leite** or **uma meia de leite**. That same size cup of black coffee will be **um duplo** – a double. A large white coffee is called **um galão**, and is served in a tall glass. If you prefer your coffee with less milk ask for it to be **escuro** – dark. Tea is, of course, available as well but will be on the weak side and without milk or lemon. If wanting it strong, ask for **chá forte** (strong tea). For milk, ask for **leite frio** to avoid being served hot milk. Lemon is **limão**. Herb tea is **tisana**. A very pleasant, fragrant caffeine-free beverage is **chá de limão** (lemon tea), consisting of boiling water poured over lemon rind. Drinking chocolate, hot or cold (**chocolate quente/frio**) is another option. In Lisbon, the chocolate at Nicola's, the famous tea/coffee house, is a must.*

▲ Specialist tea and coffee shops stock a great variety of those products, but especially coffee – Portugal's preferred drink. ▶

People go to cafés all day long, for their caffeine fix and for socialising. Cafés also serve snacks and simple meals.

▶

# BEER

*Despite the high consumption of wine, beer is a common drink, the most popular being **Sagres** and **Super Bock**. Portuguese beer is served chilled, often with a savoury snack. In Portugal beer is lager. There is no such distinction as lager, ale, bitter, etc. Draught beer is stronger (over 4%) and is sold at beer houses, **cervejarias**, where you can also find food, as a rule. A small glass of draught beer is **um fino** or **uma imperial**. A tankard (approx. 1 pint) is **uma caneca** and a litre tankard is **uma girafa**. You can also find dark ale (**cerveja preta**), bottled.*

▲ Popular beer varieties.
◀ You can also find all the big names from Britain, Germany and elsewhere, usually produced under licence in Portugal. There are now British-style pubs in more tourist areas. These will have imported stout (Guinness) and other imported beers.

▲ *Cervejaria*
Beer houses normally serve food, which is often excellent. Some are particularly well-known for their steak, normally served with a fried egg on top, and plenty of gravy-like sauce, with very good chips.

**can you recommend a good beer house?**
pode recomendar uma boa cervejaria?
*pod ruh-koo-men-**dar** ooñ **boh**-uh suhr-vay-zhar-**ee**-uh*

**I'd like a beer**
queria uma cerveja
*kree-uh oo-muh suhr-**vay**-zhuh*

**what beers do you have?**
que cervejas tem?
*kuh suhr-**vay**-zhush tayñ*

**a small beer**
uma imperial
*oo-muh eeñ-pehr-**yal***

**a pint of beer**
uma caneca
*oo-muh kuh-**nay**-kuh*

**a litre of beer**
uma girafa
*oo-muh zhee-**rah**-fuh*

talking

# WINE

*A great effort on the part of winemakers and producers over the last 15 years or so has placed Portuguese wines on a par with some of the best that Europe has to offer. Instead of concentrating mainly on the large internal market, they are now successfully producing a great variety of wines taking into account foreign trends as well. This, together with the natural flair of very competent winemakers and the quality of a vast number of interesting native grapes (with a small percentage of international varieties, such as Cabernet Sauvignon, Merlot, Pinot Noir and Chardonnay) translates into intriguing wines, generally very fruity and easy on the palate. In fact, one of the joys in Portugal is discovering its delicious wines, ideal partners to the country's flavoursome food. Restaurants will have a comprehensive wine list (**Lista dos vinhos**) but normally their house-wine (**Vinho da casa**) is trustworthy, despite its low price. This may be served in a jug, but is often bottled privately for that establishment, perhaps from vineyards belonging to the owner's family.*

*Red wine is the best, although there are many worthwhile exceptions, such as the lemony and zesty Vinho Verde (e.g. Aveleda), from the Minho region, highly suitable for seafood and for drinking on its own, well chilled. In other regions, some splendid whites are made from Bical grape, Arinto and Fernão Pires (known also as Maria Gomes). As a rule, whites are better drunk young.*

Douro table wines are normally red, made from the same grapes as port and by the same producers. They are rich and elegant, smooth and fruity, with excellent body and good tannins. They include varieties such as Quinta do Crasto, Poças, Cockburns and many others. Douro is a DOC region (**denominação de origem controlada**), meaning that it must follow very stringent controls and use only native grapes.

◀

◀ Dão, an old classic region, is improving, with more modern, interesting wines than in previous years.

Regional wines are also subject to tight controls but allow some use of grapes other than native ones, which adds extra interest. However, some are single-grape varieties, such as Bairrada's Baga, perfect for drinking with the local dish of sucking pig.

Bairrada belongs to the large Beiras region, three provinces which offer, between them, exciting, complex wines. The region also produces a number of reasonably good champagne-type wines (*espumantes*), from very dry to sweet, such as Raposeira.

Luis Pato

Vinha Pan

2000

VINHO REGIONAL
BEIRAS

*Criado e engarrafado por
Luis Pato, Anadia, Portugal*

PRODUCE OF PORTUGAL

**keywords keywords keywords**

**vinho branco**
*veen-yoo brañ-koo*
white wine

**vinho tinto**
*veen-yoo teeñ-too*
red wine

**velho**
*vel-yoo*
mature

**seco**
*seh-koo*
dry

**doce**
*dohs*
sweet

**encorpado**
*en-kor-pah-doo*
full-bodied

**natural**
*nah-too-ral*
at room temperature

**fresco**
*fresh-koo*
chilled

**the wine list, please**
a lista de vinhos, por favor
*uh leesh-tuh duh veen-yoosh poor fa-vor*

**what wines do you have?**
que vinhos tem?
*kuh veen-yoosh tayñ*

**what are the local wines?**
quais são os vinhos da região?
*kwysh sowñ oosh veen-yoosh duh ruh-zhowñ*

**can you recommend a good wine?**
pode recomendar um bom vinho?
*pod ruh-koo-meñ-dar ooñ boñ veen-yoo*

**a glass of red wine**
um copo de vinho tinto
*ooñ ko-poo duh veen-yoo teeñ-too*

**a glass of white wine**
um copo de vinho branco
*ooñ ko-poo duh veen-yoo brañ-koo*

**a bottle of...**
uma garrafa de...
*oo-muh guh-rra-fuh duh...*

**red wine**
vinho tinto
*veen-yoo teeñ-too*

**white wine**
vinho branco
*veen-yoo brañ-koo*

**another bottle**
outra garrafa
*oh-truh guh-rra-fuh*

**another glass**
outro copo
*oh-troo koh-poo*

**a glass of port**
um cálice de Porto
*ooñ kah-lee-suh duh por-too*

**talking talking talking**

The Ribatejo region, in the centre of Portugal, has a long-standing wine-making tradition. Favoured grapes include Trincadeira Preta and Castelão, also known as Periquita, which practically guarantee excellent wines, such as those by Casa Cadaval, Falua, DFJ and many other producers.

Estremadura, North of Lisbon, and the vast Alentejo region, are home to outstanding, plummy wines, with a judicious amount of oak. In Estremadura look out for wines from Alenquer, Torres Vedras, Colares and Bucelas. Reguengos, Borba and Vidigueira are some of the areas of the Alentejo where modern winemakers have been producing remarkable wines. Esporão, Cartuxa, Quinta do Carmo and Chaminé are among the region's prestigious names. South of Lisbon, the Setúbal peninsula is flanked by Terras do Sado and Palmela, with spicy, very drinkable red wines, and the excellent João Pires white. Setúbal itself is famous for its Moscatel fortified wine, made from locally grown Muscat grapes. The Alambre range is particularly good.

**is this wine produced here?**
este vinho é produzido aqui?
*esht **veen**-yoo e proh-doo-**zee**-doo a-**kee***

**is it possible to visit any vineyards?**
é possível visitar uma vinha?
*e poos-**see**-vel vee-zee-**tar** oo-muh **veen**-yuh*

Within the fortified category, Madeira and Port wines are specific to Portugal and have a long tradition associated with the UK. These wines are ideal for many occasions, from aperitif to cheese and dessert, and also with some foods, such as pâté, game, cured meats, roasts and smoked fish, as well as dried fruits, nuts and chocolate. Madeira wines comprise four styles (Sercial, Verdelho, Boal and Malvasia, or Malmsey), from dry to sweet. Their extraordinary bouquet and length makes them very special and their unique maturation system gives them exceptional keeping qualities.

Port wines can be white (dry to sweet) – these should be chilled – or red (Ruby, Tawny and Vintage). Other categories are LBV (late bottled vintage), Vintage Character, and so on. Read the label or ask for guidance. Tawnys (semi-sweet to sweet) are perhaps the most popular. The best indicate their age (10, 20, 30 years), reflected in price and quality. Grapes for Port (many exclusive to the region) are grown along the spectacular, forbidding slopes of the Douro river, in the north of Portugal. This was the very first demarcated wine region in the world, back in 1756, and is also the most difficult to cultivate.

**Caldo verde** Soup made with kale, pot[ato], olive oil and chouriço
**Pastéis de bacalhau** Salt cod cakes
**Arroz de pato** (Braga) Duck with rice
**Rojões** Cubes of marinated pork spiced with cumin
**Broa** Maize bread
**Pudim Abade de Priscos** Egg pudding flavoured with port
**Sopa dourada** Dessert of sponge cake, ground almonds and egg yolks
**Wines** vinho verde Alvarinho, Aveleda

**Rancho** Thick soup made with assorted meats, vegetables and pasta
**Bacalhau à lagareiro com batatas à murro** Baked salt cod and baked potatoes, soaked in olive oil
**Açordas** Bread dishes generally with cured meats, salt cod or shellfish
**Caldeirada de enguias** Eel stew
**Leitão assado à Bairrada** Roast suckling pig from Bairrada region
**Chanfana** Rich lamb stew
**Queijo da Serra** Buttery ewes' cheese from Estrela Mountain
**Arroz doce** Rice pudding
**Ovos moles** Soft egg sweet (yolks and sugar)
**Pastéis de Tentúgal** Egg-filled pastries
**Wines** Bical, Baga (Bairrada), Dão

**Sopa de pedra** Stone soup: meat, bean and vegetable soup
**Favas à moda do Ribatejo** Broad beans with pork, cured meats, garlic and coriander
**Cabrito assado** Roast kid
**Fatias de Tomar** Sponge slices in syrup
**Tigeladas de Abrantes** Baked egg custard
**Wines** Reds: Segada, Senda do Vale, Quinta de Lagoalva

**Açorda de marisco** Shellfish bread dish
**Rissóis de camarão** Creamy prawn rissoles
**Sardinhas assadas** Char-grilled sardines served with boiled potatoes and a tomato, onion and roast pepper salad
**Salmonetes grelhados** Grilled mullet with a butter and lemon sauce
**Amêijoas à Bulhão Pato** Clams with garlic and fresh coriander
**Bacalhau à Brás** Salt cod with onion and potatoes, bound with eggs

**Bife à café** Steak in creamy sauce topped with a fried egg
**Pastéis de nata** Rich custard tarts
**Queijadas de Sintra** Cheese and cinnamon cakes
**Wines** Periquita, Torres Vedras, J.M. Fonseca and Moscatel (Muscat) from Setúbal

PORTUGAL

•Braga
TRÁS-C[...]
MINHO
•Vila Real
Porto •

•Aveiro
BEIRAS

•Coimbra

•Leiria
ESTREMADURA
•Cast[elo]
Bran[co]

RIBATEJO
•Santarém

Lisboa
•Évora
Setúbal
TERRAS
DO SADO
ALENTEJO
•Beja

ALGARVE
Faro •

**Sopa de castanhas** *Chestnut soup with beans and rice*
**Feijoada** *Bean stew with pork*
**Cozido à Portuguesa** *Assorted fresh and cured meats cooked with vegetables*
**Presunto de Chaves** *Smoked cured ham from Chaves*
**Queijo do Monte** *Rich ewes' cheese*
**Nozes** *Walnuts*
**Azeite** *Olive oil*

**Sopa de moganga** *Pumpkin soup*
**Atum salpresado** *Salted tuna steak with red beans, sweet potatoes, corn and salad*
**Cavalas com molho de vilão** *Marinated, fried mackerel in vinegar sauce*
**Cozido à madeirense** *Boiled assorted fresh and cured meats and vegetables*
**Espetada** *Large kebab shared among the people at the table*
**Milho frito** *Fried polenta*
**Bolo de mel da Madeira** *Dark and spicy cake with molasses and nuts*
**Wine** *Madeira (Sercial, Verdelho, Bual, Malmsey)*

**Sopa azeda** *Sour soup with a dash of vinegar*
**Arroz de lapas** *Limpet rice*
**Garoupa recheada** *Stuffed grouper*
**Polvo guisado** *Stewed octopus*
**Alcatra** *Beef braised slowly in wine*
**Inhame** *Yam*
**Pudim de coalhada** *Rich cheesecake*
**Covilhetes de leite** *Custard tarts from Terceira Island*
**Wine** *Verdelho (Pico and Biscoitos)*

MADEIRA

Funchal

AZORES

**Sopa à alentejana** *Bread soup with garlic, coriander and poached egg*
**Migas** *Omelette-like bread dish generally with cured meats*
**Empadas de galinha** *Chicken pies (Évora)*
**Ensopado de borrego** *Rich lamb stew on bread slices*
**Carne de porco na cataplana** *Marinated pork cooked with clams in a cataplana*
**Bolos podres** *Cakes made with honey, olive oil and spices*
**Queijadas** *Cheese tartlets*
**Queijo de Nisa** *Strong ewes' milk cheeses*
**Queijinhos de Évora** *Small and delicious ewes' milk cheeses from Évora*
**Wines** *Cartuxa, Esporão, Cortes de Cima*

**Choquinhos com tinta** *Squid in its own ink*
**Amêijoas na cataplana** *Clams cooked with chouriço in a cataplana*
**Lulas recheadas** *Small stuffed squid*
**Arjamolho** *Gaspacho soup*
**Bolos de Dom Rodrigo** *Egg cakes in syrup*
**Bolinhos de amêndoa** *Almond cakes in fruit shapes, with egg filling*
**Morgado de figo** *Pressed dried spicy figs*
**Figos cheios** *Dried figs stuffed with almonds*

*There are times when you cannot eat some things. It is as well warning the waiter before making your choice.*

talking talking talking talking talking talking talking

**I'm vegetarian**
sou vegetariano(a)
*soh vuh-zhay-tuhr-yah-noo(-nuh)*

**I don't eat meat/pork**
não como carne/porco
*nown koh-moo karn/por-koo*

**I don't eat fish/shellfish**
não como peixe/marisco
*nown koh-moo paysh/muh-reesh-koo*

**I'm allergic to shellfish**
sou alérgico(a) a marisco
*soh a-lehr-zhee-koo(-kuh) uh muh-reesh-koo*

**I can't eat raw eggs**
não posso comer ovos crus
*nown pos-soo koo-mehr oh-voosh kroosh*

**I am on a diet**
estou de dieta
*shtoh duh dee-yeh-tuh*

**I am allergic to peanuts**
sou alérgico(a) a amendoins
*soh a-lehr-zhee-koo(-kuh) uh a-mayñ-doo-eeñsh*

**I can't eat liver**
não posso comer fígado
*nown pos-soo koo-mehr fee-guh-doo*

**I don't drink alcohol**
não tomo bebidas alcoólicas
*nown toh-moo buh-bee-dush al-koo-ol-ee-kush*

**what is this made with?**
de que é feito?
*duh kuh e fay-too*

**is it raw?**
está cru?
*shta kroo*

**is it made with unpasteurised milk?**
é feito com leite não-pasteurizado?
*e fay-too koñ layt nown-pash-tay-oo-ree-zah-doo*

**is it made with vegetable stock?**
é feito com caldo vegetal?
*e fay-too koñ kal-doo vay-zhuh-tahl*

**frito**
*free-too*
fried

**cozido**
*ko-zee-doo*
boiled

**a vapor**
*uh va-por*
steamed

**assado**
*as-sah-doo*
roast

**molho**
*mol-yoo*
sauce

**recheado**
*ruh-chay-ah-doo*
stuffed

**grelhado**
*gruhl-yah-doo*
grilled

**fumado**
*foo-mah-doo*
smoked

**guisado**
*gee-sah-doo*
stewed

**escalfado**
*shkul-fah-doo*
poached

**estufado**
*shtoo-fah-doo*
braised

**no forno**
*noo for-noo*
cooked in oven

**doce**
*doss*
sweet

**salgado**
*sal-gah-doo*
salty

# MENU READER

## A

**...à caçadora** hunter-style (poultry or game marinated in wine and garlic)

**...à jardineira** garden-style with vegetables like green beans and carrots

**...à lagareiro** baked dish made with lots of olive oil

**...à marinheira** with white wine, onions and parsley

**...à portuguesa** Portuguese fashion, i.e. with tomato sauce

**abacate** avocado

**abóbora** pumpkin
  **sopa de abóbora** pumpkin soup

*abóbora*

**açafrão** saffron

**acelga** swiss chard

**acepipes** appetisers

**acompanhamentos** side dishes

**açorda** typical Portuguese dish with bread
  **açorda com peixe frito** thick bread soup accompanying fried fish
  **açorda de alho** thick bread soup with garlic and beaten egg (generally served with fried fish in traditional restaurants)

**açorda de marisco** thick bread soup with shellfish and a beaten egg, typical of the Lisbon area

**açorda de sável** thick bread soup with shad

**açorda de Sesimbra** thick bread soup with fish, garlic and coriander

**açúcar** sugar

**adocicado** slightly sweet

**agrião** watercress

**água** water
  **água mineral com gás** sparkling mineral water
  **água mineral sem gás** still mineral water

**água tónica** tonic water

**aguardente** brandy
  **velha** old or **velhíssima** very old

**aipo** celery

**albardado** in batter

**alcachofra** artichoke
  **fundo de alcachofra** artichoke heart

**alcaparra** caper

**alcatra** braised beef, typical of the Azores

**alecrim** rosemary

**aletria** fine noodles

*alecrim*

*alho*

**alface** lettuce

**alfenim** moulded sugar, a speciality of the Azores

**alheiras** chicken and garlic sausage from Trás-os-Montes

**alho** garlic

**alho francês** leek

**almoço** lunch

**almôndegas** meatballs

**alperces** apricots

**amargo** bitter

**amarguinha** bitter-almond liqueur made in the Algarve region

**ameĩjoas** clams
 **ameĩjoas à Bulhão Pato** clams with garlic and coriander
 **ameĩjoas ao natural** steamed clams with herbs and lemon butter
 **ameĩjoas na cataplana** clams cooked in a 'cataplan' pot, with *chouriço* and herbs

*bolos de amêndoas*

**ameixa** plum
 **ameixas de Elvas** preserved greengages from Elvas (Alentejo)
 **ameixa seca** prune

**amêndoas** almonds
 **amêndoas doces** sugared almonds

**amendoim** peanut

**amora** blackberry

**ananás** pineapple

**anchovas** anchovies

**aniz** aniseed liqueur

**ao** in the style of

**aperitivo** aperitif

**areias de Cascais** small cookies from Cascais

**arenque** herring

**arjamolho** kind of gazpacho soup, typical of the Algarve

**arroz** rice
 **arroz branco** plain rice
 **arroz de Cabidela** chicken or rabbit highly seasoned risotto

**arroz de ervilhas** pea rice
 **arroz de frango** chicken with rice
 **arroz de lampreia** lamprey with rice
 **arroz de lapas** limpets with rice (typical of the Azores)
 **arroz de manteiga** rice with butter
 **arroz de marisco** shellfish with rice
 **arroz de pato** rice with duck
 **arroz de polvo** octopus with rice
 **arroz de tomate** tomato rice
 **arroz doce** rice pudding Portuguese-style made on top of stove with lemon rind, vanilla and topped with cinnamon
 **arroz no forno** rice cooked in the oven

**arrufadas de Coimbra** sweet buns from Coimbra

**assado** roasted
 **assado no forno** oven-roasted
 **assado no espeto** spit roasted

**asparagos** asparagus

*azeite*

*bacalhau com natas*

**atum** tuna fish
  **atum assado** braised tuna with onions and tomatoes
  **atum de cebolada** tuna steak with onions and tomato sauce
  **atum de conserva** canned tuna
  **atum salpresado** salted tuna dish often eaten during festivities in Madeira
**aveia** oats
**avelã** hazelnut
**aves** fowl
**azeda** sorrel
  **azedas** sharp Azorean soups, containing a little vinegar
**azedo** sour
**azeite** olive oil
**azeitonas** olives
  **preta** black
  **verde** green
**azevias** half-moon shaped cakes

# B

**bacalhau** salt cod

*bacalhau com batatas a murro*

**bacalhau à Brás** traditional dish with salt cod, onion and potatoes all bound with scrambled eggs
**bacalhau à Gomes de Sá** good salt cod dish with layers of potatoes, onions and boiled eggs, laced with olive oil and baked
**bacalhau à lagareiro** salt cod baked with lots of olive oil
**bacalhau com natas** salt cod in cream sauce au gratin
**bacalhau com todos** salt cod poached with potatoes and vegetables
**bacalhau assado** charcoal-grilled cod
**bacalhau na brasa** salt cod grilled on charcoal, served with olive oil
**bagaceira** brandy similar to eau-de-vie
**banana** banana
**banha** lard
**barriga de freira** a sweet made with yolks and sugar, slightly caramelised
**batata** potato
  **batata doce** sweet potato
  **batata doce assada** baked sweet potato
  **batatas a murro** potatoes baked in their own skins then soaked in olive oil
  **batatas assadas** baked potatoes
  **batatas fritas** chips
  **batatas cozidas** boiled potatoes

*batatas*

**batido** milkshake
 **batido de fruta** fruit milkshake
 **batido de morango** strawberry milkshake

**baunilha** vanilla

**bebida** drink
 **bebida sem álcool/não alcoólica** non-alcoholic drink

**bem passado** well done

**berbigão** cockle

**beringela** aubergine

**besugo** sea bream

**beterraba** beetroot

**bica** strong small black coffee

**bifana** pork tenderloin in a roll

**bife** steak (and chips and perhaps fried egg)
 **...bem passado** well done
 **...mal passado** medium...
 **...muito mal passado** rare
 **bife à café** steak in cream sauce topped with a fried egg (with chips)
 **bife à Portuguesa** steak in mustard sauce topped with a fried egg (with chips)
 **bife do lombo** sirloin steak

**bifes de atum** tuna steaks

**bifes de perú** turkey steaks

**bifinhos de vitela** veal fillet served with Madeira sauce

**biscoitos** biscuits/cookies
 **biscoitos de azeite** olive oil biscuits

**bitoque** small steak with fried egg and chips

**bola** layered bread and cured meat pie

**bola de Berlim** doughnut

**bolachas** biscuits
 **bolachas de água e sal** water biscuits (crackers)

**boleimas** cakes with a bread dough base with olive oil, sugar, eggs and spices

**bolinhos de bacalhau** cod croquettes

**bolo** cake
 **bolo caseiro** homemade cake

*bolo de arroz*

**bolo de arroz** sponge cake made with rice, often eaten at breakfast

**bolo de chocolate** chocolate cake

**bolo de mel** honey cake

**bolo de mel da Madeira** Madeira molasses cake made with lots of spices and eaten traditionally at Christmas

**bolo de Natal** Christmas fruitcake

**bolo podre** delicious dark cake made with honey, olive oil and spices

**bolo rei** a cake-ring made with a sweet dough with dried and crystallised fruits, eaten at Epiphany

**bolos de Dom Rodrigo** cakes made with egg yolks, sugar, almonds and cinnamon, and

*bolo podre*

sold in little pointed foil parcels to keep the syrup inside
**bolos de ovos** egg cakes
**borracho** young pigeon
**borrego** lamb
**branco** white
  **cerveja branca** white beer
  **vinho branco** white wine
**broa** a crusty rustic maize bread
**broas de mel** small honey cakes eaten at Christmas
**broas podres de Natal** small spicy cakes eaten at Christmas
**brócolos** broccoli
**Bucelas** a type of wine from the Estremadura region
**bucho** pork haggis

## C

**cabrito** kid
  **cabrito assado** roast kid with a spiced marinade
  **cabrito frito** fried kid
  **cabrito montês** roebuck
  **cabrito à ribatejana** marinated roast kid with paprika typical of Ribatejo
**caça** game
**cacau** cocoa
**cachorro** hotdog

**cachucho** small sea bream
**café** coffee
  **bica** small, strong black coffee (espresso)
  **carioca** small but slightly weaker black coffee
  **com leite** white coffee
  **duplo** large cup of coffee
  **frio** iced coffee
  **galão** large white coffee served in a tall glass
  **garoto** small white coffee
  **meia de leite** ordinary size cup of half coffee, half milk
  **sem cafeína** decaffeinated
**caipirinha** rum and lemon
**caju** cashew nut
**caldeirada** fish stew
  **caldeirada à fragateira** seafood stew, as prepared by fishermen
  **caldeirada de enguias** eel stew
  **caldeirada de peixe** fish stew
**caldo** broth
  **caldo de carne** beef broth
  **caldo de galinha** chicken broth
  **caldo verde** green broth, made with shredded kale and potatoes with a little *chouriço* and olive oil

*caldo verde*

**camarões** shrimps
**caneca** medium-sized beer glass
**canela** cinnamon
**canja** chicken soup, thickened with rice or small pasta and chicken pieces

**capão** capon

**capilé** drink made with iced coffee, lemon rind and sugar

**caracóis** snails (small, cooked in a tasty broth and served with a toothpick)

**caranguejo** crab

**carapau** horse mackerel, served whole, fried or grilled

**caril** curry

**carioca** small weak coffee

**carioca de limão** lemon infusion

**carne** meat
  **carne assada** roast meat (generally beef, sometimes pork)
  **carne de porco à alentejana** highly seasoned pork dish with clams,typical of the Alentejo
  **carne de vaca** beef
  **carne de vaca assada** roast beef
  **carne de vaca à antiga** marinated roast beef, served with new potatoes (speciality from the Azores)
  **carne de vinha d'alhos** popular festive Madeiran dish, with marinated pork, bread, sweet and new potatoes
  **carnes frias** cold meats

**carneiro** mutton

**casa de chá** tea-house

**casa de pasto** restaurant serving cheap, homely meals

*carapau*

**cataplana** shellfish dish made with pork, pepper, garlic and onion, and cooked in a cataplana pot

**cavala** mackerel
  **cavalas com molho de vilão** marinated and fried mackerel, served with a reduced marinade (Madeiran speciality)

**cebola** onion

**cebolada** fried onion garnish

**cenoura** carrot
  **sopa de puré de cenoura** carrot purée soup

**cereja** cherry

**cerveja** beer/lager
  **cerveja à pressão** draught beer
  **cerveja em garrafa** bottled beer
  **cerveja preta** dark ale

**cervejaria** beer house, serving food

**chá** tea
  **chá com leite** tea with milk
  **chá com limão** tea with lemon
  **chá forte** strong tea
  **chá de ervas/tisana** herb tea

**chanfana** rich lamb/ kid stew
  **chanfana da Bairrada** kid stew

**cherne** species of grouper with dark skin, a very prized fish normally served grilled

**chicória** endive

*cebolas*

**castanha** chestnut
  **castanhas assadas** roasted chestnuts
  **castanhas cozidas** boiled chestnuts with aniseed

*chouriço assado*

**chila** or **gila** type of pumpkin (spaghetti squash) made into jam, used as a filling for many cakes and desserts all over Portugal

**chispalhada** pig's trotters stew

**chispe com feijão** trotters with beans, cured meats and vegetables

**chocolate** chocolate
 **chocolate frio** cold chocolate
 **chocolate quente** hot chocolate

**chocos com tinta** cuttlefish in its own ink

**choquinhos** squid
 **choquinhos com tinta** squid in its ink

**chouriço** spicy smoked sausage
 **chouriço assado** baked spicy smoked sausage

**churrasco** barbecued/ cooked on charcoal

**churrasqueira** restaurant specialising in *frango à piri-piri* (chicken with piri-piri)

**clarete** light red wine

**coco** coconut

**codorniz** quail

**coelho** rabbit
 **coelho à caçadora** hunter's rabbit or hare, cooked in wine and herbs

**coentrada** with fresh coriander

**coentros** fresh coriander

**cogumelos** mushrooms

**colares** a type of wine from the Estremadura region

**colorau** sweet paprika

**comidas** meals

**cominho** cumin seed

**compota** jam or compote

**congro** conger eel

**conhaque** cognac

**conta** bill

**copo** glass

**coração** heart

**cordeiro** lamb

**costeleta** chop
 **costeletas de porco** pork chops
 **costeletas de porco grelhadas** grilled pork chops

**couve** cabbage

*coentros*

*costeletas de porco*

**couve-de-bruxelas** brussels sprouts

**couve-flor** cauliflower

**couve-lombarda** savoy cabbage

**couve portuguesa** Portuguese cabbage (a large and very tender cabbage), commonly used to accompany poached fish, when in season

**couve-roxa** red cabbage

**covilhetes de leite** custard tarts from the Azores

**cozido** boiled or poached
**cozido à Madeirense** boiled Madeira-style pork and vegetables, with pumpkin and couscous
**cozido à portuguesa** boiled assorted meats, vegetables and rice, served in a large platter

**cravinhos** cloves

**creme** custard
**creme de leite** milk custard

**criação** fowl

**croissants com fiambre** ham-filled croissants

**croissants recheados** filled croissants

**croquetes de carne** meat croquettes

**cru** raw

**cuba livre** rum and coke

# D

**damasco** apricot

**digestivo** digestive e.g. brandy

*damascos*

**dobrada** tripe
**dobrada à moda do Porto** tripe Oporto fashion in a bean stew

**DOC** (*denominação de origem controlada*) denotes a very good wine

**doce** sweet, jam
**doces de amêndoa** marzipan sweets
**doce de fruta** jam
**doce de laranja** marmalade

**dourada** sea bream

# E

**eirós** large eel generally fried and served with an *escabeche* sauce

**ementa** menu
**ementa turística** tourist menu, good-value menu based on local dishes

**empadão de batata** shepherd's pie

**empadas** small chicken or veal pies

**endívia** endive

**enguia** eel
**enguias de caldeirada** eel stew, typical of Aveiro
**enguias fritas** fried eels

**ensopado** fish or meat stew served on bread slices
**ensopado de borrego** rich lamb stew served on bread slices

**entradas** starters

**entrecosto** entrecôte steak

**erva-doce** aniseed

**ervilhas** peas
**ervilhas com paio e ovos** peas with garlic sausage and poached eggs

**escabeche** a special sauce containing vinegar, normally served with cold fried fish

**escalfado** poached
**ovo escalfado** poached egg

**espada** the name given in Madeira to *peixe espada* (scabbard fish)

**espadarte** swordfish
  **espadarte fumado** smoked swordfish

**esparguete** spaghetti

**espargos** asparagus

**esparregado** spinach purée with garlic

**especiarias** spices

**esperanças** delicate cakes from the Azores, filled with almonds

**espetada** kebab

**esplanada** open-air restaurant or café

**espinafre** spinach

**espumante** sparkling wine (champagne type)

**estragão** tarragon

**estufado** braised
  **carne estufada** braised meat

**esturjão** sturgeon

**extra-seco** extra-dry

# F

**farinha** flour

**farinheira** sausage made with flour and pork fat

**farófias** 'floating islands' made with egg whites and custard sauce

**fartes de batata** square cakes of sweet potato purée with spices and almonds

**farturas** long doughnuts, often eaten at festivals

**fataça** grey mullet

**fatias** slices
  **fatias de Tomar** sponge slices served in a light syrup
  **fatias douradas** slices of bread dipped in egg, fried and covered with sugar and cinnamon

**favada à portuguesa**
  broad beans cooked with smoked meats, onions and coriander

**favas** broad beans

**febras** thin slices of roast pork
  **febras de porco à alentejana** pork fillet with onions, *chouriço* and bacon

*favada à portuguesa*

**feijão** beans
  **feijão encarnado** red beans
  **feijão frade** black-eyed beans
  **feijão guisado** beans stewed with bacon in a tomato sauce
  **feijão preto** black beans
  **feijão verde cozido** boiled French beans

**feijoada** bean stew with pork meat and *chouriço*

**fiambre** cooked ham

**fígado** liver
  **fígado de coentrada** pork liver with coriander
  **fígado de galinha** chicken liver
  **fígado de porco de cebolada** pork liver with onions

*figos*

**figos** figs
  **figos cheios** dried figs stuffed with almonds
  **figos secos** dried figs

**filetes de pescada** hake fillet in batter

**filhós** fritters eaten at Christmas

**filhós de abóbora** pumpkin purée fritters eaten at Christmas

**filhoses** festive fried cakes sprinkled with sugar and cinnamon or dipped into honey or syrup

**fofas do Faial** choux-type pastry filled with cream or custard, typical of the Azores

**folar** a sweet loaf with spices, topped with boiled eggs and eaten at Easter

**folhados de carne** meat puff-pastries

**framboesa** raspberry

**frango** young chicken
  **frango à piri-piri** barbecued tender chicken with chilli
  **frango assado** roast tender chicken
  **frango no churrasco** barbecued tender chicken in a hot sauce (piri-piri)

**fresco** cold/chilled or fresh
  **uma cerveja muito fresca** a very cool beer

**fressura de porco guisada** pork offal casserole

**fricassé** meat or fish (generally chicken) served with an egg and lemon sauce

**frio** cold

**fritada de peixe** deep-fried mixed fish

**frito** fried

**fruta** fruit
  **fruta cristalizada** candied fruit
  **fruta da época** fruit in season
  **fruta em calda** fruit in syrup

**fumado** smoked
  **salmão fumado** smoked salmon

**fundo de alcachofra** artichoke heart

## G

**galheteiro** cruet stand

**galinha** chicken

**galinhola** woodcock

**galinhola à Alentejana** Alentejo woodcock, cooked with wine, garlic and seasonings, with a tasty filling

**galão** milky coffee served in a large glass

**gambas** large prawns
  **gambas na chapa** large prawns cooked on the hot plate

**ganso** goose

**garoto** small white coffee

*garoupa*

**garoupa** grouper
  **garoupa recheada** stuffed and baked grouper, a typical dish from the Azores

**garrafa** bottle

**gasosa** soft drink with gas

**gaspacho** cold soup with finely cut vegetables

**gelado** ice-cream

**geleia** jelly

**gelo** ice

**gengibre** ginger

**gim** gin

**ginjinha** morello-cherry liqueur typical of Portugal

**girafa** beer glass (approx.1 pint)

**goiaba** guava

**granizado de café** iced coffee

**grão** chickpeas
  **bacalhau com grão** poached salt cod with boiled chickpeas, seasonings, olive oil and boiled egg

**gratinado** au gratin
**grelhado** grilled
  **grelhado misto** mixed grill
**groselha** red currant
**guisado** stewed

## H

**hortaliça** generic name given to
vegetables
  **sopa de hortaliça** vegetable
  soup
**hortelã** mint
  **chá de hortelã** mint tea
**hortelã-pimenta** peppermint

## I

**imperial** small beer glass
**incluído** included
**inhame** yam, very popular
on some of the Azores
islands
**iscas** traditional pork liver dish
made with wine and garlic
  **iscas com elas** well-seasoned
  liver dish served with boiled
  potatoes, a Lisbon speciality

## J

**jantar** dinner
**jardineira** mixed vegetables
**jarro** carafe
**javali** wild boar
**jeropiga** fortified dessert wine
**Joaquinzinhos** small horse-
mackerel fried whole (like white-
bait), very popular in some
restaurants

## L

**lagosta** lobster
**lagostim-do-rio** freshwater
crayfish
**lagostins** king prawns
**lampreia** lamprey (an eel-like fish)
  **lampreia de ovos** egg lamprey,
  a rich dessert
**lanche** afternoon snack
consisting of tea and cakes or
buttered toast
**lapas** limpets, popular in Madeira
and the Azores
  **lapas Afonso** limpets served
  with a tasty onion sauce

*lagostins*

**laranja** orange
  **laranja descascada** peeled
  orange, normally served with a
  sprinkle of sugar
**laranjada engarrafada**
  bottled orange juice
  **laranjada natural** fresh orange
  juice
**lavagante** lobster
**lebre** hare
**legumes** vegetables
**leitão assado à moda da
  Bairrada** crisply roasted
  suckling pig from the Bairrada
  region
**leite** milk
**leite-creme** crème brûlée
**leite frio/quente** cold/hot milk
**lentilha** lentil
**licor de leite** milk liqueur
**licor de tangerina** mandarin
  liqueur
**lima** lime
**limão** lemon
**limonada** lemonade
**língua** tongue
  **língua estufada** braised tongue
**linguado** sole
  **linguado frito** fried sole
  **linguado grelhado** grilled sole
**linguiça** pork sausage with
  paprika
**lista dos vinhos** wine list
**lombinho de porco** pork loin
**lombo de porco** pork fillet
**louro** bay leaf

*maçã*

**lulas** squid
  **lulas à Algarvia** squid in garlic,
  Algarve style
  **lulas cheias** local name in the
  Algarve for *lulas recheadas*
  (stuffed squid)
  **lulas guisadas** stewed squid
  **lulas recheadas** small squid
  stuffed with rice and
  seasonings

# M

**maçã** apple
  **maçã assada** large baked russet
  apple
**maçapão** marzipan
**macarrão** macaroni
**macedónia de frutas** mixed fruit
  salad

*maçãs assadas*

*limão*

**madeira** wine from Madeira
**maduro** mature
**maionese** mayonnaise
**malagueta** hot pepper
**mal passado** rare
**mandioca** cassava root
**manga** mango
**manjar celeste** sweet made with eggs, bread crumbs, almonds and sugar
**manjericão** basil
**manteiga** butter
**mãozinhas de vitela guisadas** stewed calves' trotters
**maracujá** passion fruit
**marinado/a** marinated
**marisco** shellfish
**marisqueira** a restaurant or bar specialising solely in shellfish
**marmelada** quince jam – excellent with cheese

*marmelo*

**marmelo** quince, a popular fruit, often baked
**massa** pasta
**medalhão** medallion
**medronheira** strawberry-tree fruit liqueur
**meia-dose** half-portion
**meia garrafa** half bottle
**meio-doce** medium-sweet
**meio-seco** medium-dry
**mel** honey
  **mel de cana** molasses

*melancia*

**melancia** watermelon
**melão** melon
  **melão com presunto** melon with cured ham slices, a starter
**menu turístico** tourist menu, good-value menu based on local dishes
**merenda** afternoon snack consisting of tea and cakes or buttered toast
**merendinha** pastry filled with *chouriço* or *presunto* (ham)
**merengue** meringue
**mero** red grouper fish
**mexilhões** mussels
**migas** bread cooked with well-seasoned ingredients to form a kind of omelette
  **migas à alentejana** thick bread soup with pork meat and garlic
  **migas à lagareiro** bread cooked with cabbage, salt cod and olive oil
  **migas de pão de milho** thick maize bread soup with olive oil and garlic
**mil-folhas** mille feuille (custard pastry)
**milho** corn (maize)
  **milho doce** sweetcorn
  **milho frito** polenta fried in cubes, popular in Madeira
**miolos** brains
**misto** mixed
**moganga** pumpkin

**molho** sauce
  **molho béchamel** béchamel sauce
  **molho de caril** curry sauce
  **molho de escabeche** a special sauce containing vinegar, normally served with cold fried fish
  **molho de tomate** tomato sauce
  **molho tártaro** piquant mayonnaise with capers, gherkins and olives
**morangos** strawberries
**morcela** spicy black pudding
**morgado de figo** dried pressed figs with spices
**moscatel de Setúbal** medium-

*nozes*

**nabiça**

sweet muscat wine
**mostarda** mustard
**mousse de chocolate** chocolate mousse

# N

**...na brasa** char-grilled
**...na cataplana** stewed in cataplana vessel (typical double-wok pot used in the Alentejo and Algarve)
**...na frigideira** sautéed or fried
**nabiça** turnip greens
**nabo** turnip
**natas** cream
**nata batida** whipped cream

**natural** plain, without dressing or served at room temperature (usually wine or water)
**...no espeto** kebab/on the spit
**...no forno** roasted or cooked in the oven
**nozes** walnuts
  **nozes de Cascais** caramelised walnuts, from Cascais

# O

**óleo** vegetable oil
**omeleta** omelette
  **omeleta de cogumelos** mushroom omelette
  **omeleta de fiambre** ham omelette
  **omeleta de queijo** cheese omelette
  **omeleta simples** plain omelette
**ostras** oysters
**ouriço-do-mar** sea-urchin
**ovas** fish roe
**ovos** eggs
  **ovos cozidos** boiled eggs
  **ovos escalfados** poached eggs
  **ovos estrelados** fried eggs
  **ovos mexidos** scrambled eggs
  **ovos moles** soft egg sweet
  **ovos quentes** soft-boiled eggs

*pão*

*pastéis*

# P

**paio** thick smoked sausage made with lean meat

**palha de Abrantes** sweet made with eggs, looking like straw

**panados** slices of meat coated in egg and breadcrumbs and fried

**pão** bread
  **pão de centeio** rye bread
  **pão de forma** sliced bread for toast
  **pão-de-ló** light sponge cake
  **pão de milho** maize bread
  **pão saloio** country-style bread

**pãozinho** bread roll

**papaia** papaya

**papas** polenta soup
  **papas de milho doces** sweet polenta

**papo-seco** bread roll

**papos de anjo** small egg cakes with syrup

**pargo** red bream

**parrilhada** grilled fish

**passas de uva** raisins

**pastéis** tarts, cakes, pasties
  **pastéis de arroz** rice tarts from the Azores
  **pastéis de bacalhau** salt-cod cakes
  **pastéis de carne** meat pasties
  **pastéis de feijão** tarts made with beans, eggs and almonds
  **pastéis de nata/de Belém** egg custard tarts from Belém (Lisbon)

*pastéis de bacalhau*

**pastéis de Santa Clara** pastries with a filling of almonds, egg yolk and sugar
**pastéis de Tentugal** small pastries with an egg filling
**pastelaria** pâtisserie/pastry shop
**pastel de massa tenra** meat pasty
**pataniscas (de bacalhau)** salt-cod fritters
**paté de fígado** liver pâté
**pato** duck
**pato assado com arroz** roast duck with rice
**pé de porco com feijão** pigs' trotters with beans
**peito** breast
**peixe** fish
**peixe assado** baked fish
**peixe cozido** poached fish
**peixe frito** fried fish
**peixe grelhado** grilled fish
**peixe e marisco** fish and shellfish
**peixe espada** scabbard fish
**peixe espada frito** fried scabbard fish
**peixe espada grelhado** grilled scabbard fish
**peixe-galo** John Dory
**peixinhos da horta** French beans fried in batter
**pepino** cucumber
**pequeno almoço** breakfast
**pêra** pear

*pescada frita*

**percebes** barnacles, highly prized shellfish
**perdiz** partridge
**perdiz à Montemor** Montemor-style partridge, cooked with wine and spices
**perdiz com couve lombarda** partridge with cabbage
**perna** leg
**pernil** ham
**perú** turkey
**pescada** hake
**pescada com todos** hake poached with potatoes and vegetables
**pescadinha** small hake for frying
**pescadinhas de rabo na boca** whole rolled-up small fried hake
**pêssego** peach

*peixe espada*

*pescadinha*

*pêssego*

**pêssego careca** nectarine
**pezinhos de porco de coentrada** pork trotters with coriander and garlic
**picante** spicy
**pimenta** pepper (spice)
**pimentos** peppers
  **pimentos assados** grilled peppers
**pinhão** pine kernel
**pinhoada** pinenut brittle
**pinhões** peanuts
**piri-piri** chilli sauce
**polvo** octopus
  **polvo grelhado** grilled octopus
  **polvo guisado** stewed octopus
**pombo** pigeon
**porco** pork
  **porco à alentejana** traditional dish with pork, clams and herbs
  **porco assado** roast pork

*porco assado*

**posta à mirandesa** spit-roasted veal, Miranda-style
**pouco picante** mild
**prato** dish
  **prato do dia** dish of the day
  **prato principal** main dish
  **pratos de carne** meat dishes
**preço** price
**pregado** turbot
**prego** steak in a roll
  **prego com fiambre** steak with sliced ham
  **prego no pão** steak roll
  **prego no prato** steak with fried egg and chips served on a plate
**presunto** cured ham
**preta** dark (black)
  **cerveja preta** dark beer
**pudim** pudding
  **pudim Abade de Priscos** rich egg pudding flavoured with port and lemon
  **pudim de bacalhau** salt cod loaf served with tomato sauce
  **pudim da casa** restaurant's own dessert (often crème caramel)
  **pudim de coalhada** popular Azorean rich, fresh cheese pudding
  **pudim de pão** bread pudding
  **pudim de queijo** cheese pudding
  **pudim de requeijão** ricotta-type cheese pudding
  **pudim flan** crème caramel
  **pudim Molotov** egg-white pudding with egg sauce or caramel
**puré de batata** mashed potato

## Q

**queijadas** cheese tarts
  **queijadas de Évora** cheese tarts made with cheese from ewes' milk
  **queijadas da Madeira** small Madeiran cheese cakes
  **queijadas de requeijão** ricotta-type cheese tarts
  **queijadas de Sintra** little cheese cakes with cinnamon made in Sintra

*queijo*

**quejinhos** little cheeses
  **quejinhos de amêndoa** little almond cheeses
  **queijinhos do céu** egg yolk and sugar sweets
  **queijinhos frescos** small fresh cheeses (cows', ewes' or goats' milk)
  **queijinhos secos** small dried cheeses
**queijo** cheese
  **queijo de Alverca** small cheese from Alverca, near Lisbon
  **queijo cabreiro** goats' cheese
  **queijo cardiga** cheese made from ewes' and goats' milk
  **queijo da Ilha** cheddar-type cheese from the Azores, also known as *queijo de S. Jorge*
  **queijo de Évora** small ewes' cheese from Évora
  **queijo da Serra** buttery cheese from Estrela Mountain, soft, runny cheese made with ewes' milk
  **queijo de Azeitão** hard or soft cheese made with ewes' milk
  **queijo de cabra** goats' cheese
  **queijo de Nisa** a rich ewe's cheese from Nisa (Alentejo)
  **queijo de ovelha** small, dried ewes' milk cheeses
  **queijo fresco** fresh cheese

  **queijo saloio** small cheese made with ewes' milk or a mixture of goats' and ewes' milk
**quente** hot
**quiabo** okra

# R

**rabaçal** mild cheese from the Coimbra region
**rabanada** french toast
**rabanete** radish
**raia** skate
**rancho** a substantial soup
**recheado com…** stuffed/filled with…
**recheio** stuffing
**regiões demarcadas** demarcated wine regions

*romãs*

**repolho** cabbage
**requeijão** fresh curd cheese resembling ricotta
**rim (rins)** kidney
  **rins à Madeira** kidneys served in Madeira wine sauce
  **rins com vinho do Porto** kidneys in port wine sauce
**rissóis de camarão/peixe** shrimp or fish rissoles
**robalo** sea bass
**romãs** pomegranate
**rojões** crisp pieces of marinated pork

# S

**sal** salt
**salada** salad
  **salada de feijão frade** black-eyed bean salad, with boiled egg, olive oil and seasonings
  **salada de fruta** fruit salad
  **salada de polvo** a starter with cold octopus, seasoned with olive oil, coriander, onion and vinegar
  **salada mista** mixed salad (tomato, lettuce, cucumber, onion)
  **salada russa** Russian salad
**salgados** savouries (snacks)
**salmão** salmon
  **salmão fumado** smoked salmon

*sandes e sumo*

*sapateira*

**salmonetes grelhados** grilled red mullet in a butter and lemon sauce
**saloio** small cheese made from ewes' or goats' milk, often served as a pre-starter to a meal in the Lisbon region
**salpicão** slices of large *chouriço*
**salsa** parsley
**salsichas** sausages
**salteado** sautéed
**salva** sage
**sandes** sandwich
  **sandes de fiambre** cooked ham sandwich
  **sandes de lombo** steak sandwich
  **sandes de presunto** cured ham sandwich
  **sandes de queijo** cheese sandwich
**santola** spider crab
**sapateira** crab (generally dressed)
**sarapatel** a highly seasoned Madeiran dish made with pork blood and liver
**sarda** mackerel
**sardinhas** sardines
  **sardinhas assadas** char-grilled sardines
  **sardinhas na telha** oven-baked sardines cooked on a roof tile with olive oil and seasoning
**sável** shad

*sardinhas*

**seco** dry

**sericaia** baked custard with cinnamon

**serpa** a type of ewes' milk cheese from the Alentejo region

**serra** a creamy cheese made from ewes' milk, from the Serra de Estrela region

**serviço incluído** service included

**sidra** cider

**simples** neat (as in 'neat whisky')

**sobremesas** desserts

**solha** plaice

**sonho** doughnut-type fried cake, dipped in sugar and cinnamon

**sopa** soup
  **sopa à alentejana** soup Alentejo-style, made with chunks of bread, olive oil, fresh coriander and garlic, topped with poached egg
  **sopa azeda de feijão** bean soup with vegetables and bread, sweet potatoes, cinnamon and a spoonful of vinegar (Azores)
  **sopa de cabeça de peixe** fish head soup, using the head of a large fish, tomatoes, potatoes, stale bread and seasonings (Algarve)
  **sopa de camarão** prawn soup
  **sopa de castanhas piladas** hearty soup made with

chestnuts, beans and rice
  **sopa de ervilhas** pea soup
  **sopa de espinafres** spinach soup
  **sopa de feijão** bean soup with vegetables
  **sopa de feijão frade** black-eyed bean soup
  **sopa de feijão verde** green bean soup
  **sopa de funcho** fennel soup with beans and bacon fat (Azores)
  **sopa de grão** chickpea soup
  **sopa de legumes** vegetable soup
  **sopa de marisco** shellfish soup
  **sopa de moganga** Madeiran pumpkin soup
  **sopa de pedra** a rich soup with lots of meat, beans and vegetables
  **sopa de peixe** fish soup
  **sopa de poejos** pennyroyal soup with eggs (Alentejo)
  **sopa de rabo de boi** oxtail soup
  **sopa de tomate** tomato soup
  **sopa do dia** soup of the day
  **sopa do Espírito Santo** 'Holy Spirit' soup made with meats, vegetables, bread, herbs and spices (Azores)
  **sopa dos campinos** salt cod and tomato soup
  **sopa dourada** dessert made with egg yolks
  **sopa e um papo-seco/pãozinho** soup and roll
  **sopa seca** thick bread soup with meats

**sorvete** ice-cream

**sumo de fruta** fruit juice
  **ananás** pineapple
  **laranja** orange
  **maçã** apple
  **pêra** pear
  **pêssego** peach
  **tomate** tomato
  **uva** grape

**suspiros** meringues

*tomates*

**torta de Viana** a sponge roll filled with a rich egg sweet

**tosta** toasted sandwich
  **tosta mista** ham and cheese toasted sandwich

**toucinho** bacon
  **toucinho do céu** 'bacon from heaven', an egg and almond pudding

**tremoços** lupin seeds, commonly consumed with beer

# T

**tainha** grey mullet

**tâmara** date

**tamboril** monkfish

**tangerina** mandarin

**tarte** tart
  **tarte de amêndoa** almond tart
  **tarte de limão** lemon tart
  **tarte de maçã** apple tart

**tasca** small taverna serving cheap food and drink

**tasquinha** small taverna serving cheap food and drink

**tempero** seasoning

**tenro** tender

**tibornas** slices of freshly baked bread sprinkled with coarse sea salt and olive oil

**tigeladas de Abrantes** individually baked custards in special cups

**tinto** red wine

**tisana** herbal tea
  **tisana de camomila** camomile tea
  **tisana de Lúcia-Lima** vervaine tea

**tomate** tomato

**toranja** grapefruit

**tornedó** prime cut of beef

**torradas** toast

**Torres Vedras** red wine from the Estremadura region

**torta** sponge roll
  **torta de laranja** orange sponge roll

*uvas*

**tripas à moda do Porto** tripe stew with beans and various meats, Oporto-style

**trufa** truffle

**truta** trout
  **trutas à moda do Minho** trout cooked in wine and rich seasonings
  **truta de Barroso** traditional northern dish of fried trout stuffed with ham

**tutano** marrow

# U

**uísque** whisky

**uvas** grapes

# V

**vagens** runner beans

**variado** assorted

**verdelho** local Azorean wine

**vermute** vermouth

**vieira** scallop

*vinhos do Porto*

**vinagre** vinegar
**vinha d'alhos** marinated in wine and garlic
**vinho** wine
  **vinho abafado** locally made fortified wine
  **vinho adamado** sweet wine
  **vinho branco** white wine
  **vinho branco seco** dry white wine
  **vinho branco meio-seco** medium-dry white wine
  **vinho da casa** house wine
  **vinho espumante** sparkling wine

  **vinho generoso** fortified wine
  **vinho Moscatel** muscat wine
  **vinho regional/da região** local wine
  **vinho tinto** red wine
  **vinho tinto encorpado** full-bodied red wine, ideal with red meats
  **vinho tinto meio-encorpado** medium-bodied red wine, ideal with salted fish dishes or light meats
  **vinho tinto velho** mature red wine, ideal with red meats
  **vinho verde** dry, sparkling 'green' wine made with slightly unripe grapes from the Minho region
  **vinhos espumantes** sparkling wines
  **vinhos da Madeira** madeira wines
  **vinhos do Porto** port wines
**vitela** veal
  **vitela no espeto** veal cooked on the spit

# X

**xarope** syrup
  **xarope de groselha** blackcurrant syrup
  **xarope de morango** strawberry syrup
**xerez** sherry

# DICTIONARY

english–portuguese

portuguese–english

# A

a um (uma)
abbey a abadia
able: to be able (to) poder
abortion o aborto
about (roughly) mais ou menos
  a book about... um livro sobre...
  about ten o'clock por volta das dez
above acima de
abroad adv no estrangeiro
  to go abroad ir ao estrangeiro
abscess um abcesso
accelerator o acelerador
accent o acento
  (pronunciation) a pronúncia
to accept aceitar
  (approve of) aprovar
access o acesso
  wheelchair access o acesso para
  cadeiras de rodas
accident o acidente
accommodation o alojamento
to accompany acompanhar
account (bill) a conta
  (in bank) a conta (bancária)
account number o número da conta
accountant o/a contabilista
to ache doer
  my head aches dói-me a cabeça
  it aches dói-me
  they ache doem-me
acid o ácido
actor/actress o actor/a actriz
to adapt adaptar
adaptor (electrical) o adaptador
adder a cobra
address a morada
  what is your address? qual é a sua
  morada?
address book a agenda
admission charge/fee o preço de
  entrada
admit: to admit to hospital ingresar no
  hospital
adult o/a adulto(a)
  for adults para adultos
advance: in advance antecipadamente
advertisement o anúncio
to advise aconselhar
aerial a antena
aeroplane o avião

aerosol o aerossol
afraid: to be afraid of ter medo de
after depois
  after lunch depois do almoço
afternoon a tarde
  this afternoon esta tarde
  in the afternoon à tarde
  tomorrow afternoon amanhã à tarde
aftershave lotion o aftershave ; a loção
  após-barba
again outra vez
against prep contra
  I am against that sou contra isso
age a idade
  old age a idade avançada
agency a agência
ago: 2 days ago há 2 dias
to agree concordar
agreement o acordo
AIDS a SIDA
air bag o airbag
air bed o colchão de ar
air conditioning o ar condicionado
  is there air conditioning? tem ar
  condicionado?
air freshener o purificador do
  ambiente
airline a linha aérea
airmail a via aérea ; por avião
airplane o avião
airport o aeroporto
airport bus o autocarro do aeroporto
air ticket o bilhete de avião
aisle (plane, theatre, etc) a coxia
alarm o alarme
alarm clock o despertador
alcohol o álcool
alcohol-free sem álcool
alcoholic adj alcoólico(a)
all todo(a), todos(as)
allergic alérgico(a)
  I'm allergic to sou alérgico(a) a
allergy a alergia
alley a travessa
to allow permitir
  to be allowed estar permitido(a)
all right está bem
  are you all right? você está bem?
almond a amêndoa
almost quase
alone sozinho(a)
alphabet o alfabeto
already já
also também
altar o altar

**aluminium foil** a folha de alumínio
**always** sempre
**a.m.** da manhã
**amber** *(light)* amarelo(a)
**ambulance** a ambulância
**America** os Estados Unidos
**American** (norte)-americano(a)
**amount:** *total amount* o total
**anaesthetic** a anestesia
 *general anaesthetic* a anestesia geral
 *local anaesthetic* a anestesia local
**anchor** a âncora
**anchovy** a anchova
**ancient** antigo(a)
**and** e
**angel** o anjo
**angina** a angina de peito
**angry** zangado(a)
**animal** um animal
**aniseed** a erva-doce
**ankle** o tornozelo
**anniversary** o aniversário
**to announce** anunciar
**announcement** o anúncio
**annual** anual
**another** um(a) outro(a)
 *another beer?* mais uma cerveja?
**answer** *n* a resposta
**to answer** responder
**answerphone** o gravador de chamadas
**ant** a formiga
**antacid** o antiácido
**antibiotic** o antibiótico
**antifreeze** o anticongelante
**antihistamine** o anti-histamínico
**anti-inflammatory** o anti-inflamatório
**antiques** as antiguidades
**antique shop** a loja de antiguidades
**antiseptic** o antiséptico
**any** *(some)* algum(a)
 *(negative)* nenhum(a)
 *I haven't any money* não tenho
 dinheiro
 *have you any apples?* tem maçãs?
**anyone** *(in questions)* alguém
 *(negative)* ninguém
**anything** *(in questions)* alguma coisa
 *(negative)* nada
 *I haven't got anything* não tenho
 nada
**anywhere** *(in any place at all)* em
 qualquer parte
 *(negative)* em nenhuma parte
 *I haven't seen him anywhere* não o vi
 em nenhuma parte

**apartment** o apartamento
**aperitif** o aperitivo
**appendicitis** a apendicite
**apple** a maçã
**application form** o formulário de
 requerimento
**appointment** *(meeting)* o encontro
 (marcado)
 *(doctor)* a consulta
 *(hairdresser)* a hora marcada
 *I have an appointment* tenho un
 encontro (marcado)
**approximately** aproximadamente
**apricot** o damasco
**April** o Abril
**architect** o/a arquitecto(a)
**architecture** a arquitectura
**arm** o braço
**armbands** *(to swim)* as braçadeiras
**armchair** a poltrona
**aromatherapy** a aromaterapia
**to arrange** organizar
**to arrest** prender
**arrival** a chegada
**to arrive** chegar
**art** a arte
**art gallery** a galeria de arte
**arthritis** a artrite
**artichoke** a alcachofra
**artificial** artificial
**artist** o/a artista
**ashtray** o cinzeiro
**to ask** *(question)* perguntar
 *(to ask for something)* pedir
**asparagus** o espargo
**asleep: he/she is asleep** está
 adormecido(a)
**aspirin** a aspirina
 *soluble aspirin* aspirina efervescente
**asthma** a asma
 *I have asthma* tenho asma
**at** em ; a
 *at home* em casa
 *at 8 o'clock* às oito
 *at once* imediatamente
 *at night* à noite
**Atlantic Ocean** o oceano Atlântico
**to attack** atacar
**attractive** *(person)* atraente
**aubergine** a beringela
**auction** o leilão
**audience** a audiência**

## a                eng-por

**August** o Agosto
**aunt** a tia
**au pair** o/a au pair
**Australia** a Austrália
**Australian** australiano(a)
**author** o/a autor(a)
**automatic** automático(a)
**automatic car** o carro automático
**autumn** o outono
**available** disponível
**avalanche** a avalancha
**avenue** a avenida
**average** a média
  *adj* médio(a)
**avocado** o abacate
**to avoid** evitar
**awake: *to be awake*** estar acordado(a)
**awful** terrível
**axle** o eixo

## B

**baby** o bebé
**baby food** a comida de bebé
**baby milk** o leite infantil
**baby's bottle** o biberão
**baby seat** *(in car)* o assento do bebé
**baby-sitter** o/a babysitter
**baby-sitting service** serviço de baby-sitting
**baby wipes** as toalhitas
**bachelor** o solteiro
**back** *(of body)* as costas
**backache** a dor de costas
**backpack** a mochila
**back seat** o assento traseiro
**bacon** o toucinho ; bacon
**bad** *(weather, news)* mau (má)
  *(fruit, vegetables)* podre
**badminton** o badminton
**bag** o saco
  *(handbag)* a mala de mão
  *(case)* a mala
**baggage** a bagagem
**baggage allowance** o peso limite da bagagem
**baggage reclaim** a recolha de bagagem
**bait** *(for fishing)* a isca
**baked** assado(a)
**baker's** a padaria

**balcony** a varanda
**bald** *(person)* calvo(a)
  *(tyre)* careca
**ball** a bola
**ballet** o ballet
**balloon** o balão
**banana** a banana
**band** *(music)* a banda musical
**bandage** a ligadura
**bank** o banco
  *(river)* a margem
**bank account** a conta bancária
**banknote** a nota (bancária)
**bankrupt** falido(a)
**bar** o bar
**bar of chocolate** a barra de chocolate
**barbecue** o churrasco
  *to have a barbecue* fazer um churrasco
**barber** o barbeiro
**to bark** ladrar
**barn** o celeiro
**barrel** o barril
**basement** a cave
**basil** o manjericão
**basket** o cesto
**basketball** o basquete(bol)
**basketwork** os artigos de vime
**bat** *(animal)* o morcego
  *(for table tennis)* a raqueta
**bath** o banho
  *to have a bath* tomar banho
**bathing cap** a touca de banho
**bathroom** a casa de banho
  *with bathroom* com casa de banho
**battery** *(for car)* a bateria
  *(for torch, radio, etc)* a pilha
**bay** a baía
**bayleaf** a folha de louro
**B&B** o quarto com pequeno-almoço
  *(place)* a pensão
**to be** ser ; estar
**beach** a praia
  *private beach* a praia particular
  *sandy beach* a praia arenosa
  *nudist beach* a praia naturista
**beach hut** a barraca
**bean** o feijão
  *broad bean* a fava
  *French/green bean* o feijão verde
  *kidney bean* o feijão encarnado
  *soya bean* o feijão de soja
**bear** *(animal)* o urso
**beard** a barba
**beautiful** belo(a) ; lindo(a)
**beauty salon** o salão de beleza

**9**

**because** porque
**to become** tornar-se
**bed** a cama
  *double bed* a cama de casal
  *single bed* a cama de solteiro
  *sofa bed* o sofá-cama
  *twin beds* as camas separadas ; duas camas
**bedding** a roupa de cama
**bedclothes** a roupa de cama
**bedroom** o quarto
**bee** a abelha
**beef** a carne de vaca
**beer** a cerveja
**beetroot** a beterraba
**before** antes de
  *before breakfast* antes do pequeno-almoço
**beggar** o/a mendigo(a)
**to begin** começar
**behind** atrás
  *behind the bank* atrás do banco
**beige** bege
**to believe** acreditar
**bell** *(door)* a campainha
  *(church)* o sino
**to belong to** pertencer a
**below** debaixo de
  *(less than)* abaixo de ; menos que/de
**belt** o cinto
**bend** *(in road)* a curva
**berth** *(in ship)* o beliche
**beside** *(next to)* ao lado de
  *beside the bank* ao lado do banco
**best: the best** o/a melhor
**to bet on** apostar em
**better (than)** melhor (do que)
**between** entre
**bib** o bibe
**bicycle** a bicicleta
  *by bicycle* de bicicleta
**bicycle lock** o cadeado da bicicleta
**bicycle repair kit** o estojo de ferramentas
**bidet** o bidé
**big** grande
**bigger (than)** maior que
**bike** *(motorbike)* a moto
  *(pushbike)* a bicicleta
  *mountain bike* a bicicleta de montanha
**bikini** o bikini
**bill** *(in hotel, restaurant)* a conta
  *(for work done)* a factura
  *(gas, telephone)* a conta
**bin** o caixote do lixo

**bin liner** o saco do lixo
**binoculars** os binóculos
**bird** o pássaro
**biro** a esferográfica
**birth** o nascimento
**birth certificate** a certidão de nascimento
**birthday** o aniversário
  *happy birthday* parabéns
  *my birthday is on...* faço anos no...
**birthday card** o cartão de aniversário
**birthday present** a prenda de anos
**biscuits** as bolachas
**bit:** *a bit of* um bocado (de)
**bite** *(snack)* a merenda ; o lanche
  *(of animal)* a mordedura ; a mordida
  *(of insect)* a picada
  *let's have a bite to eat* vamos comer algo
**to bite** *(animal)* morder
  *(insect)* picar
**bitten** *(by animal)* mordido(a)
  *(by insect)* picado(a)
**bitter** amargo(a)
**black** preto(a)
**blackberry** a amora silvestre
**blackcurrant** a groselha
**blank** o espaço em branco
**blanket** o cobertor
**bleach** a lixívia
**to bleed** sangrar
**blender** *(for food)* o liquificador
**blind** *(person)* cego(a)
**blind** *(for window)* a persiana
**blister** a bolha
**block of flats** o prédio de apartamentos
**blocked** *(pipe, sink)* entupido(a)
  *(road)* cortada ao trânsito
**blond** *(person)* louro(a)
**blood** o sangue
**blood group** o grupo sanguíneo
**blood pressure** a tensão arterial
**blood test** a análise ao sangue
**blouse** a blusa
**blow-dry** o brushing
**to blow-dry** fazer um brushing
**blue** azul
  *dark blue* azul escuro
  *light blue* azul claro
**blunt** *(knife, etc)* embotado(a)
**boar** o javali

**boarding card** o cartão de embarque
**boarding house** a pensão
**boat** o barco
**boat trip** a viagem de barco
**body** o corpo
**to boil** ferver
**boiler** a caldeira
**boiled** cozido(a)
**bomb** a bomba
**bone** o osso
  *fish bone* a espinha
**bonfire** a fogueira
**bonnet** *(of car)* o capot
**book** o livro
  *book of tickets* a caderneta de bilhetes
**to book** reservar
**booking** a marcação ; a reserva
**booking office** a bilheteira
**bookshop** a livraria
**boot** *(of car)* o porta-bagagem
**boots** as botas
**border** a fronteira
**boring** aborrecido(a)
**boss** o/a chefe
  *(employer)* o patrão/a patroa
**both** ambos(as)
**bottle** a garrafa
  *a bottle of wine* uma garrafa de vinho
  *a half bottle* uma meia-garrafa
**bottle opener** o abre-garrafas
**bowl** *(for washing )* a bacia
  *(for food)* a tigela
**bow tie** o laço
**box** a caixa
**box office** a bilheteira
**boxer shorts** os boxers
**boy** o rapaz
**boyfriend** o namorado
**bra** o soutien
**bracelet** a pulseira
**brain** o cérebro
**to brake** travar
**brake fluid** o óleo dos travões
**brake light** a luz de travagem
**brake shoes** as sapatas
**brakes** os travões
**branch** *(of tree)* o ramo
  *(of business, etc)* a sucursal
**brand** *(make)* a marca
**brandy** o conhaque

**brass** o latão
**bread** o pão
  *French bread* o cacete
  *sliced bread* o pão de forma
  *wholemeal bread* o pão integral
**breadcrumbs** o pão ralado
**bread roll** o pãozinho ; o papo-seco
**to break** quebrar ; partir
**breakable** frágil
**breakdown** *(car)* a avaria
  *(nervous)* o colapso nervoso
**breakdown service** o pronto-socorro
**breakdown van** o pronto-socorro
**breakfast** o pequeno-almoço
**breast** *(chicken)* o peito
**to breastfeed** amamentar
**to breathe** respirar
**brick** o tijolo
**bride** a noiva
**bridegroom** o noivo
**bridge** a ponte
  *(game)* o bridge
**briefcase** a pasta
**bright** brilhante
**Brillo pad®** a esponja de aço
**brine** a salmoura
**to bring** trazer
**Britain** a Grã-Bretanha
**British** britânico(a)
**broad** largo(a)
**broccoli** os brócolos
**brochure** a brochura
**broken** partido(a) ; quebrado(a)
**broken down** *(car, etc)* avariado(a)
**bronchitis** a bronquite
**bronze** o bronze
**brooch** o broche
**broom** a vassoura
**brother** o irmão
**brother-in-law** o cunhado
**brown** castanho(a)
**bruise** a nódoa negra
**brush** a escova
**Brussels sprouts** as couves-de-Bruxelas
**bubble bath** a espuma para o banho
**bucket** o balde
**buffet car** o vagão restaurante
**to build** construir
**building** o edifício ; o prédio
**building site** o terreno de construção
**bulb** *(light)* a lâmpada
**bull** o touro
**bullfight** a tourada
**bullfighter** o toureiro

1 **bullring** a praça de touros
**bumbag** a carteira de cintura
**bumper** *(on car)* o pára-choques
**bunch** *(of flowers)* o ramo
   *(of grapes)* o cacho
**bureau de change** a casa de câmbio
**burger** um hambúrguer
**burglar** o ladrão/a ladra
**burglar alarm** o alarme de roubo
**burglary** o roubo
**to burn** queimar
**burnt** *(food)* queimado(a)
**burst** rebentado(a)
**bus** o autocarro
**bus pass** o passe de autocarro
**bus station** a estação de autocarros
**bus stop** a paragem de autocarros
**bus ticket** o bilhete de autocarro
**bus tour** a excursão de autocarro
**business** os negócios
   *on business* de negócios
**business card** o cartão-de-visita
**business class** a classe executiva
**businessman/woman** o homem/a
   mulher de negócios
**business trip** a viagem de negócios
**busy** ocupado(a)
   *(place)* movimentado(a)
**but** mas
**butcher's** o talho
**butter** a manteiga
**button** o botão
**to buy** comprar
**by** por
   *(near)* perto de
   *(next to)* ao lado de
   *by bus* de autocarro
   *by car* de carro
   *by ship* de barco
   *by train* de comboio
**bypass** *(road)* o desvio

# C

**cab** *(taxi)* o táxi
**cabaret** o cabaré
**cabbage** a couve
**cabin** *(on boat)* o camarote
**cabin crew** os tripulantes de cabine
**cable car** o teleférico
**cable TV** a televisão por cabo
**café** o café
   *internet café* o cibercafé
**cafetière** a cafeteira
**cake** o bolo

**cake shop** a pastelaria
**calamine lotion** a loção de calamina
**calculator** a calculadora
**calendar** o calendário
**calf** *(young cow)* a vitela
**to call** chamar
**call** *(telephone)* uma chamada
   *a long-distance call* uma chamada
   interurbana
**calm** calmo(a); tranquilo(a)
**camcorder** a camcorder
**camera** a máquina fotográfica
**camera case** o estojo da máquina
   fotográfica
**to camp** acampar
**camping gas** o gás para campismo
**camping stove** o fogão portátil; o
   fogão de campismo
**campsite** o parque de campismo
**can** *(verb – to be able)* poder
   **I/we can** posso/podemos
   **I/we cannot** não posso/não podemos
   **can I...?** posso ...?
   **can we...?** podemos ...?
**can** *n* a lata
**canned goods** as conservas
**can opener** o abre-latas
**Canada** o Canadá
**Canadian** canadense
**canal** o canal
**to cancel** cancelar
**cancellation** o cancelamento
**cancer** o cancro
**candle** a vela
**canoe** a canoa
**to go canoeing** fazer canoagem
**cap** *(hat)* o boné
   *(diaphragm)* o diafragma
**capital** *(city)* a capital
**car** o carro
   *car alarm* o alarme do carro
   *car ferry* o barco de passagem
   *car hire* o aluguer de automóveis
   *car insurance* o seguro de
   automóveis
   *car keys* as chaves do carro
   *car park* o parque de
   estacionamento
   *car parts* as peças sobressalentes
   *car radio* o rádio do carro
   *car seat* *(for children)* o banco para
   crianças
   *car wash* a lavagem automática

carafe a garrafa

caravan a caravana

carburettor o carburador

card *(business)* o cartão (de visita)
*(greetings)* o cartão
*(playing)* a carta de jogar

cardboard o cartão

cardigan o casaco de lã

careful cuidadoso(a)
*to be careful* ter cuidado
*be careful!* cuidado!

carnation o cravo

carpet a carpete
*(rug)* o tapete

carriage a carruagem

carrot a cenoura

to carry transportar

carton o pacote

case *(suitcase)* a mala

cash o dinheiro

to cash *(cheque)* levantar

cash desk a caixa

cash dispenser a caixa automática ;
o Multibanco

cashier o/a caixa

cash machine a caixa automática ;
o Multibanco

cashpoint a caixa automática ;
o Multibanco

casino o casino

casserole *(dish)* o tacho
*(meal)* o guisado (no forno)

cassette a cassette ; a fita

cassette player o toca-fitas

castle o castelo

casualty department o Serviço de
Urgência

cat o gato

cat food comida para gatos

catacombs as catacumbas

catalogue o catálogo ; o CD

to catch *(bus, train, etc)* apanhar

cathedral a catedral

Catholic católico(a)

cauliflower a couve-flor

cave a caverna

cavity *(in tooth)* a cárie dentária

CD o disco compacto

CD player o leitor de discos compactos

ceiling o tecto

celery o aipo

cellar a cave

cellphone o telefone celular

cemetery o cemitério

centimetre o centímetro

central central

central heating o aquecimento central

central locking o fecho centralizado

cent o cêntimo *(i.e. 1/100th of a euro)*

centre o centro

century o século
*19th century* o século dezanove
*21st century* o século vinte e um

ceramics a cerâmica

cereal *(for breakfast)* os cereais

certain certo(a)

certificate o certificado

chain a corrente

chair a cadeira

chairlift o teleférico

chalet o chalé

challenge o desafio

chambermaid a empregada de quarto

Champagne o champanhe

change *(loose coins)* o dinheiro trocado
*(money returned)* o troco

to change trocar ; mudar
*to change money* trocar dinheiro
*to change (clothes)* mudar de roupa
*to change (train, etc)* mudar

changing room o gabinete de provas

Channel: *the English Channel* o Canal
da Mancha

chapel a capela

charcoal o carvão

charge o custo
*cover charge* o couvert
*please charge it to my account* por
favor ponha na minha conta

charger *(for battery)* o carregador

charter flight o voo charter

cheap barato(a)

cheaper mais barato(a)

to check verificar

to check in *(at airport)* fazer o check-in
*(at hotel)* apresentar-se

check-in desk o balcão do check-in

cheek a bochecha

cheerful alegre

cheers saúde!

cheese o queijo

cheeseburger um hambúrger com
queijo

chef o cozinheiro-chefe/a cozinheira-
chefe

chemist's a farmácia

cheque o cheque

chequebook o talão de cheques

**cheque card** o cartão de cheques
**cherry** a cereja
**chess** o xadrez
**chest** *(of body)* o peito
**chestnut** a castanha
**chewing gum** a pastilha elástica
**chicken** a galinha ; o frango
**chicken breast** o peito de galinha
**chickenpox** a varicela
**child** a criança
**child safety seat** *(car)* o banco de segurança para crianças
**children** as crianças
**chilli** a malagueta
**chimney** a chaminé
**chin** o queixo
**china** a porcelana
**chips** as batatas fritas
**chocolate** o chocolate
**chocolates** os chocolates
**choice** a escolha
**choir** o coro
**to choose** escolher
**chop** *(meat)* a costeleta
**chopping board** a tábua da cozinha
**christening** o baptizado
**Christian name** o nome próprio
**Christmas** o Natal
  *merry Christmas!* feliz Natal!
**Christmas card** o cartão de Boas Festas
**Christmas Eve** a véspera de Natal
**Christmas present** a prenda de Natal
**church** a igreja
**cider** a cidra
**cigar** o charuto
**cigarette** o cigarro
**cigarette lighter** o isqueiro
**cigarette papers** as mortalhas
**cinema** o cinema
**circle** *(theatre)* o balcão
**circuit breaker** o disjuntor
**circus** o circo
**cistern** a cisterna
**citizen** o cidadão/a cidadã
**city** a cidade
**city centre** o centro (da cidade)
**claim** a reclamação
**to clap** bater palmas
**class: first class** primeira classe
  *second class* segunda classe
**clean** limpo(a)
**to clean** limpar
**cleaner** *(person)* o/a empregado (a) de limpeza
  *(product)* produto de limpeza

**cleanser** o leite de limpeza
**clear** claro(a)
**client** o/a cliente
**cliff** o rochedo
**to climb** subir
**climbing** o alpinismo
**climbing boots** as botas de alpinismo
**clingfilm®** a película aderente
**clinic** a clínica
**cloakroom** o vestiário
**clock** o relógio
**to close** fechar
**closed** fechado(a) ; encerrado(a)
**cloth** *(fabric)* o tecido
  *(rag)* o trapo
**clothes** as roupas
**clothes line** o estendal
**clothes peg** a mola da roupa
**clothes shop** a loja de roupas ; a loja de moda
**cloudy** nublado(a)
**clove** *(spice)* o cravinho
**club** o clube
**clutch** a embraiagem
**coach** a camioneta
**coach station** a rodoviária ; o terminal de camionagem
**coach trip** a viagem de camioneta
**coal** o carvão
**coast** a costa
**coastguard** a polícia marítima
**coat** o casaco
**coat hanger** o cabide
**Coca Cola®** a Coca-Cola®
**cockroach** a barata
**cocktail** o cocktail
**cocoa** o cacau
**coconut** o coco
**cod** o bacalhau
**code** *(phone)* o indicativo
**coffee** o café
  *white coffee* o café com leite
  *large white coffee* o galão
  *small black coffee* a bica ; o café
  *decaffeinated coffee* o café descafeinado
**coil** *(contraceptive)* o DIU
**coin** a moeda
**Coke®** a Coca-Cola®
**colander** o coador

**cold** frio(a)
 *I'm cold* tenho frio
 *it's cold* está frio(a)
 *cold water* a água fria
**cold** *(illness)* a constipação
 *I have a cold* tenho uma constipação
**cold sore** a herpes labial
**collar** *(of dress)* a gola
 *(of shirt)* o colarinho
**collarbone** a clavícula
**colleague** o/a colega
**to collect** coleccionar
 *(to collect someone)* ir buscar
**collection** a colecção
**colour** a cor
**colour-blind** daltónico(a)
**colour film** *(for camera)* o rolo a cores
**comb** o pente
**to come** vir
 *(arrive)* chegar
**to come back** voltar
**to come in** entrar
 *come in!* entre!
**comedy** a comédia
**comfortable** confortável
**company** *(firm)* a companhia
**compartment** o compartimento
**compass** a bússola
**to complain** queixar-se (de)
 *I want to complain of...* quero
 queixar-me de...
**complaint** uma queixa
 *complaints book* livro de reclamações
 *I wish to make a complaint* quero
 fazer uma reclamação
**complete** completo(a)
**to complete** completar
**composer** o/a compositor(a)
**compulsory** obrigatório(a)
**computer** o computador
**computer disk** *(floppy)* uma disquete
**computer game** o jogo de computador
**computer program** o programa de
 computador
**computer software** o software
**concert** o concerto
**concert hall** a sala de concertos
**concession** o desconto
**concussion** o traumatismo craniano
**condensed milk** o leite condensado
**condition** *(requirement)* a condição
 *(state)* o estado

**conditioner** o amaciador
**condom** o preservativo
**conductor** *(of orchestra)* o maestro/a
 maestrina
**cone** o cone
**conference** a conferência
**confession** a confissão
**to confirm** confirmar
 *please confirm* é favor confirmar
**confirmation** *(of booking)* a confirmação
**confused** confuso(a)
**congratulations!** parabéns!
**connection** *(flight, etc)* a ligação
**constipated** com prisão de ventre
**constipation** a prisão de ventre
**consulate** o consulado
**to consult** consultar
**to contact** pôr-se em contacto com
**contact lens cleaner** o líquido para as
 lentes de contacto
**contact lenses** as lentes de contacto
**to continue** continuar
**contraception** a anticoncepcão
**contraceptive** o preservativo ; o
 anticoncepcional
**contract** o contrato
**convenient: is it convenient?** é
 conveniente?
**convulsions** as convulsões
**to cook** cozinhar
**cooked** cozinhado(a)
**cooker** o fogão
**cookies** os biscoitos
**cool** fresco(a)
**cool box** *(for picnics)* a caixa refrigerada
**copper** cobre
**copy** a cópia
**to copy** copiar
**coriander** os coentros
**cork** *(in bottle)* a rolha
**corkscrew** o saca-rolhas
**corner** o canto
 *(outside)* a esquina
**corridor** o corredor
**cortisone** a cortisona
**cost** o custo
**to cost** custar
 *how much does it cost?* quanto
 (é que) custa?
**costume** o traje
 *(swimming – men)* os calções de banho
 *(swimming – women)* o fato de banho
**cot** o berço
**cottage** a casa de campo
**cotton** o algodão

**cotton buds** os cotonetes
**cotton wool** o algodão (hidrófilo)
**couchette** a couchette
**to cough** tossir
**cough** a tosse
**cough mixture** o xarope para a tosse
**cough sweets** as pastilhas para a tosse
**counter** *(shop, bar etc)* o balcão
**country** o país
**countryside** o campo
**couple** *(two people)* o casal
  *a couple of...* um par de...
**courgettes** as courgettes
**courier** *(tour guide)* o guia turístico/a
  guia turística
**courier service** o mensageiro
**course** *(of meal)* o prato
  *(of study)* o curso
**cousin** o/a primo(a)
**cover charge** o couvert
**cow** a vaca
**crab** o caranguejo
**crafts** o artesanato
**craftsman/woman** o artesão/a artesã
**cramps** as cãibras
**crash** *(car)* o choque
**to crash** colidir
**crash helmet** o capacete
**cream** *(for face, etc)* o creme
  *(on milk)* a nata
  *soured cream* as natas azedas
  *whipped cream* o chantilly
**creche** a creche
**credit card** o cartão de crédito
**crime** o crime
**crisps** as batatinhas fritas
**crop** a colheita
**croissant** o croissant
**to cross** *(road)* atravessar
**cross** a cruz
**crossed lines** as linhas cruzadas
**crossing** *(sea)* a travessia
**crossroads** o cruzamento
**crossword puzzle** as palavras cruzadas
**crowd** a multidão
**crowded** cheio(a) de gente
**crown** a coroa
**cruise** o cruzeiro
**crutches** as muletas
**to cry** *(weep)* chorar
**crystal** o cristal
**cucumber** o pepino
**cufflinks** os botões de punho
**cul-de-sac** o beco sem saída
**cumin** o cominho

**cup** a chávena
**cupboard** o armário
**curlers** os rolos
**currant** a passa de corinto
**currency** a moeda
**current** a corrente
**curtain** a cortina
**cushion** a almofada
**custard** o leite-creme
**custom** *(tradition)* o costume
**customer** o freguês/a freguesa
**customs** *(at airport etc)* a alfândega
**customs declaration** declaração
  alfandegária
**customs officer** o/a funcionário(a)
  aduaneiro(a)
**to cut** cortar
  *we've been cut off* foi interrompida a
  ligação
**cut** o corte
  *cut and blow-dry* cortar e secar
**cutlery** os talheres
**to cycle** andar de bicicleta
**cycle track** a pista para ciclistas
**cycling** o ciclismo
**cyst** o quisto
**cystitis** a cistite

# D

**daily** cada dia ; diariamente
**dairy produce** os lacticínios
**daisy** a margarida
**dam** a barragem
**damage** os danos
**damp** húmido(a)
**dance** o baile
**to dance** dançar
**danger** o perigo
**dangerous** perigoso(a)
**dark** o escuro
  *adj* escuro(a)
  *after dark* depois do anoitecer
**date** a data
**date of birth** a data de nascimento
**daughter** a filha
**daughter-in-law** a nora
**dawn** o amanhecer
**day** o dia
  *every day* todos os dias
  *per day* ao dia ; por dia

**dead** morto(a)

**deaf** surdo(a)

**dear** *(on letter)* querido(a)
*(expensive)* caro(a)

**death** a morte

**debt** a dívida

**decaff** o café descafeinado
*have you decaff?* tem café
descafeinado?

**decaffeinated coffee** o café
descafeinado

**December** o Dezembro

**deckchair** a cadeira de lona

**to declare:** *nothing to declare* nada a
declarar

**deep** fundo(a)

**deep freeze** o congelador

**deer** o veado

**to defrost** descongelar

**to de-ice** descongelar

**delay** a demora ; o atraso
*how long is the delay?* quanto é o
atraso?

**delayed** atrasado(a)

**delicatessen** a charcutaria

**delicious** delicioso(a)

**demonstration** *(political)* a manifestação

**dental floss** o fio dental

**dentist** o/a dentista

**dentures** a dentadura postiça

**deodorant** o desodorizante

**to depart** partir

**department** o departamento

**department store** o grande armazém

**departure lounge** a sala de embarque

**departures** as partidas

**deposit** o depósito

**to describe** descrever

**description** a descrição

**desk** a secretária
*(in hotel, airport)* o balcão

**dessert** a sobremesa

**details** os pormenores ; os detalhes

**detergent** o detergente

**detour** o desvio

**to develop** *(film)* revelar

**diabetes** a diabetes

**diabetic** *(person)* diabético(a)
*(food)* para diabéticos
*I'm diabetic* sou diabético(a)

**to dial** marcar

**dialect** o dialecto

**dialling code** o indicativo

**dialling tone** o sinal

**diamond** o diamante

**diaper** a fralda

**diaphragm** *(in body)* o diafragma
*(contraceptive)* o diafragma

**diarrhoea** a diarreia

**diary** o diário ; a agenda

**dice** os dados

**dictionary** o dicionário

**to die** morrer

**diesel** o gasóleo

**diet** a dieta
*I'm on a diet* estou de dieta
*special diet* o regime especial

**different** diferente

**difficult** difícil

**to dilute** diluir

**dinghy** o bote

**dining room** a sala de jantar

**dinner** o jantar
*to have dinner* jantar

**dinner jacket** o smoking

**diplomat** o/a diplomata

**direct** directo(a)

**directions** *(instructions)* instrucções
*to ask for directions* pedir indicações

**directory** *(phone)* a lista telefónica

**directory enquiries** as informações
telefónicas

**dirty** sujo(a)

**disability** a incapacidade

**disabled** deficiente ; incapacitado(a)
*disabled person* o/a deficiente

**to disagree** discordar

**to disappear** desaparecer

**disappointed** desiludido(a)

**disaster** o desastre

**disco** a discoteca

**discount** o desconto

**to discover** descobrir

**disease** a doença

**dish** o prato

**dishtowel** o pano de cozinha

**dishwasher** a máquina de lavar louça

**dishwasher powder** o detergente em
pó

**disinfectant** o desinfectante

**disk** *(computer)* o disco
*floppy disk* a disquete
*hard disk* o disco duro

**to dislocate** *(joint)* deslocar

**disposable** descartável

**distance** a distância

**distant** distante

**distilled water** a água destilada
**district** o distrito
**to disturb** incomodar
**to dive** mergulhar
**diver** o/a mergulhador(a)
**diversion** o desvio
**diving** mergulhar
**divorced** divorciado(a)
　*I'm divorced* sou divorciado(a)
**DIY shop** a loja de bricolaje
**dizzy** tonto(a)
**to do** fazer
**doctor** o/a médico(a)
**documents** os documentos
**dog** *(male)* o cão
　*(female)* a cadela
**dog food** comida para cães
**dog lead** a correia
**doll** a boneca
**dollar** o dólar
**domestic** doméstico(a)
**domestic flight** o voo doméstico
**dominoes** o dominó
**donor card** o cartão de dador
**donkey** o burro
**door** a porta
**doorbell** a campainha
**double** o dobro
**double bed** a cama de casal
**double room** o quarto de casal
**doughnut** a bola de Berlim
**down:** *to go down* descer
**downstairs** em baixo
**dragonfly** a libélula
**drain** *(sewer)* o esgoto
**draught** *(of air)* a corrente de ar
　*there's a draught* há uma corrente
　de ar
**draught lager** a imperial
**drawer** a gaveta
**drawing** o desenho
**dress** o vestido
**to dress (oneself)** vestir-se
**dressing** *(for food)* o tempero ; o molho
　*(for wound)* o penso
**dressing gown** o roupão
**drill** *(tool)* a broca
**drink** a bebida
**to drink** beber
**drinking chocolate** o chocolate
**drinking water** a água potável
**to drive** conduzir
**driver** o/a condutor(a)
**driving licence** a carta de condução

**drizzle** o chuvisco
**drought** a seca
**to drown** afogar
**drug** *(medicine)* o medicamento
　*(narcotic)* a droga
**drunk** bêbedo(a)
**dry** seco(a)
**to dry** secar
**dry-cleaner's** a limpeza a seco
**dryer** o secador
**duck** o pato
**due:** *when is it due?* está previsto para
　quando?
**dummy** *(for baby)* a chupeta
**during** durante
**dust** o pó
**to dust** limpar o pó
**duster** o pano do pó
**dustpan and brush** pá e vassoura
**duty** *(tax)* o imposto
**duty-free** livre de impostos ; 'duty free'
**duvet** o edredão
**duvet cover** o saco do edredão
**dye** a tinta
**dynamo** o dínamo

# E

**each** cada
**eagle** a águia
**ear** a orelha
　*(inner)* o ouvido
**earache** a dor de ouvidos
　*I have earache* doem-me os ouvidos
**earlier** mais cedo
**early** cedo
**earphones** os auscultadores
**earplugs** as borrachinhas (de ouvido)
**earrings** os brincos
**earth** *(planet)* a terra
**earthquake** o terramoto
**east** o leste
**Easter** a Páscoa
　*Happy Easter!* feliz Páscoa!
**easy** fácil
**to eat** comer
**ebony** o ébano
**echo** o eco
**economy** a economia
**edge** a beira ; a aresta
**eel** a enguia

**effective** eficaz

**egg** o ovo
  *fried egg* o ovo estrelado
  *hard-boiled egg* o ovo cozido
  *scrambled eggs* os ovos mexidos
  *soft-boiled egg* o ovo quente

**egg white** a clara de ovo

**egg yolk** a gema de ovo

**either... or...** ou... ou...

**elastic band** o elástico

**Elastoplast®** o penso

**elbow** o cotovelo

**electric** eléctrico(a)

**electric blanket** o cobertor eléctrico

**electrician** o/a electricista

**electricity** a electricidade ; a luz

**electricity meter** o contador de electricidade

**electric razor** a máquina de barbear

**electric shock** o choque eléctrico

**elevator** o elevador

**elegant** elegante

**e-mail** o correio electrónico; e-mail
  *to e-mail someone* mandar um e-mail

**e-mail address** o endereço de e-mail

**embarrassing** embaraçoso(a)

**embassy** a embaixada

**emergency** a emergência

**emergency exit** a saída de emergência

**emery board** a lixa de unhas

**empty** vazio(a)

**end** o fim

**engaged** comprometido(a)
  *(phone, toilet, etc)* ocupado(a)
  *(to be married)* noivo(a)

**engine** o motor

**engineer** o/a engenheiro(a)

**England** a Inglaterra

**English** inglês (inglesa)
  *(language)* o inglês

**Englishman** o inglês

**Englishwoman** a inglesa

**enjoy oneself** divertir-se
  *I enjoy swimming* gosto de nadar
  *I enjoy dancing* gosto de dançar
  *enjoy yourself!* diverte-te!
  *enjoy your meal!* bom apetite!

**to enlarge** aumentar

**enormous** enorme

**enough** bastante
  *that's enough* chega

**enquiries** informações

**enquiry desk** o balcão de informações

**to enter** entrar

**entertainment** a diversão

**enthusiastic** entusiástico(a)

**entrance** a entrada

**entrance fee** o bilhete ; o preço de entrada

**envelope** o envelope

**epileptic** epiléptico(a)

**epileptic fit** o ataque epiléptico

**equipment** o equipamento

**eraser** a borracha

**error** o erro ; o engano

**eruption** a erupção

**escalator** a escada rolante

**to escape** escapar

**escape ladder** a escada de salvação

**espadrilles** as alpercatas

**espresso** a bica ; o café

**essential** essencial

**estate agent** o/a agente imobiliário(a)

**estate agent's** a imobiliária

**establish** estabelecer

**euro** o euro

**Eurocheque** o Eurocheque

**Europe** a Europa

**European** europeu (européia)

**European Union** a União Européia

**eve** a véspera
  *Christmas Eve* a véspera de Natal
  *New Year's Eve* a véspera de Ano Novo

**even** *(number)* par

**evening** a noite
  *in the evening* à noite
  *this evening* esta noite
  *tomorrow evening* amanhã à noite

**evening dress** o traje de cerimónia

**evening meal** o jantar

**every** cada

**everyone** toda a gente

**everything** todas as coisas, tudo

**everywhere** por todo o lado

**examination** o exame ; a prova

**example: for example** por exemplo

**excellent** excelente

**except** excepto

**excess baggage/luggage** o excesso de bagagem

**to exchange** trocar

**exchange rate** o câmbio

**exciting** emocionante

**excursion** a excursão

**excuse** a desculpa
  *excuse me!* desculpe!

**exercise** *(physical)* o exercício

**exercise book** o caderno
**exhaust pipe** o tubo de escape
**exhibition** a exposição
**exit** a saída
**expenses** as despesas
**expensive** caro(a)
**expert** o/a perito(a)
**to expire** *(ticket, etc)* caducar
**expiry date** o vencimento
**to explain** explicar
**explosion** a explosão
**to export** exportar
**express** *(train)* o expresso
**express: to send a letter express**
mandar uma carta por correio
expresso
**extension** *(phone)* a extensão
**extra** extra
*an extra bed* uma cama adicional
**to extinguish** apagar
**eye** o olho
**eyebrows** as sobrancelhas
**eyedrops** as gotas para os olhos
**eyelashes** as pestanas
**eyeliner** o lápis para os olhos
**eyeshadow** a sombra para os olhos

# F

**fabric** o tecido
**face** a cara ; o rosto
**face cloth** a toalha de rosto
**facial** a limpeza facial
**facilities** as instalações
**factory** a fábrica
**to fail** fracassar
*(engine, brakes)* falhar
**to faint** desmaiar
**fainted** desmaiado(a)
**fair** *(hair)* louro(a)
**fair** *(just)* justo(a)
**fair** *(funfair)* o parque de diversões
*(trade)* a feira
**fairway** *(golf)* o fairway
**fake** falso(a)
**fall** *(autumn)* o Outono
**to fall** cair
*he/she has fallen* ele/ela caiu
**false teeth** os dentes postiços
**family** a família
**famous** famoso(a)
**fan** *(hand-held)* o leque
*(electric)* a ventoínha
*(football, jazz)* o/a fan
**fan belt** a correia da ventoínha

## eng-por     f

**fancy dress** o traje de Carnaval
**far** longe
*is it far?* é longe?
*how far is it to...?* qual é a distância
daqui a...?
**fare** *(train, bus, etc)* o preço (da
passagem)
**farm** a quinta
**farmer** o/a agricultor(a)
**farmhouse** a casa da quinta
**fashionable** de moda
**fast** rápido(a)
*too fast* rápido demais
**to fasten** *(seatbelt)* apertar
**fat** gordo(a)
*saturated fats* gorduras saturadas
*unsaturated fats* gorduras insaturadas
**father** o pai
**father-in-law** o sogro
**fault** *(defect)* o defeito
*it's not my fault* a culpa não é minha
**favour** o favor
**favourite** favorito(a) ; preferido(a)
**fax** o fax
*by fax* por fax
**to fax** mandar por fax
**fax number** o número de fax
**feather** a pena
**February** o Fevereiro
**to feed** alimentar
**to feel** apalpar ; sentir
*I feel sick* tenho náuseas
*I don't feel well* sinto-me mal-
disposto(a)
**feet** os pés
**fellow** o companheiro
**felt-tip pen** a caneta de feltro
**female** a mulher
**ferry** o ferry-boat
**festival** o festival
**to fetch** *(to bring)* trazer
*(to go and get)* ir buscar
**fever** a febre
**few** poucos(as)
*a few* alguns (algumas)
**fiancé(e)** o/a noivo(a)
**field** o campo
**fig** o figo
**fight** a briga
**to fight** brigar
**file** *(computer)* o ficheiro
*(nail)* a lima
*(folder)* a pasta

**filigree** a filigrana
**to fill** encher
  *fill it up!* encha o depósito!
  *to fill in* (form) preencher
**fillet** o filete
**filling** (in tooth) a obturação
**filling station** a estação de serviço
**film** (at cinema) o filme
  (for camera) o rolo de filme
  *colour film* o rolo a cores
  *black and white film* o rolo a preto e branco
**Filofax®** a agenda
**filter** o filtro
**to find** achar
**fine** (to be paid) a multa
**fine** fino(a)
**fine arts** as belas-artes
**finger** o dedo
**to finish** acabar
**finished** acabado(a) ; terminado(a)
**fire** o fogo ; o incêndio
**fire alarm** o alarme contra incêndios
**fire brigade** os bombeiros
**fire engine** o carro dos bombeiros
**fire escape** a saída de incêndios
**fire extinguisher** o extintor
**fireplace** a lareira
**fireworks** os fogos de artifício
**firm** (company) a firma ; a companhia
**first** o/a primeiro(a)
**first aid** os primeiros socorros
**first aid kit** o estojo de primeiros socorros
**first class** a primeira classe
**first-class** de primeira classe
**first floor** o primeiro andar
**first name** o próprio nome
**fish** o peixe
**to fish** pescar
  *to go fishing* ir pescar
**fisherman** o pescador
**fishing permit** a licença de pesca
**fishing rod** a cana de pesca
**fishmonger's** a peixaria
**to fit:** *it doesn't fit me* não me serve
**fit** o ataque
  *he had a fit* ele teve um ataque
**to fix** reparar ; arranjar ; consertar
  *can you fix it?* pode arranjá-lo?
**fizzy** gasoso(a) ; com gás
**flag** a bandeira

**flame** a chama
**flash** (for camera) o flash
**flashlight** a lanterna
**flask** o termo
**flat** (apartment) o apartamento
**flat** plano(a)
  (battery) descarregado
  *this drink is flat* esta bebida já perdeu o gás
**flat tyre** o furo
**flavour** sabor
  *which flavour?* de que sabor?
**flaw** a falha
**fleas** as pulgas
**fleece** (top/jacket) de fibra polar
**flesh** a carne
**flex** o cabo eléctrico
**flight** o voo
**flip flops** os chinelos
**flippers** as barbatanas
**flood** a inundação
  *flash flood* a inundação repentina
**floor** o chão
  (storey) o andar ; o piso
  *which floor?* qual é o andar?
  *ground floor* o rés-do-chão
  *first floor* o primeiro andar
  *second floor* o segundo andar
**floorcloth** o pano do chão
**floppy disk** a disquete
**florist's shop** a florista
**flour** a farinha
**flower** a flor
**flu** a gripe
**fly** a mosca
**to fly** voar
**fly sheet** o duplo-tecto
**fog** o nevoeiro
**foggy** enevoado(a)
**foil** (silver) o papel de alumínio
**to follow** seguir
**food** a comida
**food poisoning** a intoxicação alimentar
**fool** burro(a)
**foot** o pé
  *on foot* a pé
**football** o futebol
**football match** o jogo de futebol
**football pitch** o campo de futebol
**football player** o jogador de futebol
**footpath** o caminho
**for** para ; por
  *for me* para mim
  *for you* para si
  *for him/her/us* para ele/ela/nós
  *for them* para eles (elas)

**forbidden** proibido(a)
**forecast** a previsão
  *weather forecast* a previsão do tempo
**forehead** a testa
**foreign** estrangeiro(a)
**foreigner** o/a estrangeiro(a)
**forest** a floresta
**forever** para sempre
**to forget** esquecer-se de
**to forgive** perdoar
**fork** *(for eating)* o garfo
  *(in road)* a bifurcação
**form** *(document)* o formulário ; a ficha
**formal dress** o traje de cerimónia
**fortnight** a quinzena ; quinze dias
**fortress** a fortaleza
**forward(s)** para a frente
**foul** *(in football)* a falta
**fountain** a fonte
**four-wheel drive** o quatro-vezes-quatro
**fox** a raposa
**fracture** a fractura
**fragile** frágil
**fragrance** a fragrância
**frame** *(picture)* a moldura
**France** a França
**free** *(not occupied)* livre
  *(costing nothing)* grátis
**freezer** o congelador
**French** francês (francesa)
  *(language)* o francês
**French beans** o feijão-verde
**French fries** as batatas fritas
**frequent** frequente
**fresh** fresco(a)
**fresh water** a água doce
**Friday** a sexta-feira
**fridge** o frigorífico
**fried** frito(a)
**friend** o/a amigo(a)
**friendly** simpático(a)
**frog** a rã
**from** de
  *from England* da Inglaterra
  *from Scotland* da Escócia
**front** a frente
  *in front of* em frente de
**front door** a porta da frente
**frost** a geada
**frozen** congelado(a)
**fruit** a fruta
  *dried fruit* os frutos secos
**fruit juice** o sumo de frutas
**fruit salad** a salada de frutas
**to fry** fritar

**frying pan** a frigideira
**fuel** *(petrol)* a gasolina
**fuel gauge** o medidor de gasolina
**fuel pump** a bomba de gasolina
**fuel tank** o depósito (de combustível)
**full** cheio(a)
**full board** a pensão completa
**fumes** *(of car)* os fumos de escape
**fun** a diversão
**funeral** o funeral
**funfair** o parque de diversões
**funny** engraçado(a
  *(strange)* estranho(a)
**fur** a pele
**furnished** mobilado(a)
**furniture** a mobília
**fuse** o fusível
**fuse box** a caixa de fusíveis
**futon** o futon
**future** o futuro

# G

**gallery** *(art)* a galeria de arte
**gallon** = approx. 4.5 litres
**game** o jogo
  *(animal)* a caça
**garage** *(private)* a garagem
  *(for repairs)* a oficina
  *(for petrol)* a estação de serviço
**garden** o jardim
**gardener** o/a jardineiro(a)
**garlic** o alho
**to garnish** guarnecer
**gas** o gás
**gas cooker** o fogão a gás
**gas cylinder** a garrafa de gás
**gastritis** a gastrite
**gate** *(airport)* o portão
**gay** *(person)* gay
**gear** a velocidade
  *first gear* a primeira velocidade
  *second gear* a segunda velocidade
  *third gear* a terceira velocidade
  *fourth gear* a quarta velocidade
  *fifth gear* a quinta velocidade
  *neutral* o ponto morto
  *reverse* a marcha atrás
**gearbox** a caixa de velocidades
**generous** generoso(a)
**gents'** *(toilet)* Homens
  *where is the gents'?* onde é o lavabo
  dos homens?

**genuine** (leather, antique etc) autêntico(a)
**German** alemão (alemã)
  (language) o alemão
**German measles** a rubéola
**Germany** a Alemanha
**to get** (to obtain) obter
  (to receive) receber
  (to fetch) ir buscar
**to get in** (vehicle) subir em
**to get into** entrar
**to get off** descer de
**to get on** (vehicle) subir para
**gift** o presente ; a prenda
**gift shop** a loja de lembranças
**gin and tonic** um gim tónico
**ginger** o gengibre
**girl** a rapariga
**girlfriend** a namorada
**to give** dar
**to give back** devolver
**glacier** o glaciar
**glass** (substance) o vidro ; o cristal
  (to drink out of) o copo
  a glass of water um copo de água
**glasses** os óculos
**glasses case** a caixa dos óculos
**gloss** o brilho
**gloves** as luvas
**glue** a cola
**to go** ir
  I'm going to... vou para…
  we're going to... vamos para…
**to go back** voltar
**to go down** descer
**to go in** entrar
**to go out** sair
**goat** a cabra
**God** o Deus
**godchild** o/a afilhado(a)
**goggles** os óculos protectores
**gold** o ouro
**golf** o golfe
**golf ball** a bola de golfe
**golf clubs** os tacos de golfe
**golf course** o campo de golfe
**good** bom (boa)
  very good muito bom
**good afternoon** boa tarde
**goodbye** adeus
**good evening** boa tarde ; boa noite

**good morning** bom dia
**good night** boa noite
**goose** o ganso
**gooseberry** a groselha branca
**Gothic** gótico(a)
**graduate** o/a licenciado(a)
**gram** o grama
**grandchild** o/a neto(a)
**granddaughter** a neta
**grandfather** o avô
  great grandfather o bisavô
**grandmother** a avó
  great grandmother a bisavó
**grandparents** os avós
**grandson** o neto
**grapefruit** a toranja
**grapefruit juice** o sumo de toranja
**grapes** as uvas
  green grapes as uvas brancas
  black grapes as uvas pretas
**grass** a erva
**grated** (cheese, etc) ralado(a)
**grater** (for cheese, etc) o ralador
**greasy** oleoso(a) ; gorduroso(a)
**great** (big) grande
  (wonderful) óptimo(a)
**Great Britain** a Grã-Bretanha
**green** verde
**green card** (car insurance) o cartão verde
**greengrocer's** a frutaria
**greetings card** o cartão de felicitações
**grey** cinzento(a)
**grill** a grelha
**to grill** grelhar
**grilled** grelhado(a)
**grocer's** a mercearia
**ground** (earth) a terra
  (floor) o chão
**ground floor** o rés-do-chão
  on the ground floor... no rés-do-chão…
**groundsheet** a cobertura impermeável
**group** o grupo
**to grow** crescer
**guarantee** a garantia
**guard** o guarda
**guest** o/a convidado(a)
  (in hotel) o/a hóspede
**guesthouse** a pensão
**guide** o/a guia
**to guide** guiar
**guidebook** a guia
**guided tour** a excursão guiada
**guitar** a guitarra

**gun** a pistola
**gym** o ginásio
**gym shoes** os ténis

# H

**haberdasher's** a retrosaria
**haddock** o eglefim
**haemorrhoids** as hemorróidas
**hail** o granizo
**hair** o cabelo
**hairbrush** a escova de cabelo
**haircut** o corte de cabelo
**hairdresser** o/a cabeleireiro(a)
**hairdryer** o secador de cabelo
**hair dye** a tinta para o cabelo
**hair gel** o gel para o cabelo
**hairgrip** o gancho de cabelo
**hair mousse** a espuma para o cabelo
**hairspray** a laca
**hake** a pescada
**half** a metade
  *a half bottle of* meia garrafa de
  *half an hour* meia hora
**half board** a meia pensão
**half fare** meio-bilhete
**half-price** pela metade do preço
**ham** *(cured)* o presunto
  *(boiled)* o fiambre
**hamburger** o hambúrguer
**hammer** o martelo
**hand** a mão
**handbag** a mala de mão
**handicapped** *(person)* deficiente
**handkerchief** o lenço
**handle** *(of cup)* a asa
  *(of door)* a maçaneta
**handlebars** os guiadores
**hand luggage** a bagagem de mão
**hand-made** feito(a) à mão
**handsome** bonito(a), giro(a)
**to hang up** *(phone)* desligar
**hanger** o cabide
**hang gliding** a asa-delta
**hangover** a ressaca
**to happen** acontecer
  *what happened?* o que aconteceu?
**happy** feliz ; contente
  *happy birthday!* feliz aniversário!
**harbour** o porto
**hard** duro(a)
  *(difficult)* difícil
**hard disk** o disco duro
**hardware shop** a loja de ferragens
**hare** a lebre

**harm** o mal ; o dano
**harvest** a colheita
**hat** o chapéu
**to have** ter
  *I have...* eu tenho...
  *I don't have...* eu não tenho...
  *we have...* nós temos...
  *we don't have...* nós não temos...
  *do you have...?* tem...?
**to have to** ter que/de
**hay fever** a febre dos fenos
**hazelnut** a avelã
**he** ele
**head** a cabeça
**headache** a dor de cabeça
  *I have a headache* dói-me a cabeça
**headlights** os faróis
**headphones** os auscultadores
**head waiter** o chefe de mesa
**health** a saúde
**health food shop** a loja de produtos dietéticos
**healthy** saudável
**to hear** ouvir
**hearing aid** o aparelho auditivo
**heart** o coração
**heart attack** o ataque de coração
**heartburn** a azia
**heatstroke** a insolação
**to heat up** aquecer
**heater** o aquecedor
**heating** o aquecimento
**heaven** o Céu
**heavy** pesado(a)
**heel** *(of foot)* o calcanhar
  *(of shoe)* o salto
**heel bar** o sapateiro
**height** a altura
**helicopter** o helicóptero
**hello** olá
  *(on phone)* está?
**helmet** o capacete
**help** a ajuda
  *help!* socorro!
**to help** ajudar
  *can you help me?* pode-me ajudar?
**hem** a bainha
**hen** a galinha
**hepatitis** a hepatite
**herb** a erva aromática
**herbal tea** a tisana

**here** aqui
  *here is...* aqui está...
  *here is my passport* aqui está o meu passaporte
**hernia** a hérnia
**hi!** olá!
**to hide** (something) esconder
  (oneself) esconder-se
**high** (price, speed, building) alto(a)
  (number) grande
**high blood pressure** a tensão alta
**highchair** a cadeira de bebé
**high tide** a maré alta
**hill** a colina
**hill-walking** o alpinismo
**him** (direct object) o
  (indirect object) lhe
  (after preposition) ele
**hip** a anca
**hip replacement** a prótese de anca
**hire** o aluguer
  *car hire* o aluguer de carros
  *bike hire* o aluguer de bicicletas
  *boat hire* o aluguer de barcos
  *ski hire* o aluguer de esquis
**to hire** alugar
**historic** histórico(a)
**history** a história
**to hit** bater
**to hitchhike** andar à boleia
**HIV** o vírus da SIDA
**HIV positive** seropositivo(a)
**hobby** o passatempo
**to hold** (to contain) conter
**hold-up** o engarrafamento
**hole** o buraco
**holiday** as férias
  (public holiday) o feriado
  *on holiday* de férias
**holiday rep** o/a representante da agência de viagens
**hollow** oco(a)
**holy** santo(a)
**home** a casa
  *at home* em casa
  *to go home* voltar para casa
**homeopath** o/a homeopata
**homeopathic** homeopático(a)
**homeopathy** a homeopatia
**homesick:** *to be homesick* ter saudades de casa
  *I'm homesick* tenho saudades de casa
**homosexual** homossexual

**honest** honesto(a)
**honey** o mel
**honeymoon** a lua-de-mel
**hood** (of jacket) o capuz
  (of car) a capota
**hook** (for fishing) o anzol
**to hope** esperar
  *I hope so/not* espero que sim/não
**horn** (of car) a buzina
**hors d'œuvre** a entrada
**horse** o cavalo
**horse racing** as corridas de cavalo
**horse riding:** *to go horse riding* andar a cavalo
**hosepipe** a mangueira
**hospital** o hospital
**hostel** a pousada
**hot** quente
  *I'm hot* tenho calor
  *it's hot* está quente
  *it's hot* (weather) faz/está calor
**hot chocolate** o chocolate quente
**hotel** o hotel
**hot water** a água quente
**hot-water bottle** o saco de água quente
**hour** a hora
  *half an hour* meia hora
  *1 hour* uma hora
  *2 hours* duas horas
**house** a casa
**housewife/husband** a/o dona(o) de casa
**house wine** o vinho da casa
**housework** a lida da casa
**hovercraft** o hovercraft
**how** como
  *how much?* quanto(a)?
  *how many?* quantos(as)?
  *how are you?* como está?
**hundred** cem ; cento
  *five hundred* quinhentos
**hungry:** *I am hungry* tenho fome
**hunt** a caça
**to hunt** caçar
**hunting permit** a licença de caça
**hurry:** *I'm in a hurry* tenho pressa
**to hurt** doer
  *that hurts* isso dói
  *my back hurts* tenho dor de costas
**husband** o marido
**hut** a cabana
**hydrofoil** o hidrofólio
**hypodermic needle** a agulha hipodérmica

**I** eu
**ice** o gelo
  *(cube)* o cubo
  *with ice* com gelo
  *without ice* sem gelo
**ice box** o frigorífico
**ice cream** o gelado
**iced coffee** o café gelado
**iced tea** o chá gelado
**ice lolly** o gelado
**ice rink** o rinque de patinagem
**to ice-skate** patinar sobre o gelo
**ice skates** os patins de lâmina
**idea** a idéia
**identity card** o bilhete de identidade
**if** se
**ignition** a ignição
**ignition key** a chave de ignição
**ill** doente
  *I'm ill* estou doente
**illness** a doença
**immediately** imediatamente
**immersion heater** o esquentador de imersão
**immigration** a imigração
**immunisation** a imunização
**to import** importar
**important** importante
**impossible** impossível
**to improve** melhorar
**in** em
  *(within)* dentro de
  *in 10 minutes* dentro de dez minutes
  *in London* em Londres
**in front of** em frente de
**inch** = approx. 2.5 cm
**included** incluído(a)
**inconvenient** inconveniente
**to increase** aumentar
**indicator** *(on car)* o pisca-pisca
**indigestion** a indigestão
**indigestion tablets** os comprimidos para indigestão
**indoors** em casa
**inefficient** ineficiente
**infection** a infecção
**infectious** contagioso(a)
**informal** *(person)* sem formalidades
  *(costume)* informal
**information** a informação
**information desk** o balcão de informações

**information office** o departamento de informações
**ingredient** o ingrediente
**inhaler** *(for medication)* o inalador
**injection** a injecção
**to injure** lesionar
**injured** ferido(a)
**injury** a lesão
**ink** a tinta
**inn** a estalagem
**inner tube** a câmara-de-ar
**inquiries** informações
**inquiry desk** o balcão de informações
**insect** o insecto
**insect bite** a picada de insecto
**insect repellent** o repelente contra insectos
**inside** dentro
**instalment** a prestação
**instant coffee** o café instantâneo
**instead of** em vez de
**instructor** o/a instrutor(a)
**insulin** a insulina
**insurance** o seguro
**insurance certificate** a apólice de seguro
**to insure** pôr no seguro
**insured: to be insured** estar no seguro
**intelligent** inteligente
**to intend to do** tencionar fazer
**interesting** interessante
**internet** a internet
**internet café** o cibercafé
**international** internacional
**interpreter** o/a intérprete
**interval** o intervalo
**interview** a entrevista
**into** em ; a
  *into the centre* ao centro
**to introduce someone to someone** apresentar alguém a alguém
**invitation** o convite
**to invite** convidar
**invoice** a factura
**Ireland** a Irlanda
**Irish** irlandês (irlandesa)
**iron** *(metal)* o ferro
  *(for clothes)* o ferro de engomar
**to iron** passar a ferro
**ironing board** a tábua de engomar
**ironmonger's** a loja de ferragens

**island** a ilha
**it** o/a
**Italian** italiano(a)
  *(language)* o italiano
**Italy** a Itália
**itch** a comichão
**to itch** fazer comichão
  *it itches* faz comichão
**item** o artigo
**itemized bill** a factura detalhada
**ivory** o marfim

# J

**jack** *(for car)* o macaco
**jacket** o casaco
  *waterproof jacket* o casaco
  impermeável
**jackpot** o prémio (de lotaria, rifa)
**jacuzzi®** o jacuzzi
**jam** a compota
**jammed** *(stuck)* bloqueado(a)
**January** o Janeiro
**jar** o jarro ; o pote
**jaundice** a icterícia
**jaw** o queixo
**jazz** o jazz
**jealous** ciumento(a)
**jeans** as jeans ; as calças de ganga
**jelly** a gelatina
**jellyfish** a medusa ; a alforreca
**jet ski** a motonáutica
**jetty** o quebra-mar ; o cais
**jewel** a jóia
**jewellery** a joalharia
**Jewish** judeu (judia)
**job** o emprego
**to jog** ir fazer jogging
**to join** *(club)* associar-se a
**to join in** participar
**joint** *(of body)* a articulação
**joke** a piada ; a anedota
**to joke** brincar
**journalist** o/a jornalista
**journey** a viagem
**judge** o juiz (a juíza)
**jug** o jarro
**juice** o sumo
  *apple juice* o sumo de maçã
  *orange juice* o sumo de laranja
  *tomato juice* o sumo de tomate
  *a carton of juice* um pacote de sumo
**July** o Julho

**to jump** saltar
**jump leads** os cabos para ligar a bateria
**junction** o cruzamento
**June** o Junho
**just:** *just two* apenas dois
  *I've just arrived* acabo de chegar

# K

**karaoke** o karaokê
**to keep** guardar
  *(retain)* ficar com
  *keep the change!* fique com o troco!
**kennel** a casota
**kennels** *(for dogs to stay)* o canil
**kettle** a chaleira
**key** a chave
  *card key* a chave-cartão
**keyboard** o teclado
**keyring** o porta-chaves
**to kick** *(person)* dar um pontapé em
  *(ball)* chutar
**kid** *(young goat)* o cabrito
  *(child)* a criança
**kidneys** os rins
**to kill** matar
**kilo** o quilo
  *a kilo of apples* um quilo de maçãs
  *2 kilos* dois quilos
**kilogram** o quilograma
**kilometre** o quilómetro
**kind** *(person)* amável
**kind** *(sort)* a espécie
**king** o rei
**kiosk** o quiosque
**kiss** o beijo
**to kiss** beijar
**kitchen** a cozinha
**kitchen paper** o papel de cozinha
**kite** o papagaio
**kitten** o/a gatinho(a)
**knee** o joelho
**knickers** as cuecas
**knife** a faca
**to knit** fazer malha
**to knock** *(on door)* bater
**to knock down** *(with car)* atropelar
**to knock over** *(vase, glass)* derrubar
**knot** o nó
**to know** *(have knowledge of)* saber
  *(person, place)* conhecer
  *I don't know* não sei
**to know how to do something** saber
  fazer alguma coisa
  *to know how to swim* saber nadar
**kosher** kosher

**label** a etiqueta
**lace** a renda
**laces** *(for shoes)* os atacadores
**ladder** a escada
**ladies'** *(toilet)* Senhoras
**lady** a senhora
**lager** a cerveja
  *bottled lager* a cerveja de garrafa
  *draught lager* a imperial
**lake** o lago
**lamb** o cordeiro
**lame** coxo(a)
**lamp** a lâmpada
**lamppost** o poste de iluminação
**lampshade** o abajur
**land** a terra
  *(country)* o país
**to land** aterrar
**landing** *(of plane)* a aterragem
**landlady** a senhoria
**landlord** o senhorio
**landslide** o desabamento
**lane** *(on motorway)* a faixa
**language** a língua
**language school** a Escola de Línguas
**laptop** o computador portátil
**large** grande
**last** último(a)
  *the last bus* o último autocarro
  *the last train* o último comboio
  *last night* ontem à noite
  *last week* a semana passada
  *last year* o ano passado
  *the last time* a última vez
**late** tarde
  *the train is late* o comboio está atrasado
  *sorry we are late* desculpe o atraso
**later** mais tarde
**to laugh** rir
**launderette** a lavandaria automática
**laundry service** o serviço de lavandaria
**lavatory** o lavabo
**lavender** a alfazema
**law** a lei
**lawn** o relvado
**lawyer** o/a advogado(a)
**laxative** o laxante
**layby** a berma
**lazy** preguiçoso(a)
**lead** *(electrical)* o cabo
  *(for dog)* a correia
**lead** *(metal)* o chumbo

**lead-free** sem chumbo
**leaf** a folha
**leak** *(of gas, liquid)* o escape ; o derrame
  *(roof)* o infiltração
**to leak:** *it's leaking (pipe)* está a verter
**to learn** aprender
**lease** o arrendamento
**least:** *at least* pelo menos
**leather** o couro
**leather goods** os cabedais
**to leave** *(leave behind)* deixar
  *(train, bus etc)* partir
  *when does it leave?* a que horas parte?
  *when does the bus leave?* a que horas parte o autocarro?
  *when does the train leave?* a que horas parte o comboio?
**leek** o alho francês
**left:** *on/to the left* à esquerda
**left-handed** canhoto(a)
**left luggage** *(office)* o depósito de bagagens
**left luggage locker** o cacifo
**leg** a perna
**legal** legal
**lemon** o limão
**lemonade** a limonada
**lemon tea** o carioca de limão ; o chá de limão
**to lend** emprestar
**length** o comprimento
**lens** *(of glasses)* a lente
  *(of camera)* a objectiva
**lenses** *(contact lenses)* as lentes de contacto
**lesbian** a lésbica
**less** menos
  *less than* menos do que
**lesson** a lição
**let** *(allow)* deixar
  *(lease)* alugar
**letter** a carta
  *(of alphabet)* a letra
**letterbox** a caixa do correio
**lettuce** a alface
**level crossing** a passagem de nível
**library** a biblioteca
**licence** a licença
  *(driving)* a carta de condução
**lid** a tampa
**lie** *(untruth)* a mentira
**to lie down** deitar-se

**life** a vida
**lifebelt** o cinto salva-vidas
**lifeboat** o barco salva-vidas
**lifeguard** o (guardo) salva-vidas
**life insurance** o seguro de vida
**life jacket** o colete de salvação
**life raft** a bolsa salva-vidas
**lift** *(elevator)* o elevador
  *(in car)* a boleia
**light** a luz
  *have you a light?* tem lume?
**light** *(not heavy)* leve
  *(colour)* claro(a)
**light bulb** a lâmpada
**lighter** o isqueiro
**lighthouse** o farol
**lightning** os relâmpagos
**like** como
  *it's like this* é assim
**to like** gostar de
  *I like coffee* gosto de café
  *I don't like...* não gosto de...
  *I'd like to...* gostava de...
  *we'd like to...* gostávamos de...
**lilo** o colchão de ar
**lime** a lima
**line** *(row, queue)* a fila
  *(phone)* a linha
**linen** *(cloth)* o linho
  *(bed linen)* a roupa de cama
**lingerie** a roupa interior
**lion** o leão
**lip reading** a leitura de lábios
**lips** os lábios
**lip salve** a pomada para os lábios
**lipstick** o batom
**liqueur** o licor
**list** a lista
**to listen to** ouvir
**litre** o litro
  *a litre of milk* um litro de leite
**litter** *(rubbish)* o lixo
**little** pequeno(a)
  *a little...* um pouco de...
**to live** viver ; morar
  *I live in Edinburgh* moro em
  Edimburgo
  *he lives in London* ele vive em
  Londres
  *he lives in a flat* ele vive num
  apartamento; ele mora num
  apartamento
**liver** o fígado

**living room** a sala de estar
**lizard** o lagarto
**loaf** *(of bread)* o pão
**lobster** a lagosta
**local** local
**to lock** fechar com chave
**lock** a fechadura
  *the lock is broken* a fechadura está
  quebrada
  *bike lock* o cadeado da bicicleta
**locker** *(luggage)* o depósito de
  bagagem
**locksmith** o/a serralheiro(a)
**log** o tronco
**log book** *(for car)* a documentação do
  carro
**lollipop** o chupa-chupa
**London** Londres
  *in London* em Londres
  *to London* a Londres
**long** comprido(a) ; longo(a)
  *for a long time* durante muito tempo
**long-sighted** presbíope
**to look after** cuidar de
**to look at** olhar
**to look for** procurar
**loose** solto(a)
  *it's come loose* soltou-se
**lorry** o camião
**to lose** perder
**lost** perdido(a)
  *I have lost my wallet* perdi a minha
  carteira
  *I am lost* estou perdido(a)
**lost property office** a secção de
  perdidos e achados
**lot:** *a lot (much)* muito(a)
  *(many)* muitos(as)
**lotion** a loção
**lottery** a lotaria
**loud** *(noisy)* barulhento(a)
  *(volume)* alto(a)
**lounge** *(in hotel)* a sala de estar
  *(in house)* a sala de estar
  *(in airport)* o salão
**to love** amar
  *I love swimming* gosto muito de
  nadar
  *I love you* amo-te
**lovely** encantador(a)
**low** baixo(a)
**low-fat** magro(a)
**low tide** a maré baixa
**luck** a sorte
**lucky:** *to be lucky* ter sorte
**luggage** a bagagem

**39**  **luggage rack** o porta-bagagens
**luggage tag** a etiqueta de bagagem
**luggage trolley** o carrinho
**lump** *(swelling)* o inchaço
  *(on head)* o galo
**lunch** o almoço
**lunch break** a hora do almoço
**lung** o pulmão
**luxury** o luxo

# M

**machine** a máquina
**mad** *(insane)* louco(a)
  *(angry)* furioso(a)
**madam** a senhora
**magazine** a revista
**maggot** a larva
**magnet** o íman
**magnifying glass** a lupa
**magpie** a pega
**maid** a empregada
**maiden name** o nome de solteira
**mail** o correio
  *by mail* pelo correio
**main** principal
**main course** *(of meal)* o prato principal
**main road** a estrada principal
**mains** *(electrical)* a rede eléctrica
**to make** *(generally)* fazer
  *(meal)* preparar
**make-up** a maquilhagem
**male** masculino(a)
**mallet** o maço
**man** o homem
**to manage** *(cope)* arranjar-se ;
  conseguir
**manager** o/a gerente
**managing director** o/a director(a) geral
**manual** manual
**many** muitos(as)
**map** o mapa
**marathon** a maratona
**marble** o mármore
**March** o Março
**margarine** a margarina
**marina** a marina
**marinated** marinado(a)
**marjoram** o orégão
**mark** *(stain)* a nódoa
**market** o mercado
  *where is the market?* onde (é que)
  fica o mercado?
  *when is the market?* quando (é que)
  há mercado?

**marketplace** o mercado
**marmalade** o doce de laranja
**married** casado(a)
  *I'm married* sou casado(a)
  *are you married?* é casado(a)?
**marry: to get married** casar(-se)
**marsh** o pântano
**marzipan** o maçapão
**mascara** o rímel®
**mashed potato** o puré de batata
**Mass** *(church service)* a missa
**mast** o mastro
**masterpiece** a obra-prima
**match** o fósforo
  *(game)* o jogo
**matches** os fósforos
**material** o material
  *(cloth)* o tecido
**to matter:** *it doesn't matter* não tem
  importância ; não importa
  *what is the matter?* o que (é que) se
  passa?
**mattress** o colchão
**maximum** o máximo
**May** o Maio
**mayonnaise** a maionese
**mayor** o presidente da Câmara
**me** me
  *(after preposition)* mim
  *me too* eu também
**meadow** o prado
**meal** a refeição
**to mean** significar
  *what does this mean?* o que (é que)
  quer dizer isto?
**measles** o sarampo
**to measure** medir
**meat** a carne
  *white meat* as carnes brancas
  *red meat* as carnes vermelhas
  *I don't eat meat* não como carne
**mechanic** o/a mecânico(a)
**medical insurance** o seguro de doença
**medicine** o medicamento
**medieval** medieval
**Mediterranean** o Mediterrâneo
**medium** médio(a)
  *medium rare (meat)* meio-passado(a)
**to meet** *(by chance)* encontrar
  *(by arrangement)* encontrar-se com
  *pleased to meet you* prazer em
  conhecê-lo(a)
**meeting** a reunião

**meeting point** o ponto de encontro

**melon** o melão

**to melt** derreter

**member** (of club, etc) o/a sócio(a)

**membership card** o cartão de sócio(a)

**memory** a memória
  *(thing remembered)* a lembrança

**men** os homens

**to mend** arranjar ; consertar

**meningitis** a meningite

**menu** a ementa
  *set menu* a ementa fixa
  *à la carte menu* a ementa a la carte

**meringue** o merengue

**message** a mensagem ; o recado

**metal** o metal

**meter** o contador

**metre** o metro

**microwave oven** o micro-ondas

**midday** o meio-dia
  *at midday* ao meio-dia

**middle** o meio

**middle-aged** de meia-idade

**midge** o mosquito

**midnight** a meia-noite
  *at midnight* à meia-noite

**migraine** a enxaqueca
  *I've a migraine* tenho uma enxaqueca

**mild** *(climate)* temperado(a)
  *(taste)* suave

**mile** a milha

**milk** o leite
  *fresh milk* o leite fresco
  *full-cream milk* o leite gordo
  *hot milk* o leite quente
  *long-life milk* o leite ultrapasteurizado
  *powdered milk* o leite em pó
  *semi-skimmed milk* o leite meio-gordo
  *skimmed milk* o leite magro
  *soya milk* o leite de soja
  *with milk* com leite
  *without milk* sem leite

**milkshake** o batido de leite

**millenium** o milénio

**millimetre** o milímetro

**million** o milhão

**mince** *(meat)* a carne picada

**mind** *n* a mente

**to mind** *vb (take care of)* ocupar-se de
  *(object to)* objectar
  *do you mind if...?* importa-se … se?
  *I don't mind* não me importo

**mineral water** a água mineral

**minibar** o minibar

**minimum** o mínimo

**minister** *(political)* o ministro
  *(church)* o pastor

**mink** o vison

**minor road** a estrada secundária

**mint** *(herb)* a hortelã
  *(sweet)* o rebuçado de mentol

**minute** o minuto

**mirror** o espelho

**to misbehave** comportar-se mal

**miscarriage** o aborto (espontâneo)

**Miss...** Menina… ; Senhora…

**to miss** *(plane, train, etc)* perder

**missing** *(lost)* perdido(a)
  *my son is missing* o meu filho desapareceu

**mistake** o erro

**misty: it's misty** há nevoeiro

**misunderstanding** o mal-entendido

**to mix** misturar

**mixer** a batedeira

**mobile phone** o telemóvel

**modem** o modem

**modern** moderno(a)

**moisturizer** o creme hidratante

**mole** *(on skin)* o sinal

**moment: just a moment** um momento

**monastery** o mosteiro

**Monday** a segunda-feira

**money** o dinheiro
  *I've no money* não tenho dinheiro

**money order** o vale postal

**monkey** o macaco

**month** o mês
  *this month* este mês
  *last month* o mês passado
  *next month* o mês que vem

**monthly** mensalmente

**monument** o monumento

**moon** a lua

**mooring** o atracadouro

**mop** a esfregona

**moped** a motocicleta

**more** mais
  *more than 3* mais de três
  *more bread* mais pão
  *more wine* mais vinho

**morning** a manhã
  *in the morning* de manhã
  *this morning* esta manhã
  *tomorrow morning* amanhã de manhã

**morning-after pill** a pílula abortiva

**mosque** a mesquita

**mosquito** o mosquito
**mosquito net** o mosquiteiro
**mosquito repellent** o repelente contra mosquitos
**most:** *most of* a maioria de
**moth** a borboleta
*(clothes)* a traça
**mother** a mãe
**mother-in-law** a sogra
**motor** o motor
**motorbike** a moto
**motorboat** o barco a motor
**motorcycle** a motocicleta
**motorway** a auto-estrada
**mould** *(mildew)* o bolor
**mountain** a montanha
**mountain bike** a bicicleta de montanha
**mountain rescue** o socorro para alpinistas
**mountaineering** o alpinismo
**mouse** o rato
**mousse** *(food)* a mousse
*(hair)* a espuma
**moustache** o bigode
**mouth** a boca
**mouthwash** o desinfectante para a boca
**to move** mexer ; mover
*it isn't moving* não se mexe ; não se move
**movie** o filme
**to mow** cortar
**Mr** Senhor
**Mrs** Senhora
**Ms** Senhora
**much** muito(a)
*too much* demais ; demasiado(a)
**mud** a lama
**muddy** *(road)* lamacento(a)
*(clothes)* enlameado(a)
**mugging** o assalto
**mumps** a papeira
**muscle** o músculo
**museum** o museu
**mushroom** o cogumelo
**music** a música
**musical** o musical
**mussel** o mexilhão
**must** *(to have to)* dever
*I must* devo
*we must* devemos
*I mustn't* não devo
*we mustn't* não devemos
**mustard** a mostarda
**mutton** o carneiro
**my** meu (minha)

# N

**nail** *(metal)* o prego
*(on finger)* a unha
**nailbrush** a escova das unhas
**nail clippers** o corta-unhas
**nail file** a lima para as unhas
**nail polish** o verniz das unhas
**nail polish remover** a acetona
**nail scissors** as tesouras para as unhas
**name** o nome
*my name is...* o meu nome é…
*what's your name?* como (é que) se chama?
**nanny** a ama
**napkin** o guardanapo
**nappy** a fralda
**narrow** estreito(a)
**national** nacional
**national park** o parque nacional
**nationality** a nacionalidade
**natural** natural
**nature** a natureza
**nature reserve** a reserva natural
**navy blue** azul-marinho
**near** perto
*near the bank* perto do banco
*is it near?* fica perto?
**necessary** necessário(a)
**neck** o pescoço
**necklace** o colar
**nectarine** a nectarina
**to need** precisar de
*I need...* preciso de
*we need...* precisamos de
*I need to go* tenho que ir
**needle** a agulha
*a needle and thread* uma agulha e a linha
**negative** *(photo)* o negativo
**neighbour** o/a vizinho(a)
**nephew** o sobrinho
**nest** o ninho
**net** a rede
**nettle** a urtiga
**never** nunca
*I never drink wine* nunca bebo vinho
**new** novo(a)
**news** as notícias
*(on television)* o telejornal
**newsagent** a tabacaria
**newspaper** o jornal

**newsstand** o quiosque
**New Year** o Ano Novo
  *happy New Year!* Feliz Ano Novo!
**New Year's Eve** a véspera de Ano Novo
**New Zealand** a Nova Zelândia
**next** próximo(a)
  *next to* ao lado de
  *next week* a semana que vem
  *the next bus* o próximo autocarro
  *the next stop* a próxima paragem
  *the next train* o próximo comboio
**nice** *(person, holiday)* simpático(a) agradável
  *(place)* bonito(a)
**niece** a sobrinha
**night** a noite
  *at night* à noite
  *last night* ontem à noite
  *per night* por noite
  *tomorrow night* amanhã à noite
**nightclub** a boite
**nightdress** a camisa de noite
**night porter** o porteiro da noite
**no** não
  *no entry* entrada proibida
  *no smoking* proibido fumar
  *no thanks* não, obrigado(a)
  *(without)* sem
  *no sugar* sem açúcar
  *no ice* sem gelo
**nobody** ninguém
**noise** o barulho
**noisy** barulhento(a)
  *it's very noisy* há muito barulho
**nonalcoholic** não-alcoólico(a)
**none** nenhum(a)
  *there's none left* não sobrou nada
**non-smoker** o/a não-fumador(a)
**non-smoking** não-fumador(a)
**north** o norte
**Northern Ireland** a Irlanda do Norte
**North Sea** o Mar do Norte
**nose** o nariz
**not** não
**note** *(banknote)* a nota
  *(letter)* a nota
**note pad** o bloco-notas
**nothing** nada
  *nothing else* mais nada
**notice** o aviso
**noticeboard** o placar
**novel** o romance

**now** agora
**nowhere** *(be)* em nenhum lugar
  *(go)* a lugar nenhum
**nuclear** nuclear
**nudist beach** a praia para nudistas
**number** o número
**numberplate** *(car)* a matrícula
**nurse** o/a enfermeiro(a)
**nursery** *(creche)* a creche
**nursery slope** a rampa para principiantes
**nut** *(to eat)* a noz
  *(for bolt)* a porca
**nutmeg** a noz moscada

# O

**oak** o carvalho
**oar** o remo
**oats** a aveia
**to obtain** obter
**obvious** óbvio(a)
**occasionally** às vezes
**occupation** *(work)* a ocupação
**ocean** o oceano
**October** o Outubro
**octopus** o polvo
**odd** *(number)* ímpar
**of** de
  *a bottle of water* uma garrafa de água
  *a glass of wine* um copo de vinho
  *made of...* feito(a) de...
**off** *(radio, engine, etc)* desligado(a)
  *(milk, food, etc)* estragado(a)
  *this meat is off* esta carne está estragada
**to offer** oferecer
**office** o escritório
**often** muitas vezes
  *how often?* quantas vezes?
**oil** o óleo
**oil filter** o filtro do óleo
**oil gauge** o indicador do óleo
**ointment** a pomada
**OK** está bem
**old** velho(a)
  *how old are you?* quantos anos tem? ; que idade tem?
  *I'm ... years old* tenho ... anos
**old age pensioner** o/a reformado(a)
**olive** a azeitona
**olive oil** o azeite
**omelette** a omeleta
**on** *(light, TV)* aceso(a)
  *(engine)* a trabalhar

**143**

on em ; em cima de
*on the table* na mesa
*on time* a horas
**once** uma vez
*at once* imediatamente
**one** um (uma)
**one-way** de sentido único
**onion** a cebola
**only** somente
*adj* único(a)
**open** *adj* aberto(a)
**to open** abrir
**opera** a ópera
**opera house** o teatro da ópera
**operation** *(surgical)* a operação
**operator** *(phone)* o/a telefonista
**opposite:** *opposite (to)* em frente de
*opposite the hotel* em frente do
hotel
**optician's** o oculista
**or** ou
*tea or coffee?* chá ou café?
**orange** *(fruit)* a laranja
*(colour)* cor-de-laranja
**orange juice** o sumo de laranja
**orchestra** a orquestra
**order:** *out of order* fora de serviço ;
avariado(a)
**to order** *(in restaurant)* pedir
*can I order?* posso pedir?
**oregano** o orégão
**organic** biológico(a)
**to organize** organizar
**original** original
**ornament** o ornamento
**other:** *the other one* o/a outro(a)
*have you any others?* tem outros(as)?
**ounce** = approx. 30 g
**our** nosso(a)
**out** fora
*he's gone out* ele saiu
*he's out* não está
**out of order** fora de serviço
**outdoor** ao ar livre
**outside:** *it's outside* está lá fora
**oven** o forno
**oven gloves** as luvas de cozinha
**ovenproof** refratário(a)
**over** *(on top of)* sobre
**to be overbooked** ter mais reservas
que lugares
**to overcharge** cobrar demais
**overcoat** o sobretudo
**overdone** *(food)* cozido demais
**overdose** a dose excessiva
**to overheat** aquecer demasiado

**to overload** sobrecarregar
**to oversleep** dormir além da hora
**to overtake** *(in car)* ultrapassar
**to owe** dever
*you owe me...* deve-me...
*I owe you...* devo-lhe...
**owl** a coruja
**owner** o/a dono(a)
**oxygen** o oxigénio
**oyster** a ostra

# P

**pace** o passo
**pacemaker** o pacemaker
**to pack bags** fazer as malas
**package** o embrulho
**package tour** a viagem organizada
**packet** o pacote
**padded envelope** o envelope
almofadado
**paddling pool** a piscina para crianças
**padlock** o cadeado
**page** a página
**paid** pago(a)
**pain** a dor
**painful** doloroso(a)
**painkiller** o analgésico
**to paint** pintar
**paintbrush** o pincel
**painting** a pintura
*(picture)* o quadro
**pair** o par
**palace** o palácio
**pale** pálido(a)
**pan** *(frying)* a frigideira
*(saucepan)* a caçarola
**pancake** a panqueca
**panniers** *(for bike)* as bolsas para a
bicicleta
**pants** *(briefs)* as cuecas
**panty liner** os pensos higiénicos
**paper** o papel
*(newspaper)* o jornal
**paper hankies** os lenços de papel
**paper napkins** os guardanapos de
papel
**papoose** *(for carrying baby)* a mochila
para levar o bebé
**paracetamol** o paracetamol
**paraffin** o óleo de parafina
**paragliding** para-pente

## p            eng-por

**paralysed** paralisado(a)
**parcel** a encomenda
**pardon** desculpe!
  *I beg your pardon?* desculpe-me!
**parents** os pais
**park** o parque
**to park** estacionar
**parking disk** o disco de estacionamento
**parking meter** o parquímetro
**parking ticket** a multa (por estacionamento em lugar proibido)
**parsley** a salsa
**part** a parte
**partner** *(business)* o/a sócio(a)
  *(friend)* o/a companheiro(a)
**party** *(celebration)* a festa
  *(political)* o partido
**pass** *(mountain)* o desfiladeiro
  *(train, bus)* o passe
**passenger** o/a passageiro(a)
**passport** o passaporte
**passport control** o controle de passaportes
**pasta** as massas
**pastry** *(dough)* a massa
  *(cake)* o bolo
**pâté** o paté
**path** o caminho
**patient** o/a paciente; o/a doente
  *adj* paciente
**pavement** o passeio
**to pay** pagar
  *I'd like to pay* queria pagar
  *where do I pay?* onde é que se paga?
  *I've paid* já paguei
**payment** o pagamento
**payphone** o telefone público
**peace** a paz
**peach** o pêssego
**peak rate** a taxa alta
**peanut** o amendoim
**peanut allergy** a alergia a amendoins
**peanut butter** a manteiga de amendoim
**pear** a pêra
**pearls** as pérolas
**peas** as ervilhas
**pedal** o pedal
**pedal boat** o barco de pedáis
**pedestrian** o/a peão
**pedestrian crossing** a passadeira para peões

**to pee** fazer xixi
**to peel** *(fruit)* descascar
**peg** *(clothes)* a mola
  *(tent)* a estaca
**pen** a caneta
**pencil** o lápis
**penfriend** o/a correspondente
**penicillin** a penicilina
**penis** o pénis
**penknife** o canivete
**pension** a pensão
**pensioner** o/a reformado(a)
**people** as pessoas
**pepper** *(spice)* a pimenta
  *(vegetable)* o pimento
**per** por
  *per day* por dia
  *per hour* por hora
  *per week* por semana
  *per person* por pessoa
  *50 km per hour* 50 km por hora
**perch** *(fish)* a perca
**perfect** perfeito(a)
**performance** a representação
  *the next performance* a próxima representação/sessão
**perfume** o perfume
**perhaps** talvez
**period** *(menstruation)* a menstruação
**perm** a permanente
**permit** a licença
**person** a pessoa
  *per person* por pessoa
**personal organizer** a agenda
**personal stereo** o Walkman®
**pet** o animal doméstico
**pet food** a comida para animais domésticos
**pet shop** a loja para animais domésticos
**petrol** a gasolina
  *4-star petrol* a gasolina super
  *unleaded petrol* a gasolina sem chumbo
**petrol cap** a tampa do depósito de gasolina
**petrol pump** a bomba de gasolina
**petrol station** a estação de serviço
**petrol tank** o depósito da gasolina
**pewter** o estanho
**pharmacy** a farmácia
**pheasant** o faisão
**phone** o telefone
  *mobile telephone* o telemóvel
**to phone** telefonar
**phonebook** a lista telefónica

**phonebox** a cabine telefónica
**phonecard** o credifone
**photocopy** a fotocópia
  *I need a photocopy* preciso duma fotocópia
**photograph** a fotografia
  *to take a photograph* tirar uma fotografia
**phrase book** o guia de conversação
**piano** o piano
**to pick** *(fruit, flowers)* colher
  *(to choose)* escolher
**pickled** de conserva
**pickpocket** o/a carteirista
**picnic** o piquenique
  *to have a picnic* fazer um piquenique
**picnic area** a zona de piqueniques
**picnic hamper** o cesto para piqueniques
**picnic rug** a manta
**picnic table** a mesa para piqueniques
**picture** *(painting)* o quadro
  *(photo)* a foto
**pie** *(savoury)* a empada
  *(sweet)* a torta
**piece** o bocado ; o pedaço
**pier** o cais
**pig** o porco
**pill** o comprimido
  *to be on the Pill* tomar a pílula
**pillow** a almofada
**pillowcase** a fronha
**pilot** o/a piloto(a)
**pin** o alfinete
  *safety pin* o alfinete de segurança
**pineapple** o ananás
**pink** cor-de-rosa
**pint** = approx. 0.5 litre
  *a pint of beer* uma caneca de cerveja
**pipe** *(for smoking)* o cachimbo
  *(drain, etc)* o tubo ; o cano
**pity:** *what a pity!* que pena!
**pizza** a pizza
**place** o lugar
**place of birth** o lugar de nascimento
**plain** *(yoghurt, etc)* natural
  *(obvious)* claro(a)
**plait** a trança
**plan** o plano
**to plan** planear
**plane** o avião
**plant** a planta
**plaster** *(sticking)* o adesivo
  *(for broken limb)* o gesso
**plastic** o plástico
**plastic bag** o saco de plástico

**plate** o prato
**platform** *(railway)* a linha
  *which platform?* qual é a linha?
**play** *(at theatre)* a peça
**to play** jogar
  *(instrument)* tocar
**playground** o pátio de recreio
**play park** o parque infantil
**playroom** o quarto de brinquedos
**pleasant** agradável
**please** por favor ; faz favor
**pleased:** *pleased to meet you* prazer em conhecê-lo(a) ; muito prazer
**plenty:** *plenty of (much)* muito(a)
  *(many)* muitos(as)
**pliers** o alicate
**plug** *(electric)* a ficha ; a tomada
  *(for sink)* a válvula
**to plug in** ligar
**plum** a ameixa
**plumber** o canalizador
**plumbing** *(pipes)* a canalização
**plunger** *(for sink)* o desentupidor
**p.m.** *(afternoon/evening)* de tarde
  *(night)* de noite
**poached** *(fish)* cozido(a)
  *poached egg* o ovo escalfado
**pocket** o bolso
**points** *(in car)* os platinados
**poison** o veneno
**poisonous** venenoso(a)
**police** *(force)* a polícia
**police officer** o/a polícia
**police station** a esquadra
**polish** *(for shoes)* a pomada para o calçado
  *(for furniture)* a cera
**pollen** o pólen
**polluted** poluído(a)
**pollution** a poluição
**pony** o pónei
**pony trekking** o passeio a cavalo
**pool** a piscina
**pool attendant** o/a empregado(a) da piscina
**poor** pobre
**poorly:** *he feels poorly* ele não se sente bem
**pope** o papa
**poppy** a papoila
**pop socks** as peúgas
**popular** popular

**pork** a carne de porco

**port** *(wine)* o vinho do porto
*(seaport)* o porto

**porter** *(for door)* o porteiro
*(for luggage)* o carregador

**portion** a porção

**Portugal** Portugal

**Portuguese** português (portuguesa)
*(language)* o português

**possible** possível

**post:** *by post* pelo correio

**to post** pôr no correio

**postbox** a caixa do correio

**postcard** o postal

**postcode** o código postal

**poster** o póster
*(advertising)* o cartaz

**postman/woman** o/a carteiro(a)

**post office** os correios

**to postpone** adiar

**pot** *(for cooking)* a panela

**potato** a batata
*baked potato* a batata assada
*boiled potatoes* as batatas cozidas
*fried potatoes* as batatas fritas
*mashed potatoes* o puré de batata
*roast potatoes* as batatas assadas
*sautéed potatoes* as batatas
salteadas

**potato masher** o passe-vite

**potato peeler** o descascador de
batatas

**potato salad** a salada de batata

**pothole** o buraco

**pottery** a cerâmica

**pound** *(money)* a libra
*(weight)* = approx. 0.5 kilo

**to pour** deitar

**powdered:** *in powdered form* em pó

**powdered milk** o leite em pó

**power** o poder

**power cut** o corte de energia

**pram** o carrinho do bebé

**prawn** o lagostim

**to pray** rezar

**prayer** a oração

**to prefer** preferir

**pregnant** grávida
*I'm pregnant* estou grávida

**to prepare** preparar

**to prescribe** receitar

**prescription** a receita médica

**present** *(gift)* o presente ; a oferta ;
a prenda

**preservative** o preservativo

**president** o/a presidente

**press** *(newspapers)* a imprensa

**pressure** a pressão
*blood pressure* a tensão arterial
*tyre pressure* a pressão dos pneus

**pretty** bonito(a) ; lindo(a)

**price** o preço

**price list** a lista de preços

**priest** o padre

**prince** o príncipe

**princess** a princesa

**print** *(photo)* a cópia

**printer** a impressora

**prison** a prisão

**private** privado(a)

**prize** o prémio

**probably** provavelmente

**problem** o problema
*no problem* não tem problema

**programme** o programa

**professor** o/a professor(a)
catedrático(a)

**prohibited** proibido(a)

**promise** a promessa

**to promise** prometer

**pronounce** pronunciar
*how is this pronounced?* como se
pronuncia isto?

**protein** a proteína

**Protestant** protestante

**to provide** fornecer

**prune** a ameixa seca

**public** público(a)

**public holiday** o feriado

**publisher** o/a editor(a)

**pudding** o pudim

**to pull** puxar
*I've pulled a muscle* distendi o
músculo

**to pull over** *(car)* encostar

**pullover** o pulóver

**pump** a bomba

**pumpkin** a abóbora

**puncture** o furo

**puncture repair kit** o estojo de
ferramentas

**puppet** o fantoche

**puppet show** o teatro de marionetes ;
os fantoches

**puppy** o cachorro

**purple** roxo(a)

**purpose:** *on purpose* de propósito

**purse** o porta-moedas
**to push** empurrar
**pushchair** o carrinho
**to put** pôr
**to put back** *(replace)* repor
**pyjamas** o pijama

# Q

**quail** a codorniz
**quality** a qualidade
**quantity** a quantidade
**quarantine** a quarentena
**to quarrel** discutir
**quarter** o quarto
**quay** o cais
**queen** a rainha
**query** a pergunta
**question** a pergunta
**queue** a fila ; a bicha
**to queue** fazer fila
**quick** rápido(a)
**quickly** depressa
**quiet** *(place)* sossegado(a)
  *a quiet room* um quarto tranquilo
**quilt** o edredão
**quite:** *it's quite good* é bastante bom
  *quite expensive* é muito caro
**quiz** o concurso
**quiz show** *(TV)* o concurso televisivo

# R

**rabbit** o coelho
**rabies** a raiva
**race** *(sport)* a corrida
  *(human)* a raça
**race course** o hipódromo
**rack** *(luggage)* o porta-bagagens
**racket** a raqueta
**radiator** *(car)* o radiador
  *(heater)* o radiador
**radio** o rádio
**radish** o rabanete
**raffle** a rifa
**rag** o trapo
**railcard** o passe do comboio
**railway** o caminho-de-ferro
**railway station** a estação de comboio
**rain** a chuva
**to rain:** *it's raining* está a chover
**rainbow** o arco-íris
**raincoat** o impermeável ; a gabardina
**raisin** a passa de uva

**rake** o ancinho
**rape** a violação
**to rape** violar
**raped:** *I've been raped* fui violado(a)
**rare** *(unique)* raro(a)
  *(steak)* mal passado(a)
**rash** *(skin)* a urticária
**raspberries** as framboesas
**rat** a ratazana
**rate** *(price)* a taxa
**rate of exchange** o câmbio
**raw** cru(a)
**razor** a máquina de barbear
**razorblades** as lâminas de barbear
**to read** ler
**ready** pronto(a)
  *to get ready* preparar-se
**real** real
**to realize** perceber
**rearview mirror** o retrovisor
**reason** a razão
**receipt** o recibo
**receiver** *(phone)* o auscultador
**recently** recentemente
**reception (desk)** a recepção
**receptionist** o/a recepcionista
**to recharge** recarregar
**recipe** a receita
**to recognize** reconhecer
**to recommend** recomendar
**record** *(music)* o disco
**to record** *(facts)* registar
  *(music)* gravar
**to recover** *(from illness)* recuperar
**to recycle** reciclar
**red** vermelho(a) ; encarnado(a)
**redcurrants** as groselhas
**to reduce** reduzir
**reduction** o desconto
**reel** *(fishing)* o carretel
**to refer to** referir-se a
**referee** o/a árbitro(a)
**refill** *(pen, lighter)* a recarga
**refund** o reembolso
**to refuse** recusar
**regarding** com relação a
**region** a região
**to register** *(at hotel)* preencher o registo
**registered** *(letter)* registado(a)
**registration form** a folha de registo

**regulations** os regulamentos
**to reimburse** reembolsar
**relation** *(family)* o/a parente
**relationship** *(personal)* as relações
  *(family)* o parentesco
**relative** *(family)* o/a parente
**to relax** repousar ; relaxar
**reliable** de confiança
**to remain** ficar
**to remember** lembrar-se de
  *I don't remember* não me lembro
**remote control** o comando
**removal firm** a companhia de
  mudanças
**to remove** retirar
**rent** *(house)* a renda; o aluguer
  *(car)* o aluguer
**to rent** *(house, car)* alugar
**rental** o aluguer
**repair** a reparação
**to repair** reparar ; consertar
**to repeat** repetir
**to reply** responder
**report** o relatório
**to report** *(crime, person)* comunicar
**request** o pedido
**to request** pedir
**to require** precisar de
**to rescue** salvar
**reservation** a reserva
**to reserve** reservar
**reserved** reservado(a)
**resident** *(at hotel)* o/a hóspede
**resort** a estância
**rest** *(repose)* o descanso
  *(remainder)* o resto
  *the rest of the wine* o resto do vinho
**to rest** descansar
**restaurant** o restaurante
**restaurant car** o vagão restaurante
**to retire** reformar-se
**retired** reformado(a)
  *I'm retired* estou reformado(a)
**to return** *(to go back)* voltar
  *(to give something back)* devolver
**return ticket** o bilhete de ida e volta
**to reverse** fazer marcha atrás
**to reverse the charges** fazer uma
  chamada pagável no destino
**reverse-charge call** a chamada pagável
  no destino
**reverse gear** a marcha atrás

**rheumatism** o reumatismo
**rhubarb** o ruibarbo
**rib** a costela
**ribbon** a fita
**rice** o arroz
**rich** *(person)* rico(a)
  *(food)* suculento(a)
**to ride** *(horse)* montar a cavalo
  *(in a car, bus, etc)* viajar
**right** *(correct)* certo(a)
  *to be right* ter razão
**right:** *on/to the right* à direita
**right-handed** destro(a)
**right of way** a preferência ; a
  prioridade
**ring** *(for finger)* o anel
**to ring** *(bell)* tocar
  *(phone)* telefonar
  *it's ringing* está a tocar
**ring road** a circunvalação
**ripe** maduro(a)
**river** o rio
**road** a estrada
**road map** o mapa das estradas
**road sign** o sinal de trânsito
**roadworks** as obras na estrada
**roast** assado(a)
**robber** o ladrão (a ladra)
**robin** o pintarroxo
**roll** *(bread)* o pãozinho
**rollerblades** os patins em linha
**rollers** os rolos
**roller skates** os patins de rodas
**rolling pin** o rolo da massa
**romance** *(novel)* o romance
**Romanesque** românico(a)
**romantic** romântico(a)
**roof** o telhado
**roof rack** o tejadilho
**room** *(in house, hotel)* o quarto
  *(space)* o espaço
  *double room* o quarto de casal
  *family room* o quarto de família
  *single room* o quarto individual
**room number** o número do quarto
**room service** o serviço de quarto
**root** a raíz
**rope** a corda
**rose** a rosa
**rosemary** o alecrim
**rosé wine** o vinho rosé
**rotten** *(fruit, etc)* podre ; estragado(a)
**rough** *(surface)* áspero(a)
  *(sea)* agitado(a)
**round** *(shape)* redondo(a)

**roundabout** *(traffic)* a rotunda
**route** a rota ; o percurso
**row** *(line)* a fila
**to row** *(boat)* remar
**rowing** *(sport)* o remo
**rowing boat** o barco a remos
**royal** real
**rubber** *(eraser)* a borracha
  *(material)* a borracha
**rubber band** o elástico
**rubber gloves** as luvas de borracha
**rubbish** o lixo
**rubella** a rubéola
**rucksack** a mochila
**rudder** o leme
**rug** o tapete
**ruins** as ruínas
**ruler** *(for measuring)* a régua
**rum** o rum
**to run** correr
**rush hour** a hora de ponta
**rusty** ferrugento(a)
**rye** o centeio

# S

**saccharin** a sacarina
**sad** triste
**saddle** *(bike)* o selim
  *(horse)* a sela
**safe** *(for valuables)* o cofre
**safe** seguro(a)
  *is it safe?* é seguro?
**safety belt** o cinto de segurança
**safety pin** o alfinete de segurança
**sage** *(herb)* a salva
**to sail** *(sport, leisure)* velejar
**sailboard** a prancha
**sail(ing)** a vela
**sailing boat** o barco à vela
**saint** o/a santo(a)
**salad** a salada
  *green salad* a salada verde
  *mixed salad* a salada mista
  *potato salad* a salada de batatas
  *tomato salad* a salada de tomate
**salad dressing** o tempero da salada
**salami** o salame
**salary** o salário
**sale(s)** o saldo
**salesman/woman** o/a vendedor(a)
**sales rep** o/a representante de vendas
**salmon** o salmão
  *smoked salmon* o salmão fumado
**salt** o sal

**salt water** a água salgada
**salty** salgado(a)
**same** mesmo(a)
**sample** a amostra
**sand** a areia
**sandals** as sandálias
**sandwich** a sandes ; a sanduíche
  *toasted sandwich* a tosta
**sanitary towel** o penso higiénico
**sardine** a sardinha
**satellite dish** a antena parabólica
**satellite TV** a televisão via satélite
**Saturday** o sábado
**sauce** o molho
  *tomato sauce* o molho de tomate
**saucepan** a caçarola
**saucer** o pires
**sauna** a sauna
**sausage** a salsicha
**to save** *(life)* salvar
  *(money)* poupar
**savoury** saboroso(a)
**savouries** os salgados
**saw** a serra
**to say** dizer
**scales** *(weighing)* a balança
**scallops** as vieiras
**scampi** as gambas panadas
**scarf** *(woollen)* o cachecol
  *(headscarf)* o lenço (de pescoço)
**scenery** a paisagem
**schedule** o programa
**school** a escola
  *primary school* a escola primária
  *secondary school* o colégio
**scissors** a tesoura
**score** *(of match)* o resultado
**to score** marcar
**Scot** o/a escocês (escocesa)
**Scotland** a Escócia
**Scottish** escocês (escocesa)
**scouring pad** a palha de aço
**screen** *(computer, TV)* o ecrã
**screenwash** o detergente para o pára-
  brisas
**screw** o parafuso
**screwdriver** a chave de parafusos
  *phillips screwdriver®* a chave
  phillips®
**scuba diving** mergulhar
**sculpture** a escultura

sea o mar
seafood o marisco
seagull a gaivota
seal a foca
seam *(of dress)* a costura
to search for procurar
seasick enjoado(a)
  *I get seasick* enjoo
seasickness o enjoo
seaside a praia
  *at the seaside* na praia
season *(of year)* a estação
  *(holiday)* a temporada
  *in season* da época
season ticket o passe
seasoning o tempero
seat *(chair)* a cadeira
  *(on bus, train, etc)* o lugar
seatbelt o cinto de segurança
seaweed a alga marinha
second segundo(a)
second class a segunda classe
second-class *adj* de segunda classe
second-hand em segunda mão ;
  usado(a)
secretary o/a secretário(a)
security guard o guarda de segurança
sedative o sedativo
to see ver
seed a semente
to seize agarrar
self-catering com cozinha
self-employed que trabalha por conta
  própria
self-service o auto-serviço
to sell vender
  *do you sell...?* vende...?
sell-by date... usar antes de...
Sellotape® a fita-cola
semi-skimmed milk o leite meio-gordo
to send mandar
senior citizen o/a reformado(a)
sensible sensato(a)
separated separado(a)
separately: *to pay separately* pagar
  separadamente
September o Setembro
septic tank a fossa séptica
sequel *(film, book)* a continuação; a
  sequela
serious sério(a)
  *(illness)* grave

to serve servir
service *(in church)* o serviço religioso
  *(in restaurant)* o serviço
  *is service included?* o serviço está
  incluído?
service charge o serviço
service station a estação de serviço
serviette o guardanapo
set menu a ementa fixa
settee o sofá
several vários(as)
to sew coser
sewer o esgoto
sex *(gender)* o sexo
  *(intercourse)* o sexo
shade a sombra
  *in the shade* à sombra
to shake *(bottle)* sacudir
shallow pouco profundo(a)
shampoo o champô
shampoo and set a lavagem e mise
to share dividir
to share out distribuir
sharp *(razor, knife)* afiado(a)
to shave fazer a barba
shaving cream o creme de barbear
shawl o xaile
she ela
sheep a ovelha
sheet *(for bed)* o lençol
shelf a prateleira
shell *(seashell)* a concha
  *(egg, nut)* a casca
shellfish o marisco
sheltered abrigado(a)
shepherd o pastor
sherry o xerez
to shine brilhar
shingles *(illness)* o herpes zóster
ship o barco
shirt a camisa
shock absorber o amortecedor
shoe o sapato
shoelaces os cordões (de sapato)
shoe polish a graxa ; a pomada
shoe repairer's o sapateiro
shoe shop a sapataria
shop a loja
shop assistant o/a vendedor(a)
shop window a montra
shopping: *to go shopping* ir às
  compras
shopping centre o centro comercial
shore a costa

**short** curto(a)
**short circuit** o curto-circuito
**short cut** o atalho
**shortage** a escassez
**shorts** os calções
**short-sighted** míope
**shoulder** o ombro
**to shout** gritar
**show** o espectáculo
**to show** mostrar
**shower** o duche ; o chuveiro
   *to have a shower* tomar um duche
   *(rain)* o chuveiro ; o aguaceiro
**shower cap** a touca de banho
**shower curtain** a cortina do chuveiro
**shower gel** o gel para banho
**shrimps** os camarões
**to shrink** encolher
**shrub** o arbusto
**shut** *(closed)* fechado(a) ; encerrado(a)
**to shut** fechar
**shutters** as persianas ; as gelosias
**shuttle service** o serviço de ligação
**shy** tímido(a)
**sick** *(ill)* doente
   *I feel sick* sinto-me mal-disposto(a)
**side** o lado
**side dish** o acompanhamento
**sidelight** o farolim
**sidewalk** o passeio
**sieve** *(for liquids)* o coador
   *(for flour)* a peneira
**to sightsee** fazer turismo
**sightseeing** o turismo
   *to go sightseeing* fazer turismo
**sightseeing tour** a excursão
**sign** *(road-, notice, etc)* o sinal
**to sign** assinar
**signature** a assinatura
**signpost** a sinalização
**silk** a seda
**silver** a prata
**similar:** *similar to* semelhante a
**simple** simples
**since** *(time)* desde que
   *(because)* porque
   *since Saturday* desde sábado
**to sing** cantar
**single** *(not married)* solteiro(a)
   *(not double)* simples
**single bed** a cama de solteiro
**single room** o quarto individual
**single ticket** o bilhete de ida ; o bilhete
   simples

**sink** o lava-louça ; a pia
**sir** senhor
**sister** a irmã
**sister-in-law** a cunhada
**to sit** sentar-se
   *please, sit down* faça o favor de se
   sentar
**size** *(clothes)* o tamanho
   *(shoes)* o número
**to skate** patinar
**skates** *(ice)* os patins de lâmina
   *(roller)* os patins de rodas
**skating rink** o rinque de patinagem
**ski** o esqui
   *skis* os esquis
**to ski** esquiar
**ski boots** as botas de esquiar
**skiing** o esqui
   *to go skiing* ir esquiar
**ski instructor** o/a instructor(a) de esqui
**ski jump** a pista para saltos de esqui
**ski lift** o ski lift
**ski pole** a vara de esqui
**ski run** a pista de esqui
**ski stick** a vara de esqui
**ski suit** o traje de esqui
**skimmed milk** o leite magro
**skin** a pele
**skindiving** o mergulho
**skirt** a saia
**sky** o céu
**slang** o calão
**sledge** o trenó
**to sleep** dormir
**to sleep in** dormir até tarde
**sleeper** *(on train)* a carruagem-cama
**sleeping bag** o saco cama
**sleeping car** a carruagem-cama
**sleeping pill** o comprimido para dormir
**slice** a fatia
**slide** *(photograph)* o diapositivo
**to slip** escorregar
**slippers** os chinelos
**slow** lento(a)
**small** pequeno(a)
**smaller** mais pequeno(a)
**smell** o cheiro
**smile** o sorriso
**to smile** sorrir
**smoke** o fumo

**to smoke** fumar
 *I don't smoke* não fumo
 *can I smoke?* posso fumar?

**smoke alarm** o alarme contra incêndios

**smoked** fumado(a)

**smokers** os fumadores

**smoking:** *no smoking* proibido fumar

**smooth** liso(a) ; macio(a)

**snack** o lanche
 *to have a snack* comer qualquer coisa

**snack bar** o snack-bar

**snake** a cobra

**snake bite** a mordida de cobra

**to sneeze** espirrar

**to snore** ressonar

**snorkel** o tubo de ar

**snow** a neve

**to snow** nevar
 *it's snowing* está a nevar

**snowboard** o snowboard

**snowboarding:** *to go snowboarding* fazer snowboarding

**snow chains** as correntes para a neve

**snowed up** coberto de neve

**snowman** o boneco-de-neve

**snowplough** a máquina limpa-neve

**snow tyres** os pneus para a neve

**so** portanto
 *so much* tanto(a)

**soap** o sabão

**soap powder** o sabão em pó

**sober** sóbrio(a)

**socket** *(electrical)* a tomada

**socks** as peúgas

**soda water** a água com gás ; a soda

**sofa** o sofá

**sofa bed** o sofá-cama

**soft** macio(a)

**soft drink** o refrigerante

**software** o software

**soldier** o soldado

**sole** *(fish)* o linguado
 *(of shoe)* a sola

**soluble** solúvel

**some** alguns (algumas)

**someone** alguém

**something** alguma coisa

**sometimes** às vezes

**son** o filho

**son-in-law** o genro

**song** a canção

**soon** em breve
 *as soon as possible* o antes possível

**sore** magoado(a)

**sore throat:** *I have a sore throat* dói-me a garganta

**sorry:** *I'm sorry!* lamento ; desculpe!

**sort:** *what sort of cheese?* que tipo de queijo?

**sound** o som

**soup** a sopa

**sour** azedo(a)

**soured cream** as natas azedas

**south** o sul

**souvenir** a recordação ; a lembrança

**spa** as termas

**space** o espaço

**spade** a enxada

**Spain** a Espanha

**Spanish** espanhol(a)
 *(language)* o espanhol

**spanner** a chave inglesa

**spare parts** as peças sobressalentes

**spare room** o quarto de hóspedes

**spare tyre** o pneu sobressalente

**spare wheel** a roda sobressalente

**sparkling** espumoso(a)
 *sparkling water* a água com gás
 *sparkling wine* o espumante

**spark plug** a vela

**to speak** falar
 *do you speak English?* fala inglês?
 *I don't speak Portuguese* não falo português

**special** especial

**specialist** o/a especialista

**speciality** a especialidade

**speech** a fala
 *(address)* o discurso

**speed** a velocidade

**speedboat** a lancha

**speeding** o excesso de velocidade

**speeding ticket** a multa por excesso de velocidade

**speed limit** o limite de velocidade
 *to exceed the speed limit* ultrapassar o limite de velocidade

**speedometer** o conta-quilómetros

**spell:** *how do you spell it?* como se escreve?

**to spend** *(money)* gastar

**spices** as especiarias

**spicy** picante

**spider** a aranha

**to spill** entornar

**spinach** o espinafre

**53** **spin-dryer** a secadora
**spine** a coluna
**spirits** as bebidas alcoólicas
**splinter** a falha ; a lasca
**spoke** *(wheel)* o raio
**sponge** a esponja
**spoon** a colher
**sport** o desporto
**sports centre** o centro de desportos;
centro desportivo
**sports shop** a loja de artigos
desportivos
**spot** *(pimple)* a borbulha
**to sprain:** *to sprain one's ankle* torcer
o tornozelo
**spring** *(season)* a primavera
*(coil)* a mola
**spring onion** a cebolinha
**square** *(in town)* a praça ; o largo
**squash** *(drink)* o sumo
*(game)* o squash
**to squeeze** apertar
**squid** as lulas
**stadium** o estádio
**staff** o pessoal
**stage** o palco; a cena
**stain** a nódoa
**stained glass** o vitral
**stain remover** o tira-nódoas
**stairs** a escada
**stale** *(bread)* duro(a)
**stalls** *(in theatre)* a plateia
**stamp** *(postage)* o selo
**to stand** estar em pé
**to stand up** levantar-se
**star** *(in sky, in films)* a estrela
**starfish** a estrela-do-mar
**to start** começar
**starter** *(in meal)* a entrada
*(in car)* o motor de arranque
**station** a estação
**stationer's** a papelaria
**statue** a estátua
**stay** a estadia ; a visita
**enjoy your stay!** desfrute da sua
visita!
**to stay** ficar
*I'm staying at a hotel* fico num hotel
**steak** o bife
*medium steak* o bife ao ponto
*well-done steak* o bife bem-passado
*rare steak* o bife mal-passado
**to steal** roubar
**to steam** cozer no vapor
**steamed** cozido(a) a vapor

**steel** o aço
**steep:** *is it steep?* custa a subir?
**steeple** o campanário
**steering wheel** o volante
**step** *(stair)* o degrau
**stepdaughter** a enteada
**stepfather** o padrasto
**stepmother** a madrasta
**stepson** o enteado
**stereo** o estéreo
*personal stereo* o Walkman®
**sterling** *(pounds)* esterlino(a)
**stew** o guisado
**steward** *(on plane)* o comissário de
bordo
**stewardess** *(on plane)* a hospedeira de
bordo
**to stick** *(with glue)* colar
**sticking plaster** o adesivo
**still** *(not moving)* imóvel
*(not sparkling)* sem gás
*(yet)* ainda
**sting** a picada
**to sting** picar
**stitches** *(surgical)* os pontos
**stock cube** o cubo de caldo
**stockings** as meias
**stolen** roubado(a)
**stomach** o estômago
**stomach upset** o mal-estar de
estômago
**stone** a pedra
*(weight)* = approx. 6.5 kg
**to stop** *(come to a halt)* parar
*(stop doing something)* deixar de fazer
alguma coisa
**stop sign** o sinal de paragem
**store** *(shop)* a loja
**storey** o andar
**storm** a tempestade
**story** a história
**straightaway** imediatamente
**straight on** sempre em frente
**strainer** o coador
**strange** estranho(a)
**straw** *(for drinking)* a palha
**strawberry** o morango
**stream** o riacho
**street** a rua
**street map** o mapa das ruas
**strength** a força

stress o stress
strike *(of workers)* a greve
  *to be on strike* estar em greve
string o cordel
striped às riscas
stroke *(medical)* a trombose
  *to have a stroke* ter uma trombose
strong forte
  *strong coffee* o café forte
  *strong tea* o chá forte
stuck: *it's stuck* está preso(a)
student o/a estudante
student discount o desconto para
  estudantes
stuffed recheado(a)
stung picado(a)
stupid estúpido(a)
subscription a assinatura
subtitles as legendas
subway *(underpass)* a passagem
  subterrânea
suddenly de repente
suede a camurça
sugar o açúcar
  *icing sugar* o açúcar em pó
sugar-free sem açúcar
to suggest sugerir
suit *(men's and women's)* o fato
suitcase a mala
sum a soma
summer o verão
summer holidays as férias de verão
summit o cume
sun o sol
to sunbathe tomar banhos de sol
sunblock o protector solar
sunburn a queimadura de sol
Sunday o domingo
sunflower o girassol
sunflower oil o óleo de girassol
sunglasses os óculos de sol
sunny: *it's sunny* está sol
sunrise o nascer do sol
sunroof o tecto de abrir
sunscreen o filtro solar
sunset o pôr do sol
sunshade o guarda-sol; a sombra; o
  toldo
sunstroke a insolação
suntan o bronzeado
suntan lotion a loção de bronzear

supermarket o supermercado
supper a ceia
supplement o suplemento
to supply abastecer
surcharge a sobretaxa
sure seguro(a)
  *I'm sure* estou seguro(a)
to surf fazer surfe
  *to surf the Net* navegar a Internet
surfboard a prancha de surf
surgery *(operation)* a cirurgia
  *(building)* o consultório
surname o apelido
  *my surname is...* o meu apelido é...
surprise a surpresa
surrounded by rodeado(a) por
suspension a suspensão
to survive sobreviver
to swallow engolir
swan o cisne
to swear *(bad language)* blasfemar;
  praguejar
  *(in court)* jurar
to sweat suar
sweater o pulóver
sweatshirt a sweatshirt ; o sweat
sweet *(not savoury)* doce
sweet *(dessert)* a sobremesa
sweetener o adoçante
sweets os doces ; os rebuçados
to swell *(injury etc)* inchar
to swim nadar
swimming pool a piscina
swimsuit o fato de banho
swing *(for children)* o baloiço
Swiss suíço(a)
switch o interruptor
to switch off apagar ; desligar
to switch on acender ; ligar
Switzerland a Suíça
swollen *(finger, ankle, etc)* inchado(a)
swordfish o espadarte
synagogue a sinagoga
syringe a seringa

# T

table a mesa
tablecloth a toalha de mesa
tablespoon a colher de sopa
tablet *(pill)* o comprimido
table tennis o ping-pong
table wine o vinho de mesa
tail o rabo ; a cauda

**tailor's** a alfaiataria
**take** *(carry)* levar ; transportar
*(to grab, seize)* agarrar
*(medicine etc)* tomar
*(to take someone to)* levar
*how long does it take?* quanto tempo demora?
**take-away** *(food)* para levar
**to take off** levantar voo
**to take out** *(of bag etc)* tirar
**talc** o talco
**to talk to** conversar com
**tall** alto(a)
**tame** *(animal)* manso(a)
**tampons** os tampões
**tangerine** a tangerina
**tank** *(car)* o depósito
*(fish)* o aquário
**tap** a torneira
**tap water** a água da torneira
**tape** *(video)* a cassette de vídeo
**tape measure** a fita métrica
**tape recorder** o gravador
**target** o alvo
**tarragon** o estragão
**tart** a tarte
**tartar sauce** o molho tártaro
**taste** o sabor
**to taste** provar
*can I taste it?* posso provar?
**tax** o imposto
**taxi** o táxi
**taxi driver** o/a taxista
**taxi rank** a praça de táxis
**tea** o chá
*herbal tea* a tisana
*lemon tea* o chá de limão
*strong tea* o chá forte
*tea with milk* o chá com leite
**teabag** o saquinho de chá
**to teach** ensinar
**teacher** o/a professor(a)
**team** a equipa
**teapot** o bule
**tear** *(in eye)* a lágrima
*(in material)* o rasgão
**teaspoon** a colher de chá
**teat** *(on baby's bottle)* o tetina
**tea towel** o pano de cozinha
**teenager** o/a adolescente
**teeshirt** a T-shirt
**teeth** os dentes
**teething** dentição
**telegram** o telegrama

**telephone** o telefone
*mobile telephone* o telemóvel
**to telephone** telefonar
**telephone box** a cabine telefónica
**telephone call** a chamada
**telephone card** o cartão telefónico
**telephone directory** a lista telefónica
**telephone number** o número de telefone
**television** a televisão
**television set** o televisor
**telex** o telex
**to tell** dizer
**temperature** a temperatura
*to have a temperature* ter febre
**temple** o templo
**temporary** temporário(a)
**tenant** o/a inquilino(a)
**tendon** o tendão
**tennis** o ténis
**tennis ball** a bola de ténis
**tennis court** o campo de ténis
**tennis racket** a raqueta de ténis
**tent** a tenda
**tent peg** a estaca
**terminal** *(airport)* o terminal
**terrace** a esplanada ; o terraço
**terracotta** a terracota ; o barro
**terrorist** o/a terrorista
**to test** *(try out)* testar
**testicles** os testículos
**tetanus** o tétano
**than** que
*better than* melhor do que
*more than you* mais do que você
*more than five* mais de cinco
**to thank** agradecer
**thank you/thanks** obrigado(a)
*thank you very much* muito obrigado(a)
*no thanks* não, obrigado(a)
**that one** aquele (aquela)
**that one** esse (essa)
**the** *(sing)* o (a)
*(plural)* os (as)
**theatre** o teatro
**theft** o roubo
**their** seu (sua)
**them** *(direct object)* os (as)
*(indirect object)* lhes
*(after preposition)* eles (elas)
**then** então

**there** *(over there)* ali ; lá
**there is/there are** há
**thermometer** o termómetro
**these** estes (estas)
  *these ones* estes (estas)
**they** eles (elas)
**thick** grosso(a)
**thief** o/a ladrão (ladra)
**thigh** a coxa
**thin** magro(a)
**thing** a coisa
  *my things* as minhas coisas
**to think** pensar
  *(to be of opinion)* achar
**third** terceiro(a)
**thirsty:** *I'm thirsty* tenho sede
**this** este (esta)
  *this one* este (esta)
**thorn** o espinho
**those** aqueles (aquelas)
  esses (essas)
  *those ones* aqueles (aquelas)
**thousand** mil
**thread** a linha
**thriller** *(film)* o filme de suspense
  *(book)* o livro de suspense
**throat** a garganta
**throat lozenges** as pastilhas para a garganta
**through** através de ; por
**to throw away** deitar fora; descartar
**thrush** *(candida)* a candidíase vaginal
**thumb** o polegar
**thunder** o trovão
**thunderstorm** o temporal; a trovoada
**Thursday** a quinta-feira
**thyme** o tomilho
**ticket** *(bus, train, etc)* o bilhete
  *(for cinema, theatre etc)* a entrada
  *a single ticket* um bilhete de ida
  *a return ticket* um bilhete de ida e volta
  *a tourist ticket* um bilhete de turista
  *a book of tickets* uma caderneta de bilhetes
**ticket collector** o/a revisor(a)
**ticket inspector** o/a inspector(a) de bilhetes
**ticket office** a bilheteira
**tide** *(sea)* a maré
  *low tide* a maré baixa
  *high tide* a maré alta
**tidy** arrumado(a)

**to tidy up** arrumar
**tie** a gravata
**tight** apertado(a)
**tights** os collants
**tile** *(floor)* o ladrilho
  *(wall)* o azulejo
**till** *(cash desk)* a caixa
**till** *(until)* até
  *till 2 o'clock* até às duas
**time** o tempo
  *(clock)* as horas
  *what time is it?* que horas são?
  *this time* esta vez
**timetable** o horário
**tin** *(can)* a lata
**tinfoil** a folha de alumínio
**tin-opener** o abre-latas
**tip** a gorjeta
**to tip** dar uma gorjeta
**tipped** *(cigarette)* com filtro
**Tippex®** o fluido corrector
**tired** cansado(a)
**tissues** os lenços de papel
**to** a ; para
  *to London* para Londres
  *to the airport* ao aeroporto
**toadstool** o cogumelo venenoso
**toast** *(to eat)* a torrada
  *(raising glass)* brindar
**tobacco** o tabaco
**tobacconist's** a tabacaria
**today** hoje
**toddler** a criança (que começa a andar)
**toe** o dedo do pé
**together** juntos
**toilet** a casa de banho ; o lavabo
  *disabled toilets* a casa de banho para deficientes
**toilet brush** a escova da sanita
**toilet paper** o papel higiénico
**toiletries** os artigos de toilette
**token** *(for bus)* o bilhete ; a senha
**toll** *(motorway)* a portagem
**tomato** o tomate
  *tinned tomatoes* os tomates em lata
**tomato juice** o sumo de tomate
**tomato purée** o concentrado de tomate
**tomato sauce** o molho de tomate
**tomato soup** a sopa de tomate
**tomorrow** amanhã
  *tomorrow morning* amanhã de manhã
  *tomorrow afternoon* amanhã à tarde
  *tomorrow evening* amanhã ao fim da tarde/à noite
  *tomorrow night* amanhã à noite

**tongue** a língua
**tonic water** a água tónica
**tonight** esta noite ; hoje à noite
**tonsillitis** a amigdalite
**too** *(also)* também
  *too big* grande demais
  *too small* pequeno(a) demais
  *too hot (food)* quente demais
  *too noisy* demasiado barulhento(a)
**tool** a ferramenta
**toolkit** o jogo de ferramentas
**tooth** o dente
**toothache** a dor de dentes
**toothbrush** a escova de dentes
**toothpaste** a pasta dentífrica
**toothpick** o palito
**top:** *the top floor* o último andar
**top** *(of hill)* a parte de cima
  *on top of...* em cima de...
**topless:** *to go topless* fazer topless
**torch** *(flashlight)* a lanterna
**torn** rasgado(a)
**total** *(amount)* o total
**to touch** tocar
**tough** *(meat)* duro(a)
**tour** *(trip)* a excursão
  *(of museum etc)* a visita
  *guided tour* a visita guiada
**tour guide** o/a guia turístico(a)
**tour operator** a empresa de viagens
**tourist** o/a turista
**tourist information** a informação turística
**tourist office** a oficina de turismo ; o turismo
**tourist route** a rota turística
**tourist ticket** o bilhete turístico
**to tow** rebocar
**towbar** o gancho de reboque
**towel** a toalha
**tower** a torre
**town** a cidade
**town centre** o centro da cidade
**town hall** a Câmara Municipal
**town plan** o mapa da cidade
**towrope** o cabo de reboque
**toxic** tóxico(a)
**toy** o brinquedo
**toy shop** a loja de brinquedos
**tracksuit** o fato de treino
**traditional** tradicional
**traffic** o trânsito
**traffic jam** o engarrafamento
**traffic lights** o semáforo
**traffic warden** o/a guarda de trânsito

**trailer** o reboque
**train** o comboio
  *by train* de comboio
  *the next train* o próximo comboio
  *the first train* o primeiro comboio
  *the last train* o último comboio
**trainers** os (sapatos de) ténis
**tram** o eléctrico
**tranquillizer** o calmante
**to transfer** transferir
**to translate** traduzir
**translation** a tradução
**to travel** viajar
**travel agent** o agente de viagens
**travel documents** os documentos de viagem
**travel guide** o/a guia turístico(a)
**travel insurance** o seguro de viagem
**travel sickness** o enjoo
**traveller's cheque** o cheque de viagem
**tray** o tabuleiro ; a bandeja
**tree** a árvore
**trip** a viagem
**trolley** *(luggage, shopping)* o carrinho
**trouble** os problemas
  *to be in trouble* estar em dificuldades
**trousers** as calças
**trout** a truta
**truck** o camião
**true** verdadeiro(a)
**trunk** *(luggage)* o baú ; a mala grande
**trunks** *(swimming)* os calções de banho
**truth** a verdade
**to try** *(attempt)* tentar
**to try on** *(clothes, shoes)* provar
**T-shirt** a T-shirt
**Tuesday** a terça-feira
**tulip** a túlipa
**tumble dryer** a máquina de secar roupa
**tuna** o atum
**tunnel** o túnel
**turkey** o peru
**to turn** voltar ; girar
  *to turn around* voltar-se
**to turn off** *(light etc)* apagar
  *(engine)* desligar
  *(tap)* fechar
**to turn on** *(light etc)* acender
  *(engine)* ligar
  *(tap)* abrir
**turnip** o nabo

**turquoise** (colour) turquesa

**tweezers** a pinça

**twice** duas vezes

**twin-bedded room** o quarto com duas camas

**twins** os gémeos
*identical twins* os gémeos idênticos

**to type** escrever à máquina

**typical** típico(a)

**tyre** o pneu

**tyre pressure** a pressão dos pneus

# U

**ugly** feio(a)

**ulcer** a úlcera

**umbrella** o guarda-chuva; a sombrinha
(sunshade) o guarda-sol

**uncle** o tio

**uncomfortable** incómodo(a)

**unconscious** inconsciente

**under** debaixo de

**undercooked** mal cozido(a)

**underground** (metro) o metropolitano

**underpants** as cuecas

**underpass** a passagem subterrânea

**to understand** compreender ; perceber
*I don't understand* não percebo
*do you understand?* percebe?

**underwear** a roupa interior

**underwater** debaixo da água

**to undo** desfazer

**to undress** despir-se

**unemployed** desempregado(a)

**to unfasten** desapertar

**unhappy** triste; infeliz
*to be unhappy with...* não estar satisfeito(a) com...

**United Kingdom** o Reino Unido

**United States** os Estados Unidos

**university** a universidade

**unleaded petrol** a gasolina sem chumbo

**unlikely** improvável

**to unlock** destrancar

**unlucky** infeliz ; sem sorte

**to unpack** (suitcases) desfazer as malas

**unpleasant** desagradável
(person) antipático(a)

**to unplug** desligar

**to unscrew** desaparafusar

**until** até
*until 2 o'clock* até às duas

**unusual** insólito(a)

**up: to get up** levantar-se

**upside down** invertido(a)

**upstairs** em cima

**urgent** urgente

**urine** a urina

**us** nos
(after preposition) nós
*with us* connosco

**USA** os EUA

**to use** utilizar

**useful** útil

**usual** habitual

**usually** geralmente

**U-turn** a meia-volta

# V

**vacancies** (in hotel etc) os quartos vagos
(jobs) as vagas

**vacant** livre
(hotel room) o quarto vago

**vacation** as férias
*on vacation* de férias

**vaccination** a vacinação

**vacuum cleaner** o aspirador

**vagina** a vagina

**valid** válido(a)

**valley** o vale

**valuable** valioso(a)

**valuables** os objetos de valor

**value** o valor

**valve** a válvula

**van** a carrinha

**vanilla** a baunilha

**vase** (for flowers) a jarra

**VAT** o IVA

**veal** a carne de vitela

**vegan** vegetalista
*I'm vegan* sou vegetalista

**vegetables** os legumes; os vegetais

**vegetarian** vegetariano(a)
*I'm vegetarian* sou vegetariano(a)

**vehicle** o veículo

**vein** a veia

**Velcro®** o Velcro®

**velvet** o veludo

**vending machine** a máquina de venda automática

**venereal disease** a doença venérea

**venison** a carne de veado

**ventilator** o ventilador

**very** muito

**vest** a camisola interior
**vet** o/a veterinário(a)
**via** por
**video** o vídeo
**to video** *(from TV)* gravar
**video camera** a câmara de vídeo
**video cassette** a videocassete
**video game** o jogo de vídeo
**video phone** o videofone
**video recorder** o gravador de video
**view** a vista
**village** a aldeia
**vinaigrette** a vinagreta
**vinegar** o vinagre
**vineyard** a vinha
**violet** *(flower)* a violeta
**viper** a víbora
**virus** o vírus
**visa** o visto
**visit** a visita
**to visit** visitar
**visiting hours** *(hospital)* as horas de visita
**visitor** a visita
**vitamin** a vitamina
**vodka** a vodka
**voice** a voz
**volcano** o vulcão
**volleyball** o voleibol
**voltage** a voltagem
**to vomit** vomitar
**voucher** o vale ; o recibo

# W

**wage** o salário
**waist** a cintura
**waistcoat** o colete
**to wait for** esperar por
**waiter** o empregado de mesa
**waiting room** a sala de espera
**waitress** a empregada de mesa
**to wake up** acordar
**Wales** o País de Gales
**to walk** andar
**walk** o passeio
**Walkman®** o Walkman®
**walking boots** as botas de montanha
**walking stick** a bengala
**wall** *(inside)* a parede
*(outside)* o muro
**wallet** a carteira
**walnut** a noz

**to want** querer
*I want...* quero...
*we want...* queremos...
**war** a guerra
**ward** *(in hospital)* a enfermaria
**wardrobe** o guarda-fato
**warehouse** o armazém
**warm** quente
*I'm warm* estou com calor
*it's warm (weather)* está calor ; quente
**to warm up** aquecer
**warning triangle** o triângulo de sinalização
**wash: to have a wash** lavar-se
**to wash** lavar
**wash and blow-dry** lavar e secar
**washbasin** o lavatório
**washing machine** a máquina de lavar roupa
**washing powder** o detergente para a roupa
**washing-up bowl** o lava-louças
**washing-up liquid** o detergente para a louça
**wasp** a vespa
**waste bin** o balde do lixo
**watch** o relógio
**to watch** ver ; observar
**watchstrap** a pulseira de relógio
**water** a água
*bottled water* a água mineral (engarrafada)
*cold water* a água fria
*drinking water* a água potável
*fresh water* a água corrente
*hot water* a água quente
*mineral water* a água mineral
*salt water* a água salgada
*sparkling water* a água com gás
*still water* a água sem gás
**watercress** o agrião
**waterfall** a queda de água
**water heater** o esquentador
**watermelon** a melancia
**waterproof** impermeável
**to waterski** fazer esqui aquático
**water-skiing** o esqui aquático
**waterwings** as braçadeiras
**waves** as ondas
**wax** a cera
**waxing** *(hair removal)* depilação com cera

**way** *(path)* o caminho
*(manner)* a maneira
**way in** *(entrance)* a entrada
**way out** *(exit)* a saída
**we** nós
**weak** fraco(a)
*(tea, etc)* aguado(a)
**to wear** vestir
**weather** o tempo
**weather forecast** a previsão do tempo
**website** o website
**wedding** o casamento
**wedding anniversary** o aniversário de casamento
**wedding cake** o bolo de casamento
**wedding dress** o vestido de noiva
**wedding present** a prenda de casamento
**wedding ring** a aliança de casamento
**Wednesday** a quarta-feira
**week** a semana
*last week* a semana passada
*next week* a semana que vem
*per week* por semana
*this week* esta semana
*during the week* durante a semana
**weekday** o dia útil
**weekend** o fim-de-semana
*next weekend* o próximo fim-de-semana
*this weekend* este fim-de-semana
**weekly** por semana
*weekly ticket* o bilhete semanal
**to weigh** pesar
**weight** o peso
**welcome** bem-vindo(a)
**well** bem
*he's not well* ele não se sente bem
**well** *(for water)* o poço
**well-done** *(steak)* bem-passado(a)
**wellington boots** as galoshas
**Welsh** galês (galesa)
*(language)* o galês
**west** o oeste
**wet** molhado(a)
*(weather)* chuvoso(a)
**wetsuit** o fato de mergulhador
**what** que
*what is it?* o que é?
**wheat** o trigo
**wheel** a roda
**wheelchair** a cadeira de rodas

**wheel clamp** o imobilizador
**when?** quando?
**where?** onde?
**which:** *which is it?* qual é?
**while** enquanto
*in a while* dentro de pouco
**whipped cream** o chantilly
**whisky** o uísque
**white** branco(a)
**who:** *who is it?* quem é?
**whole** inteiro(a)
**wholemeal bread** o pão integral
**whose:** *whose is it?* de quem é?
**why?** porquê?
**wide** largo(a)
**widow** a viúva
**widower** o viúvo
**width** a largura
**wife** a mulher ; a esposa
**wig** a peruca
**to win** ganhar
**wind** o vento
**windbreak** o guarda-vento
**windmill** o moínho
**window** a janela
*(shop)* a montra
**windscreen** o pára-brisas
**windscreen wipers** o limpa-pára-brisas
**to windsurf** fazer windsurf
**windsurfing** o wind-surf
**windy:** *it's windy* está vento
**wine** o vinho
*red wine* o vinho tinto
*white wine* o vinho branco
*rosé wine* o vinho rosé
*dry wine* o vinho seco
*sweet wine* o vinho doce
*sparkling wine* o vinho espumante
*house wine* o vinho da casa
*table wine* o vinho de mesa
**wine list** a lista de vinhos
**wing** a asa
**wing mirror** o retrovisor exterior
**winter** o inverno
**wire** a arame
*(electric)* o fio (eléctrico)
**with** com
*with ice* com gelo
*with milk* com leite
*with sugar* com açúcar
**without** *milk* sem leite
*without sugar* sem açúcar
**witness** a testemunha
**wolf** o lobo
**woman** a mulher

**wonderful** maravilhoso(a)
**wood** *(substance)* a madeira
**woods** a floresta
**wool** a lã
**word** a palavra
**to work** *(person)* trabalhar
  *(machine)* funcionar
  *it doesn't work* não está a funcionar ;
  não funciona
**work permit** a autorização de trabalho
**world** o mundo
**worldwide** no mundo inteiro
**worried** preocupado(a)
**worse** pior
**worth:** *it's worth...* vale...
**to wrap** *(parcel, etc)* embrulhar
**wrapping paper** o papel de embrulho
**wrinkles** as rugas
**wrist** o pulso
**to write** escrever
  *please write it down* escreva-o, por
  favor
**writing paper** o papel de carta
**wrong** errado(a)
**wrought iron** o ferro forjado

# X

**x-ray** a radiografia
**to x-ray** radiografar

# Y

**yacht** o iate
**year** o ano
  *last year* o ano passado
  *next year* o ano que vem
  *this year* este ano
**yearly:** *twice yearly* duas vezes por
  ano
**yellow** amarelo(a)
**Yellow Pages** as Páginas Amarelas
**yes** sim
**yesterday** ontem
**yet:** *not yet* ainda não
**yoghurt** o iogurte
  *plain yoghurt* o iogurte natural
**yolk** a gema
**you** você/tu/o senhor (a senhora)
  vocês/vós/os senhores (as senhoras)
**young** novo(a)
  *(person)* o/a jovem
**your** teu (tua)/seu (sua)
**youth hostel** o albergue de juventude ;
  a pousada de juventude

# Z

**zebra crossing** a passadeira para
  peões
**zero** o zero
**zip** o fecho éclair
**zone** a zona
**zoo** o jardim zoológico
**zoom lens** o zoom

# A

**a** to ; the *(feminine)*
**abadia** *f* abbey
**abaixo** down ; below
**aberto(a)** open
  *aberto todo o ano* open all year round
**abre-garrafas** *m* bottle-opener
**abre-latas** *m* tin/can-opener
**Abril** *m* April
**abrir** to open ; to unlock *(door)*
**acabar** to end ; to finish
**acampar** to camp
**aceitar** to accept
**acelerador** *m* accelerator
**acender** to switch/turn on ; to light
  *(fire, cigarette)*
  *acenda as luzes* switch on the lights
**acepipes** *m* titbit ; starters
**aceso(a)** on *(light, etc)*
**acesso** *m* access
**achar** to think ; to find
  *acha bem?* do you think it's all right?
**acidente** *m* accident
**acima** above
**aço** *m* steel
  *aço inoxidável* stainless steel
**açorda** *f* bread-based dish
**acordo** *m* agreement
**Açores** *mpl* the Azores archipelago
**actual** present(-day) ; current
**actualizar** to modernize ; to update
**açúcar** *m* sugar
**adega** *f* wine cellar
**adesivo** *m* plaster *(for cut)*
**adeus** goodbye
**adiantado(a)** fast *(watch)* ; early *(train, etc)*
**adulto(a)** adult
**Advento** *m* advent
**advogado(a)** *m/f* lawyer
**aéreo(a):** *a linha aérea* airline
  *via aérea* air mail
**aeroporto** *m* airport
**agência** *f* agency
  *agência de viagens* travel agents
**agente** *m/f* agent
**agora** now
**Agosto** *m* August
**agradável** pleasant
**agradecer** to thank
**água** *f* water
  *água destilada* distilled water
*água potável* drinking water
*água com gás* fizzy water
*água sem gás* still water
**aguardente** *f* spirit brandy
**agudo(a)** sharp *(pain)*
**ajudar** to help
**albergue** *m* hostel
  *albergue de juventude* youth hostel
**alcoólico(a)** alcoholic
**aldeia** *f* small village
**alegre** jolly
**Alemanha** *f* Germany
**alemão (alemã)** German
**alérgico(a) a** allergic to
**alface** *f* lettuce
**alfaiate** *m* tailor
**alfândega** *f* customs
**alfinete** *m* pin
**alforreca** *f* jellyfish
**algodão** *m* cotton
**algum(a)** some ; any
  *alguns (algumas)* a few ; some
  *mais alguma coisa?* anything else?
**alho** *m* garlic
**alhos-porros** *mpl* leeks
**ali** there
**alimentação** *f* food
**alívio** *m* relief
**almoço** *m* lunch
  *pequeno-almoço* breakfast
**almofada** *f* pillow ; cushion
**alojamento** *m* accommodation
**alpinismo** *m* climbing
**alto!** stop!
**alto(a)** high ; tall ; loud
  *a estação alta* high season
**altura** *f* height
**alugar** to hire ; to rent
  *aluga-se* to rent
  *alugam-se quartos* rooms to let
**aluguer** *m* rental
**amanhã** tomorrow
**amarelo(a)** yellow
**amargo(a)** bitter
**ambulância** *f* ambulance
**amêijoa** *f* clam ; cockle
**ameixa** *f* plum
  *ameixa seca* prune
**amêndoa** *f* almond
  *amêndoa amarga* bitter almond liqueur
**amendoim** *m* peanut
**amigo(a)** *m/f* friend
**amora** *f* blackberry ; mulberry
**amortecedor** *m* shock absorber
**amostra** *f* sample
**analgésico** *m* painkiller

ananás m pineapple
anchovas fpl anchovies
andar to walk
andar m floor ; storey
  *o primeiro andar* first floor
anel m ring
anis m aniseed liqueur
aniversário m anniversary ; birthday
ano m year
  *Ano Novo* New Year
antes de before
antiguidades fpl antiques
apagado(a) off *(radio, etc)* ; out *(light, etc)*
apagar to switch/turn off *(light, etc)*
aparelho m gadget ; machine ; apparatus
  *aparelho para a surdez* hearing aid
apartamento m apartment ; flat
apelido m surname
  *apelido de solteira* maiden name
apenas only
apertado(a) tight
apetite m appetite
  *bom apetite!* enjoy your meal!
apólice de seguro f insurance certificate
aquecedor m heater ; electric fire
aquecimento m heating
aqui here
ar m air ; choke *(car)*
  *ar condicionado* air conditioning
arder to burn
areia f sand
arenque m herring
armário m cupboard ; closet
armazém m warehouse
  *grande armazém* department store
arrendar to let
arroz m rice
  *arroz doce* rice pudding
artesanato m handicrafts
artigo m item
  *artigos de ménage* household goods
  *artigos de vime* wickerwork
árvore f tree
ascensor m lift
Ascensão Ascension Day
assado(a) roast ; baked
assinar to sign
assinatura f signature
assistência f audience ; assistance
Assunção Assumption Day
atacadores mpl laces
até until ; as far as
aterrar to land
atrás behind

atrasado(a) late *(for appointment)*
atrasar to delay
atraso m delay
atravessar to cross
atum m tuna (fish)
autocarro m bus ; coach
  *a paragem de autocarro* bus stop
auto-estrada f motorway
automobilista m/f driver
automóvel m car
autorização f licence ; permit
avaria f breakdown
avariado(a) out of order *(machine)*; broken down *(car)*
ave f bird
avelã f hazelnut
avenida f avenue
avião m plane
aviso m warning
avô m grandfather
avó f grandmother
azedo(a) sour
azeite m olive oil
azeitona f olive
azul blue
azulejo m ornamental tile

# B

bacalhau m dried salt cod
  *bacalhau à Brás* dried salt cod with eggs, onion and potatoes
bagaceira f eau de vie
bagaço m eau de vie
bagagem f luggage ; baggage
Bairrada region producing full-bodied red and aromatic white wines
bairro m quarter ; district
Baixa f commercial centre of Lisbon
baixar to lower
baixo: *em baixo* below
balança f scales *(weighing machine)*
balcão m shop counter ; circle in theatre
banco m bank ; seat *(in car, etc)*
bandeira f flag ; banner
bandeja f tray ; salver
bandido m gangster ; robber
banheira f bath-tub
banheiro m lifeguard
banho m bath
  *a casa de banho* bathroom
  *tomar banho* to have a bath

**banquete** m banquet ; sumptuous dinner
**barato(a)** cheap
**barba** f beard
  *fazer a barba* to shave
**barbeiro** m barber
**barco** m boat ; ship
  *barco a remos* rowing boat
  *barco à vela* sailing boat
**barraca** f hut *(shed)* ; beach hut
**barreira** f trench ; obstacle ; barrier
**barriga** f belly
**barro** m pottery ; terracotta
**barulho** m noise
**bastante** enough
**batata** f potato
  *batatas fritas* chips ; crisps
**bater** to beat ; to knock
  *bata à porta* please knock
**bateria** f battery *(for car)*
**batido de leite** m milk shake
**baunilha** f vanilla
**bebé** m baby
**beber** to drink
**bebida** f drink
**beco** m alley
**belo(a)** beautiful
**bem** well
  *está bem* OK
  *bem passado(a)* well done *(steak)*
**bem-vindo(a)** welcome
**bengaleiro** m cloakroom *(at theatre)* ; hat and umbrella stand
**benzer** to bless
**beringela** f aubergine
**berma** f hard shoulder
  *bermas baixas* steep verge – no hard shoulder
**berço** m crib ; cradle ; cot
**besugo** m sea bream
**beterraba** f beetroot
**bexiga** f bladder
**bica** f espresso coffee
**bicha** f queue
  *fazer bicha* to queue
**bicicleta** f bicycle
**bife** m steak
  *bife com batatas fritas* steak and chips
**bifurcação** f junction
**bilhar** m billiards
**bilhete** m ticket ; fare
  *bilhete de entrada* admission ticket
  *bilhete de identidade* identity card

**bilheteira** f ticket office
**binóculos** mpl binoculars
**boa** see bom
**boca** f mouth
**bocado:** *um bocado* a bit ; a portion
**boîte** f nightclub
**bola** f ball
  *bola de Berlim* doughnut
**bolacha** f biscuit
**bolo** m cake
  *bolo-rei* ring-shaped fruit cake eaten at Christmas
**bolsa** f stock exchange ; handbag
**bom (boa)** good ; fine *(weather)* ; kind
  *bom dia* good morning
  *boa noite* good evening ; good night
  *boa tarde* good afternoon
**bomba** f bomb ; pump *(petrol)*
**bomba de gasolina** f petrol station
**bombeiros** mpl fire brigade
**bondade** f kindness
**boneco(a)** doll ; puppet toy
**bonito(a)** pretty
**borbulha** f spot ; pimple
**bordados** mpl embroidered items
**borrego** m lamb
**bosque** m small forest ; woodland
**bota** f boot *(to wear)*
**botão** m button; bud
**braço** m arm
**branco(a)** white
  *vinho branco* white wine
**breve** brief
  *em breve* soon
**brigada de trânsito** f traffic police
**brincos** mpl earrings
**brinquedo** m toy
**britânico(a)** British
**broa** f corn (maize) bread
  *broas* corn (maize) cakes
**bronzeador** m suntan oil
**brushing** m blow-dry
**bugigangas** fpl bric-à-brac
**burro(a)** m/f ass ; donkey ; stupid person
**buscar** to look for ; to fetch
**bússola** f compass
**buzinar** to toot *(car horn)*

# C

**cá** here ; in this place
**cabana** f shack ; hut
**cabeça** f head
**cabedais** mpl leather goods
**cabeleireiro(a)** m/f hairdresser
**cabelo** m hair

**cabide** m coat hanger ; peg *(for clothes)*
**cabine** f cabin ; booth
  *cabine telefónica* phone box
**cabo** m knife handle ; electric lead
  *cabos de emergência* jump leads
  *cabo de reboque* tow rope
**cabra** f goat
  *queijo de cabra* goat's cheese
**cabrito** m kid (goat)
**caça** f game *(to eat)* ; hunting
**caçador** m hunter
**cachorro** m hot dog ; puppy
**cada** each ; every
**cadeado** m padlock
**cadeia** f jail ; chain
**cadeira** f chair
  *cadeira de bebé* high chair ; push-chair
  *cadeira de lona* deck chair
  *cadeira de rodas* wheelchair
**cadela** f female dog
**café** m (black) coffee ; café
**cãibra** f cramp
**cair** to fall ; to fall over
**cais** m quay
**caixa** f cash desk
  *caixa automática* cash machine
  *caixa do correio* letterbox
**caixão** m coffin
**caixote** m bin ; wooden box ; container
**calar** to stop talking ; to keep silent
**calçado** m footwear
**calças** fpl trousers
**calções** mpl shorts
  *calções de banho* swimming trunks
**calços para travões** mpl brake pads
**calcular** to estimate ; to calculate
**caldeirada** f fish stew
**caldo** m stock *(for soup)*
  *caldo verde* cabbage soup
**calor** m heat
**calorífero** m heater
**cama** f bed
  *cama de casal* double bed
  *cama de bebé* cot
  *cama de criança* child's bed
  *cama de solteiro* single bed
  *a roupa de cama* bedding
**câmara de ar** f inner tube
**câmara municipal** f town hall
**camarão** m shrimp
**camarote** m cabin ; box *(theatre)*
**cambiar** to exchange ; to change money
**câmbio** m exchange rate
  *casa de câmbios* f money exchange shop

**camião** m lorry
**caminho** m path ; way ; route
**camioneta** f coach
**camisa** f shirt
  *camisa de noite* nightdress
**camomila** f camomile *(tea)*
**campaínha** f bell *(on door)*
**campismo** m camping
**campo** m field ; countryside
**campo de golfe** m golf course
**camurça** f suede
**cancelar** to cancel
**canela** f cinnamon
**caneta** f pen
**cano de esgoto** m drain
**canoagem** f canoeing
**cansaço** m fatigue
**cansado(a)** tired
**cantar** to sing
**cantina** f canteen
**canto** m corner
**cão** m dog
**capacete** m crash helmet
**capela** f chapel
**capitão** m captain
**capot** m bonnet *(of car)*
**cara** f face
**caracóis** mpl snails ; curls *(hair)*
**caramelos** mpl toffees
**caranguejo** m crab
**carapau** m horse mackerel
**caravana** f caravan
**carburador** m carburettor
**carga** f refill ; load
**caril** m curry
**carioca** m weak coffee
  *carioca de limão* lemon infusion
**Carnaval** Carnival
**carne** f meat
  *carne de borrego* spring lamb
  *carne picada* mince
  *carne de porco* pork
  *carne de vaca* beef
  *carne de vitela* veal
  *carnes frias* cold meats
**carneiro** m mutton ; lamb
**caro(a)** expensive
  *caro(a) amigo(a)* dear friend
**caroço** m pip ; stone
**carregamento** m cargo ; load
**carrinha** f van
**carrinho** m trolley
  *carrinho de bebé* pram ; carry cot

**carro** *m* car
**carruagem** *f* carriage *(railway)*
  *carruagem-cama* sleeper *(railway)*
**carruagem-restaurante** *f* restaurant car
**carta** *f* letter
**cartão** *m* card ; business card
  *cartão bancário* cheque card
  *cartão de crédito* credit card
  *cartão de embarque* boarding card
  *cartão de felicitações* greetings card
  *cartão garantia* cheque card
**cartaz** *m* poster ; billboard
**carteira** *f* wallet
**carteirista** *m* pickpocket
**carteiro** *m* postman
**carvalho** *m* oak tree
**carvão** *m* coal
**casa** *f* home ; house
  *casa de banho* toilet ; bathroom
**casaco** *m* jacket ; coat
**casado(a)** married
**casal** *m* couple
**casamento** *m* wedding
**caso** *m* case
  *em caso de…* in case of…
**castanha** *f* chestnut
  *castanhas assadas* roast chestnuts
  *castanhas piladas* dried chestnuts
**castanho(a)** brown
**castelo** *m* castle
**catedral** *f* cathedral
**causa** *f* cause
  *por causa de* because of
**cautela** take care
**cavala** *f* mackerel
**cavalheiro** *m* gentleman
**cavalo** *m* horse
**cave** *f* cellar
**cebola** *f* onion
**cedo** early
**cego(a)** *adj* blind
  *m/f* blind man/woman
**ceia** *f* supper
**célebre** famous
**cem** one hundred
**cemitério** *m* cemetery
**cenoura** *f* carrot
**centígrado** *m* centigrade
**centímetro** *m* centimetre
**cêntimo** *m* cent
**cento: por cento** per cent
**centro** *m* centre
  *centro da cidade* city centre
  *centro comercial* shopping centre
  *centro de saúde* health centre

**cera** *f* wax
**cerâmica** *f* pottery
**cérebro** *m* brain
**cereja** *f* cherry
**certeza** *f* certainty
  *ter a certeza* to be sure
**certificado** *m* certificate
**certo(a)** right *(correct, accurate)* ; certain
**cerveja** *f* beer ; lager
  *cerveja preta* bitter *(beer)*
**cervejaria** *f* beer house
**cesto** *m* basket
**céu** *m* sky
**chá** *f* tea
  *chá de limão* lemon tea
**chamada** *f* telephone call
  *chamada gratuita* free call
  *chamada internacional* international call
  *chamada pagável no destino* reverse charge call
**chamar** to call
**champô** *m* shampoo
**chão** *m* floor
**chapa de matrícula** *f* number plate
**chapéu** *m* hat
  *chapéu de sol* sunhat
**charcutaria** *f* delicatessen
**chave** *f* key
  *fechar à chave* to lock up
**chávena** *f* cup
**chefe** *m/f* boss
  *chefe de cozinha* chef
**chega!** that's enough!
**chegadas** *fpl* arrivals
**chegar** to arrive
**cheio(a)** full
**cheirar** to smell
**cheiro** *m/f* smell
  *mau cheiro* bad smell
**cheque** *m* cheque
  *cheque de viagem* traveller's cheque
  *levantar um cheque* to cash a cheque
**cherne** *m* black jewfish or grouper
**chispalhada** *f* bean stew with pig's trotters
**chispe** *m* pig's trotters
**chocos** *mpl* cuttlefish
  *chocos com tinta* cuttlefish cooked in their ink
**chouriço** *m* spicy sausage
**churrascaria** *f* barbecue restaurant
**churrasco** *m* barbecue
  *no churrasco* barbecued
**chuva** *f* rain
**chuveiro** *m* shower *(bath)*
**Cia.** *see* companhia

cidadão (cidadã) m/f citizen
cidade f town ; city
cigarro m cigarette
cima: em cima de on (top of)
cinco five
cinto m belt
  cinto de salvação lifebelt
  cinto de segurança seat belt
Cinzas (Quarta feira de Cinzas)
  Ash Wednesday
cinzento(a) grey
circuito m circuit
cirurgia f surgery (operation)
claro(a) light (colour) ; bright
classe f class
cliente m/f client
clínica f clinic
clube m club
cobertor m blanket
cobrar to charge
cobrir to cover
código m code ; dialling code
  código postal postcode
codorniz f quail
coelho m rabbit
coentro m coriander
cofre m safe
cogumelo m mushroom
coisa f thing
cola f glue
colar n necklace
colar vb to stick
colcha f bedspread
colchão m mattress
colecção f collection (of stamps etc)
colégio m (secondary) school
colete de salvação m life jacket
colher f spoon
colina f hill
collants mpl tights
colorau m paprika
coluna f pillar
  coluna vertebral spine
com with
comandos mpl controls
comboio m train
combustível m fuel
começar to begin ; to start
comer to eat
comida f food
comissário de bordo m steward ;
  purser
como as ; how
  como disse? I beg your pardon?
  como está? how are you?
comodidade f comfort

companheiro(a) m/f live-in partner
companhia (Cia.) f company
compartimento m compartment
completar to complete
completo no vacancies (sign in hotel etc)
compota f jam
compra f purchase
  ir às compras to go shopping
comprar to buy
compreender to understand
comprido(a) long
comprimento m length
comprimido m pill ; tablet
computador m computer
concelho m council
concordar to agree
concorrente m/f candidate
concurso m competition
condução f driving
  a carta de condução driving licence
condutor m driver ; chauffeur
conduzir to drive
conferência f conference
conferir to check
congelado(a) frozen (food)
congelar to freeze
  não congelar do not freeze
conhaque m cognac
conhecer to know (person, place)
conselho m advice
consertos mpl repairs
conservar to keep ; to preserve
  conservar no frio store in a cold place
constipação f cold (illness)
consulado m consulate
consulta f consultation ; appointment
consultório m surgery
consumir antes de... best before...
  (label on food)
conta f account; bill
contador m meter (electricity, water)
conter to contain
  não contem... does not contain...
contra against
contraceptivo m contraceptive
contrato m contract
convidado(a) m/f guest
convidar to invite ; to ask (invite)
convite m invitation
copo m glass (container)
cor f colour
coração m heart

**cordeiro** m lamb
**cor-de-laranja** orange (colour)
**cor-de-rosa** pink
**Corpo de Deus** Corpus Christi
**corpo** m body
**correia** f strap
  *correia de ventoinha* fan belt
**correio** m post office
  *pelo correio* by post
**corrente** f chain ; current
**correr** to flow ; to run (person)
**correspondência** f mail
**corrida** f race
  *corrida de touros* bullfight
  *corridas de cavalos* races
**cortar** to cut ; to cut off
  *cortar e fazer brushing* to cut and
  blow-dry
**corte** m cut
**cortiça** f cork
**costa** f shore ; coastline
**costela** f rib
**costeleta** f chop (meat) ; cutlet
**cotovelo** m elbow
**couro** m leather
**couve** f cabbage
  *couves-de-Bruxelas* Brussels sprouts
**couve-flor** f cauliflower
**couvert** m cover charge
**coxia** f aisle
**cozer** to boil
**cozido(a)** boiled
  *mal cozido* underdone
**cozinha** f kitchen
**cozinhar** to cook
**cozinheiro(a)** m/f cook
**cravinhos** mpl cloves
**cravo** m carnation
**creme** m custard
  *creme de barbear* shaving cream
  *creme para bronzear* suntan cream
  *creme hidratante* moisturizer
  *creme de limpeza* cleansing cream
**criança** f child
**cru(a)** raw
**cruz** f cross
**cruzamento** m junction (crossroads)
**cruzar** to cross
**cruzeiro** m cruise
**cuecas** fpl briefs ; pants
**cuidado** m care (caution)
**cumprimento** m greeting
  *cumprimentos* regards

**cunhado(a)** m/f brother-in-law/sister-in-law
**curso** m course
**curto(a)** short
**curva** f bend ; turning ; curve
  *curva perigosa* dangerous bend
**custar** to cost
**custo** m charge ; cost

# D

**damasco** m apricot
**dança** f dance
**dano** m damage
**Dão** fruity red and white wines from the north of Portugal
**dar** to give
  *dar prioridade* to give way
**data** f date
  *data de nascimento* date of birth
**de** of ; from
**debaixo de** under
**decidir** to decide
**dedo** m finger
**dedo do pé** m toe
**defeito** m flaw
**deficiente** disabled
**degrau** m step (stair)
**deitar-se** to lie down
**deixar** to let (allow) ; to leave behind
**delito** m crime
**demais** too much ; too many
**demasia** f change (money) ; excess
**demorado(a)** late
**demorar** to delay
**dente** m tooth
**dentes** mpl teeth
**dentes postiços** mpl false teeth
**dentista** m/f dentist
**dentro** inside
**depois** after(wards)
**depósito** m deposit (in bank)
  *depósito de bagagens* left-luggage
  *depósito da gasolina* petrol tank
**depressa** quickly
**desafio** m match ; game (sport) ; challenge
**desaparecido(a)** missing
**desapertar** to loosen
**descafeinado** m decaffeinated
**descansar** to rest
**descartável** throw-away ; disposable
**descer** to go down
**descoberta** f discovery
**descongelar** to defrost (food) ; to de-ice

**9**

**desconhecido(a)** m/f stranger
**desconhecido(a)** adj unknown
**desconto** m discount ; reduction
**desculpe** excuse me ; sorry
**desejar** to desire ; to wish
**desembarcar** to disembark
**desempregado(a)** unemployed
**desenho** m design ; drawing
**desinchar** to go down (swelling)
**desinfectante** m disinfectant
**desligado(a)** off (engine, gas)
**desligar** to hang up (phone) ; to switch
  off (engine, radio)
**desligue o motor** switch off your engine
**desmaiar** to faint
**desodorizante** m deodorant
**despachante** m shipper ; transport
  agent
**despesa** f expense
**desporto** m sport
**destinatário** m addressee
**desvio** m bypass ; detour ; diversion
**detergente** m detergent
**detergente para a louça** washing-up
  liquid
**detergente para a roupa** washing
  powder
**devagar** slowly ; slow down (sign)
**dever: eu devo** I must
**deve-me...** you owe me...
**devolver** to give back ; to return
**Dezembro** m December
**dia** m day
  dias da semana weekdays
  dia útil working day
  Dia da Liberdade Liberty Day
  Dia de Portugal Portugal Day
  dia de anos birthday
**diabético(a)** diabetic
**diante de** in front of (place)
**diário(a)** daily
**diarreia** f diarrhoea
**dieta** f diet ; special diet
**diferença** f difference
**difícil** difficult
**digestão** f digestion
**diluir** to dilute
**diminuir** to reduce
**dínamo** m dynamo
**dinheiro** m money ; cash
**direcção** f direction ; address ; steering
**directo(a)** direct
**direita** f right(-hand side)
  à direita on/to the right
  para a direita to the right
**direito(a)** straight ; right(-hand)
  Dto. on right-hand side (address)

**direitos** mpl duty (tax) ; rights
**dirigir** to direct
**disco** m record (music, etc)
  disco de estacionamento parking
  disk
**disponível** available
**dissolver** to dissolve
**distância** f distance
**distrito** m district
**divã-cama** m bed settee
**diversões** fpl entertainment
**divertir-se** to enjoy oneself ; to have
  fun
**dívida** f debt
**divisas** fpl foreign currency
**dizer** to say
**dobrada** f tripe
**dobrado(a)** bent
**dobro** m double
**doce** adj sweet (taste)
**doce** m dessert ; jam
**documentos** mpl documents
**doente** ill ; sick
**doer** to ache ; to hurt
**dólar** m dollar
**domicílio** m residence
**domingo** m Sunday
**dono(a)** m/f owner
  dona de casa housewife
**dor** f ache ; pain
**dormir** to sleep
**Douro** region producing port
**Dto.** see direito(a)
**duche** m shower
**duplo(a)** double
**durante** during
**durar** to last
**duro(a)** hard ; stiff ; tough (meat)
**dúzia** f dozen

# E

**e** and
**é** he/she/it is ; you are
**economizar** to save
**écrã** m screen
**edifício** m building
**edredão** m duvet ; quilt
**educado(a)** polite
**eixo de roda** m axle
**ela** she ; her ; it
**elas** they (feminine)
**elástico** m elastic band

**ele** he ; him ; it
**eles** they *(masculine)*
**electricista** *m* electrician
**eléctrico** *m* tram
**electrodomésticos** *mpl* electrical appliances
**elevador** *m* lift
**em** at ; in *(with towns, countries)* ; into
**embaixada** *f* embassy
**embarcar** to board *(ship, plane)*
**embarque** *m* embarkation ; time of sailing
**embraiagem** *f* clutch
**ementa** *f* menu
  *ementa fixa* set menu
  *ementa turística* tourist menu
**emergência** *f* emergency
**empregado(a)** *m/f* waiter(ess) ; maid ; attendant *(at petrol station)* ; assistant *(in shop)* ; office worker
**emprego** *m* job ; employment
**empurrar** to push
  *empurre* push *(sign)*
**EN** *see* estrada
**encaracolado(a)** curly
**encarnado(a)** red
**encerrado(a)** closed
**encher** to fill up ; to pump up *(tyre)*
**enchidos** *mpl* processed meats ; sausages
**encomenda** *f* parcel
**encontrar** to meet ; to find
**encontro** *m* date ; meeting
**encosta** *f* hill *(slope)*
**endereço** *m* address
**energia** *f* energy
  *o corte de energia* power cut
**enfermeiro(a)** *m/f* nurse
**enganar-se** to make a mistake
**engano** *m* mistake
**engolir** to swallow
  *não engolir* do not swallow
**engraxar** to polish *(shoes)*
**enguia** *f* eel
**enjoar** to be sick
**ensinar** to teach
**ensopado** *m* stew served on slice of bread
**enorme** big ; huge
**entender** to understand
**entorse** *f* sprain
**entrada** *f* entrance ; starter *(in meal)*
  *entrada livre* admission free

**entrar** to go in ; to come in ; to get into *(car, etc)*
**entre** among ; between
**entregar** to deliver
**entrevista** *f* interview
**enviar** to send
**enxaqueca** *f* migraine
**época** *f* period *(time)*
**equipamento** *m* equipment
**equitação** *f* horse riding
**erro** *m* mistake
**erva** *f* grass ; herb
**ervilhas** *fpl* peas
**escada** *f* ladder ; stairs
**escada rolante** *f* escalator
**escalfado(a)** poached *(egg)*
**escape** *m* exhaust
**escocês (escocesa)** Scottish
**Escócia** *f* Scotland
**escola** *f* school
**escova** *f* brush
**escova de dentes** *f* toothbrush
**escrever** to write
**escrito:** *por escrito* in writing
**escritório** *m* office
**escuro(a)** dark *(colour)*
**escutar** to listen to
**esferográfica** *f* ballpoint pen
**esgotado(a)** sold out *(tickets)* ; exhausted
**esgoto** *m* drain
**esmalte** *m* enamel
**espaço** *m* space
**espadarte** *m* swordfish
**espalhar** to scatter
**Espanha** *f* Spain
**espanhol** *m* Spanish *(language)*
**espanhol(a)** Spanish
**espargo** *m* asparagus
**esparguete** *m* spaghetti
**esparregado** *m* puréed spinach
**especialidade** *f* speciality
**especiarias** *fpl* spices
**espectáculo** *m* show *(in theatre etc)*
**espelho** *m* mirror
  *espelho retrovisor* driving mirror
**esperar** to expect ; to hope
  *esperar (por)* to wait for
**espetada** *f* kebab
**espinafre** *m* spinach
**esplanada** *f* terrace
**esposa** *f* wife
**espumante** *m* sparkling wine
**espumoso(a)** sparkling *(wine)*
**Esq.** *see* esquerda

**esquadra** f police station
**esquentador** m water heater
**esquerda** f left(-hand side)
  *à esquerda* on the left
  *Esq.* on left(-hand) side *(address)*
**esqui** m ski
**esquina** f corner *(outside)*
**está** he/she/it is ; you are
**estação** f station
  *estação alta* high season
  *estação baixa* low season
  *estação do ano* season
  *estação de autocarros* bus station
  *estação de serviço* service station
  *estação do comboio* railway station
**estacionamento** m parking
**estacionar** to park *(car)*
**estádio** m stadium
**estado** m state
  *estado civil* marital status
**Estados Unidos (EUA)** mpl United
  States
**estalagem** f inn
**estância termal** f spa
**estar** to be
**este/esta** m/f this
  *estes/estas* m/f these
**estômago** m stomach
  *o mal-estar de estômago* stomach
  upset
**estores** mpl blinds
**estrada** f road
  *estrada em mau estado* uneven road
  surface
  *estrada nacional (EN)* major road ;
  national highway
  *estrada sem saída* no through road
  *estrada secundária* minor road
**estrangeiro(a)** m/f foreigner
  *ao estrangeiro* abroad ; overseas
**estranho(a)** strange
**estreito(a)** narrow
**estudante** m/f student
**estufado(a)** braised
**etiqueta** f ticket ; label ; etiquette
**eu** I
**EUA** see Estados Unidos
**euro** m euro
**europeu (europeia)** European
**evitar** to avoid
**excepto** except
  *excepto aos domingos* Sundays
  excepted
**excesso de bagagem** m excess
  luggage ; excess baggage
**excursão** f excursion ; tour
  *excursão guiada* guided tour
**exemplo** m example
  *por exemplo* for example

**expirar** to expire
**explicar** to explain
**exportação** f exportation
**exportar** to export
**exposição** f exhibition
**extintor** m fire extinguisher
**extremidade** f edge ; extremity

# F

**fábrica** f factory
**fabricado(a) em ...** made in ...
**faca** f knife
**fácil** easy
**facilidade** f facility ; ease
**factura** f invoice
**fado** m traditional Portuguese song
**faiança** f pottery
**faisão** m pheasant
**faixa** f lane *(in road)*
**falar** to speak
**falecido(a)** deceased
**falésias** fpl cliffs
**falta** f lack
  *falta de corrente* power cut
**família** f family
**farinha** f flour
**farinheira** f sausage made with pork fat
  and flour
**farmácia** f chemist's
  *farmácia permanente* duty chemist
  *farmácias de serviço* emergency
  chemists'
**faróis** mpl headlights
**farol** m headlight ; lighthouse
**farolim** m sidelight
**fatia** f slice
**fato** m suit *(man's)*
  *fato de banho* swimsuit
  *fato de treino* tracksuit
**favas** fpl broad beans
**favor** m favour
  *faz favor* please
  *por favor* please
**fazer** to do ; to make
**febras de porco** fpl thin slices of roast
  pork
**febre** f fever
  *febre dos fenos* hay fever
  *ter febre* to have a temperature
**fechado** closed
  *fechado Domingos e Feriados* closed
  Sundays and Bank holidays
**fechar** to shut ; to close

**feijão** *m* beans
**feijão-verde** *m* French beans
**feijoada** *f* bean stew with pork and spicy sausage
**feio(a)** awful ; ugly
**feira** *f* fair *(commercial)* ; market
  *Feira Santa* Holy Day
**feito(a) à mão** handmade
**feliz** happy
**feriado** *m* public holiday
  *feriado nacional* bank holiday
**férias** *fpl* holidays
**ferido(a)** injured
**ferragens** *fpl* ironware
**ferro** *m* iron
  *ferro de engomar* iron *(for clothes)*
**ferver** to boil
**festa** *f* party *(celebration)*
  *Festa do Trabalho* Labour Day
**Fevereiro** *m* February
**fiambre** *m* ham
**ficar** to stay ; to be ; to remain
  *ficar bem* to suit
**ficha** *f* plug *(electrical)* ; registration card *(in hotel, clinic)*
  *ficha dupla/tripla* adaptor *(electrical)*
**fígado** *m* liver
**figo** *m* fig
  *figos secos* dried figs
**fila** *f* row *(line)* ; queue
**filete** *m* fillet steak ; tenderloin
**filha** *f* daughter
**filho** *m* son
**filial** *f* branch *(of bank, etc)*
**filigranas** *fpl* filigree work
**fim** *m* end
  *fim-de-semana* weekend
**fio** *m* wire
**fita** *f* tape ; ribbon
  *fita métrica* tape measure
**flor** *f* flower
**floresta** *f* forest
**florista** *f* florist
**fogão** *m* cooker
**fogo** *m* fire
  *fogos de artifício* fireworks
**folha** *f* leaf
  *folha de alumínio* aluminium foil
  *folha de estanho* tinfoil
**folhados** *mpl* puff pastries
**folheto** *m* leaflet
**fome** *f* hunger
  *tenho fome* I'm hungry
**fonte** *f* fountain ; source

**fora** out ; outside
**força** *f* power *(strength)* ; force
**formiga** *f* ant
**fornecer** to supply
**forno** *m* oven
**fortaleza** *f* fortress
**forte** strong
**forte** *m* fortress
**fósforo** *m* match
**fotografia** *f* photograph ; print
**fraco(a)** weak
**fralda** *f* nappy
**framboesa** *f* raspberry
**França** *f* France
**francês** *m* French *(language)*
**francês (francesa)** French
**frango** *m* chicken *(young and tender)*
  *frango assado* roast chicken
**frase** *f* sentence
**freguês (freguesa)** *m/f* customer
**frente** *f* front
  *em frente de* in front of ; opposite
**fresco(a)** fresh ; cool ; crisp
  *sirva fresco* serve cool
**frigorífico** *m* fridge
**frio(a)** cold
**fritar** to fry
**frito(a)** fried
**fronha** *f* pillow case
**fronteira** *f* border *(frontier)*
**fruta** *f* fruit
**frutaria** *f* fruit shop
**fruto** *m* fruit
**fuga** *f* leak ; escape
**fugir** to run away
**fumadores** *mpl* smokers
  *para não fumadores* non-smoking *(compartment, etc)*
**fumar** to smoke
  *não fumar* no smoking
**fumo** *m* smoke
**funcionar** to work *(machine)*
  *não funciona* out of order *(sign)*
**funcionário(a)** *m/f* employee ; civil servant
**fundo** *m* bottom
**fundo(a)** deep
**furar** to pierce
**furnas** *fpl* caverns
**furto** *m* theft
**fusível** *m* fuse
**futebol** *m* football

# G

**gabinete de provas** *m* changing room
**gado** *m* cattle
  *gado bravo* beware – unfenced bulls

**gaivota** f seagull ; pedal boat
**galão** m large white coffee ; gallon
**galeria** f gallery
**Gales: o País de Gales** Wales
**galês (galesa)** Welsh
**galinha** f hen ; chicken
**gamba** f prawn
**ganhar** to earn ; to win
**ganso** m goose
**garagem** f garage
**garantia** f guarantee
**gare** f platform
**garfo** m fork
**garganta** f throat
**garoto** m boy ; small white coffee
**garrafa** f bottle
**garrafão** m two or five-litre bottle
**gás** m gas
  **a botija de gás** gas cylinder
**gasóleo** m diesel
**gasolina** f petrol
**gasosa** f fizzy sweetened water
**gastar** to spend
**gaveta** f drawer
**gelado** m ice cream ; ice lolly
**gelar** to freeze
**gelataria** f ice cream parlour
**geleia** f jelly
**gelo** m ice
**gémeo(a)** m/f twin
**género** m kind ; type
  **o meu género de filme** my kind of film
**gengibre** m ginger
**gengivas** fpl gums
**genro** m son-in-law
**gente** f people
  **toda a gente** everybody
**geral** f gallery (in theatre)
**geral** adj general
  **em geral** generally
**geralmente** usually
**gerente** m/f manager
**ginjinha** f morello cherry liqueur
**gira-discos** m record player
**girassol** m sunflower
**gola** f collar
**golfe** m golf
  **o taco de golfe** golf club (stick)
**gordo(a)** fat
**gorjeta** f tip (to waiter, etc)
**gostar de** to like
**gosto** m taste
**governo** m government
**Grã-Bretanha** f Britain
**grama** m gramme
**grande** big ; large ; great

**grão** m chickpeas
**grátis** free (costing nothing)
**gravador** m tape recorder
**gravata** f tie
**grávida** pregnant
**gravura** f print (picture)
**grelhado(a)** grilled
**greve** f strike (industrial)
  **em greve** on strike
**gripe** f flu
**groselha** f (red)currant
**grosso(a)** thick
**grupo** m group ; party (group)
  **grupo sanguíneo** blood group
**grutas** fpl caves
**guarda** m/f police officer
**guarda-chuva** m umbrella
**guarda-lamas** m mudguard
**guardanapo** m napkin
**guardar** to keep ; to watch over
**guarda-sol** m sunshade
**guia** m/f guide
**guiché** m window (at post office, bank)
**guisado** m stew
**guitarra** f guitar (electric)

# H

**há** there is ; there are
**habitação** f residence ; home
**habitar** to reside
**história** f history ; story
**hoje** today
**homem** m man
  **o wc dos Homens** gents' toilet
**hora** f hour ; time (by the clock)
  **hora de chegada** time of arrival
  **hora de partida** departure time
  **hora de ponta** rush hour
  **que horas são?** what time is it?
**horário** m timetable
**hortelã** f mint (herb)
**hortelã-pimenta** f peppermint
**hóspede** m/f guest
**hospedeira** f hostess
  **hospedeira de bordo** flight attendant

# I

**iate** m yacht
**icterícia** f jaundice
**ida** f visit ; trip
  **um bilhete de ida** single ticket
  **ida e volta** return trip

**idade** f age
**identificação** f identification
**idosos** mpl the elderly ; old people
**ignição** f ignition ; starter (in car)
**igreja** f church
**igual** equal ; the same as
**ilha** f island
**Imaculada Conceição** Immaculate Conception
**impedir** to prevent
**impedido(a)** engaged (phone)
**imperial** m draught beer
**impermeável** m raincoat
    *adj* waterproof
**importação** f importation
**importância** f importance ; amount (money)
**importante** important
**imposto** m tax ; duty
    *impostos* duty ; tax
**impressão digital** f fingerprint
**impresso** m form (to fill in)
**imprevisto(a)** unexpected
**impulso** m unit of charge (for phone) ; impulse
**incêndio** m fire
**inchado(a)** swollen
**incluído(a)** included
**incomodar** to disturb
    *não incomodar* do not disturb
**indicativo** m dialling code
**indigestão** f indigestion
**infecção** f infection
**infeccioso(a)** infectious (illness)
**inflamação** f inflammation
**informação** f information
**infracção** f offence
**Inglaterra** f England
**inglês** m English (language)
**inglês (inglesa)** English
**iniciais** fpl initials
**iniciar** to begin
**início** m beginning
**inquilino** m tenant
**inscrever** to register
**insecto** m insect
**insolação** f heatstroke ; sunstroke
**instalações** fpl facilities
**instituto** m institute
**insuflável** inflatable
**inteiro(a)** whole
**interdito(a)** forbidden

**interessante** interesting
**interior** inside
**interno(a)** internal
**intérprete** m/f interpreter
**interruptor** m switch
**intervalo** m interval (in theatre)
**intestinos** mpl bowels
**intoxicação** f food poisoning
**introduzir** to introduce
**inundação** f flood
**inverno** m winter
**iogurte** m yoghurt
**ir** to go
**Irlanda** f Ireland
    *a Irlanda do Norte* Northern Ireland
**irlandês (irlandesa)** Irish
**irmã** f sister
**irmão** m brother
**iscas** fpl marinated pig's liver with potatoes
**isqueiro** m lighter
**isso** that
**isto** this
**Itália** f Italy
**italiano(a)** Italian
**itinerário** m route ; itinerary
**IVA** m VAT

# J

**já** already ; now
**jamais** never
**Janeiro** m January
**janela** f window
**jantar** m dinner ; evening meal
**jardim** m garden
**joalharia** f jeweller's ; jewellery
**joelho** m knee
**jogar** to play
**jogo** m match ; game ; play
**jóia** f jewel
**jornal** m newspaper
**jovem** young
**judeu (judia)** m/f Jew ; Jewish
**juiz(a)** m/f judge
**julgamento** m verdict ; sentence
**Julho** m July
**Junho** m June
**juntar** to join
**junto** near
**justiça** f justice
**juventude** f youth

# K

**kg.** *see* quilo(grama)

# L

**lã** f wool
**lábio** m lip
**laço** m bow (ribbon, string) ; bow-tie
**lado** m side
**ao lado de** next to
**ladrão (ladra)** m/f thief
**lagarto** m lizard
**lago** m lake
**lagosta** f lobster
**lagostim** m king prawn
**lâminas de barbear** fpl razor blades
**lâmpada** f light bulb
**lampreia** f lamprey
**lançar** to throw
**lanchar** to go for a snack
**lanche** m light mid-afternoon snack
**lápis** m pencil
 *lápis de cera* crayons (wax)
**lar** m home
**laranja** f orange
 *o doce de laranja* marmalade
**largo** m small square
**largo(a)** broad ; loose (clothes) ; wide
**largura** f width
**lata** f tin ; can (of food)
**latão** m brass
**lavabo** m lavatory ; toilet
**lava-louça** m sink
**lavandaria** f laundry
 *lavandaria automática* launderette
 *lavandaria a seco* dry-cleaner's
**lavar** to wash (clothes, etc)
**lavar a louça** to wash up
**lavar à mão** to handwash
**lavável** washable
**lebre** f hare
**legumes** mpl vegetables
**lei** f law
**leilão** m auction
**leitão** m sucking pig
**leite** m milk
 *com leite* white (coffee)
 *leite desnatado* skimmed milk
 *leite evaporado* evaporated milk
 *leite gordo* full-cream milk
 *leite magro* skimmed milk
 *leite meio-gordo* semi-skimmed milk
**lembranças** fpl souvenirs
**lembrar-se** to remember
**leme** m rudder ; helm
**lenço** m handkerchief ; tissue
**lençol** m sheet
**lente** f lens
 *lentes de contacto* contact lenses

**lento(a)** slow
**leque** m fan (hand-held)
**ler** to read
**leste** m east
**letra** f letter (of alphabet)
 *letra maiúscula* capital letter
**levantar** to draw (money) ; to lift
**levantar-se** to stand up ; get up (from bed)
**levar** to take ; to carry
**leve** light (not heavy)
**libra** f pound
 *libras esterlinas* pounds sterling
**lição** f lesson
**licença** f permit
**liceu** m secondary school
**licor** m liqueur
**ligação** f connection (trains, etc)
**ligado(a)** on (engine, gas, etc) ; connected
**ligeiro(a)** light
**lima** f lime (fruit)
**lima** f file
 *lima das unhas* nail file
**limão** m lemon
**limite** m limit
 *limite de velocidade* speed limit
**limonada** f lemonade
**limpar** to wipe ; to clean
**limpeza** f cleaning
 *limpeza a seco* dry-cleaning
**limpo(a)** clean
**língua** f language ; tongue
**linguado** m sole (fish)
**linguiça** f narrow spicy pork sausage
**linha** f line ; thread ; platform (railway)
**linho** m linen
**liquidação** f (clearance) sale
**Lisboa (Lx)** Lisbon
**liso(a)** smooth ; straight
**lista** f list
 *lista de preços* price list
 *lista telefónica* telephone directory
**litro** m litre
**livraria** f bookshop
**livre** free ; vacant ; for hire
**livro** m book
**lixívia** f bleach
**lixo** m rubbish
**loção** f lotion
**loja** f shop
**lombo** m loin (cut of meat)
**Londres** London

**longe** far
  *é longe?* is it far?
**longo(a)** long
**lotaria** f lottery
**louça** f dishes ; crockery
**louro(a)** fair (hair)
**louro** m bay leaf (herb)
**lua** f moon
**lua-de-mel** f honeymoon
**lugar** m seat (theatre) ; place
**lulas** fpl squid
**luvas** fpl gloves
**luxo** m luxury
**luz** f light
  *luzes de presença* sidelights
  *luzes de perigo* hazard lights
**Lx** see Lisboa

# M

**M.** underground (metro)
**má** see mau
**maçã** f apple
**macho** m male (animal)
**macio(a)** soft ; smooth
**maço** m packet (of cigarettes)
**Madeira** f Madeira
**madeira** f wood
**Madeira** m Madeira wine
**madrugada** f early morning
**maduro(a)** ripe
**mãe** f mother
**magro(a)** thin
**Maio** m May
**maior** larger ; largest
  *a maior parte de* the majority of
**mais** more
  *o/a mais* the most
**mal** m wrong ; evil
**mala** f suitcase ; bag ; trunk
**malagueta** f chilli
**mal-entendido** m misunderstanding
**mal-estar** m discomfort
**mancha** f stain
**mandar** to send ; to order
**maneira** f way (method)
**manga** f sleeve ; mango
**manhã** f morning
**manteiga** f butter
**manter** to keep ; to maintain
**mão** f hand
**mapa** m map
  *mapa das estradas* road map
  *mapa das ruas* street plan

**máquina** f machine
  *máquina fotográfica* camera
**mar** m sea
**maracujá** m passion fruit
**marca** f brand ; mark
**marcação** f booking ; dialling
**marcar** to dial (phone) ; to mark
**marcha-atrás** f reverse (gear)
**Março** m March
**marco do correio** m pillar box
**maré** f tide
  *maré alta* high tide
  *maré baixa* low tide
**marfim** m ivory
**marido** m husband
**marisco** m seafood ; shellfish
**marmelada** f quince jam
**marmelo** m quince
**mármore** m marble (substance)
**Marrocos** m Morocco
**mas** but
**massa** f dough
  *massas* pasta
  *massa folhada* puff pastry
**matrícula** f number plate
**mau (má)** bad ; evil
**máximo(a)** maximum
**mazagrã** m iced coffee and lemon
**me** me ; to me
**mecânico** m mechanic
**média** f average
**medicamento** m medicine
**médico(a)** m/f doctor
**medida** f measure ; size
**médio(a)** medium
**medusa** f jellyfish
**meia** f stocking ; half
**meia-hora** f half-hour
**meia-noite** f midnight
**meio** m middle
  *no meio de* in the middle of
**meio(a)** half
  *meia garrafa* a half bottle
  *meia de leite* cup of milky coffee
  (half milk, half coffee)
  *meia pensão* half board
**meio-dia** m midday ; noon
**meio-seco** medium sweet (wine)
**mel** m honey
**melancia** f watermelon
**melão** m melon
**melhor** better
  *o/a melhor* the best
**meloa** f small round melon
**menina** f Miss ; girl
**menino** m boy
**menor** smaller ; minor (underage)

**menos** least ; less
**mensagem** f message
**mensal** monthly
**menstruação** f period (menstruation)
**mercado** m market
**mercearia** f grocer's
**merengue** m meringue
**mês** m month
**mesa** f table
**mesmo(a)** same
**mesquita** f mosque
**metade** f half
  *pela metade do preço* half-price
**meter** to put in
**metro** m metre ; underground (rail)
**metropolitano** m tube (underground)
**meu (minha)** my ; mine
**mexer** to move
  *não mexer* do not touch
**mexilhão** m mussel
**migas à alentejana** bread dish with pork meats
**mil** thousand
**milhão** m million
**milho** m maize ; corn
**mim** me (after prepositions)
**minha** see meu
**mínimo(a)** minimum
**minúsculo(a)** tiny
**missa** f Mass (church service)
**mobília** f furniture
**mochila** f backpack ; rucksack
**moda** f fashion
**moeda** f coin ; currency
**moído(a)** ground (coffee, etc)
**moinho** m windmill
  *moinho de café* coffee grinder
**mola** f peg ; spring (coiled metal)
**molhado(a)** wet
**molho** m sauce ; gravy
**momento** m moment
**montanha** f mountain
**montante** m amount (total)
**montra** f shop window
**morada** f address
**moradia** f villa
**morango** m strawberry
**morar** to live ; to reside
**morcela** f black pudding
**mordedura** f bite (animal)
**morder** to bite
  *fui mordido(a) por um cão* I was bitten by a dog
**mordida** f bite
**moreno(a)** tanned ; dark-skinned
**morrer** to die

**mortadela** f cold meat
**mosaicos** mpl mosaic tiles
**mosca** f fly (insect)
**mostarda** f mustard
**mosteiro** m monastery
**mostrador** m dial ; glass counter
**mostrar** to show
**motocicleta** f motorbike
**motor** m engine ; motor
  *motor de arranque* starter motor
**motorista** m driver
**motorizada** f motorbike
**muçulmano(a)** m/f Muslim
**mudar** to change
  *mudar-se* to move house
**muito** very ; much ; quite (rather)
**muitos(as)** a lot (of) ; many ; plenty (of)
**mulher** f female ; woman ; wife
**multa** f fine
**multidão** f crowd
**mundial** worldwide
**mundo** m world
**muralhas** fpl ramparts
**muro** m wall (outside)
**museu** m museum
**música** f music

# N

**nabo** m turnip
**nacional** national
**nacionalidade** f nationality ; citizenship
**nada** nothing
  *nada a declarar* nothing to declare
**nadar** to swim
**namorada** f girlfriend
**namorado** m boyfriend
**não** no ; not
**nariz** m nose
**nascer** to be born
**nascimento** m birth
**nata** f cream
**natação** f swimming
**Natal** m Christmas
**naturalidade** f place of birth
**natureza** f nature
**navio** m ship
**neblina** f mist
**negar** to refuse
**negativo(a)** negative
**negócios** mpl business
**negro(a)** black

**nem:** *nem... nem...* neither... nor...
**nenhum(a)** none
**neta** f granddaughter
**neto** m grandson
**neve** f snow
**nevoeiro** m fog
**ninguém** nobody
**nível** m level
**nó** m knot
**No.** see número
**nocivo(a)** harmful
**nódoa** f stain
**noite** f evening ; night
  *à noite* in the evening/at night
  *boa noite* good evening/night
**noivo(a)** *adj* engaged (to be married)
  *m/f* bride/groom; fiancé(e)
**nome** m name
  *nome próprio* first name
**nora** f daughter-in-law
**nordeste** m north east
**normalmente** usually
**noroeste** m north west
**norte** m north
**nós** we ; us
**nosso(a)** our
**nota** f note ; banknote
**notar** to notice
**notícia** f piece of news
**Nova Zelândia** f New Zealand
**Novembro** m November
**novo(a)** new ; young ; recent
**noz** f nut ; walnut
**noz-moscada** f nutmeg
**nu(a)** naked
**nublado(a)** dull (weather) ; cloudy
**número (No.)** m number ; size (of
  clothes, shoes)
**nunca** never
**nuvem** f cloud

# O

**o** the (masculine)
**objeto** m object
  *objetos perdidos* lost property
**obra-prima** f masterpiece
**obras** fpl roadworks ; repairs
**obrigado(a)** thank you
**oceano** m ocean
**ocidental** western
**oculista** m/f optician
**óculos** mpl glasses
  *óculos de sol* sunglasses

**ocupado(a)** engaged (phone, toilet)
  also: busy (person)
**oeste** m west
**oferecer** to offer ; to give something
  *ofereço este livro* I give this book
**oferta** f offer ; gift
**olá** hello
**olaria** f pottery
**óleo** m oil
  *óleo dos travões* brake fluid
**oleoso(a)** greasy ; oily
**olhar para/por** to look at/after
**olho** m eye
**onda** f wave (on sea)
**onde** where
**ontem** yesterday
**óptimo(a)** excellent
**ora** now ; well now
**orçamento** m budget
**ordem** f order
**ordenado** m wage
**orelha** f ear
**organizado(a)** organized
**orquídea** f orchid
**osso** m bone
**ostra** f oyster
**ou** or
**ourivesaria e joalharia** goldsmith's and
  jeweller's
**ouro** m gold
  *de ouro* gold (made of gold)
**outono** m autumn
**outro(a)** other
  *outra vez* again
**Outubro** m October
**ouvido** m inner ear
**ouvir** to hear ; to listen (to)
**ovelha** f sheep
**ovo** m egg
**oxigénio** m oxygen

# P

**padaria** f baker's
**pagamento** m payment
  *pagamento a pronto* payment in full
**pagar** to pay
**página** f page
  *páginas amarelas* Yellow Pages
**pago(a)** paid
**pai** m father
  *pais* parents
**país** m country
**palácio** m palace
**palavra** f word
**pálido(a)** pale
**palito** m toothpick

**panado(a)** fried in egg and breadcrumbs
**pane** f breakdown *(car)*
**panela** f pan ; pot
**pano** m cloth
**pão** m bread ; loaf
  *pão de centeio* rye bread
  *pão integral* wholemeal bread
  *pão de ló* sponge cake
  *pão de milho* maize bread
  *pão torrado* toasted bread
  *pão de trigo* wheat bread
**papel** m paper
  *papel de carta* writing paper
  *papel de embrulho* wrapping paper
  *papel higiénico* toilet paper
**papelaria** f stationer's
**papo-seco** m roll *(of bread)*
**par** m pair ; couple
**para** for ; towards ; to
**parabéns** mpl congratulations ; happy birthday
**pára-brisas** f windscreen
**pára-choques** m bumper
**parafuso** m screw
**paragem** f stop *(for bus, etc)*
**parar** to stop
**pare** stop *(sign)*
  *pare ao sinal vermelho* stop when lights are red
**parede** f wall *(inside)*
**parente** m/f relation *(family)*
**pargo** m sea bream
**parque** m park
**parquímetro** m parking meter
**parte** f part
  *parte de frente* front
  *parte de trás* back
**particular** private
**partidas** fpl departures
**partir** to break ; to leave
  *a partir de...* from...
**Páscoa** f Easter
**passa** f raisin
**passadeira** f zebra crossing
**passado** m the past
**passado(a):** *mal passado(a)* rare *(steak)*
  *bem passado(a)* well done *(steak)*
**passageiro** m passenger
**passagem** f fare ; crossing
  *passagem de nível* level-crossing
  *passagem de peões* pedestrian crossing
  *passagem proibida* no right of way
  *passagem subterrânea* underpass
**passaporte** m passport
**passar** to pass ; to go by
**pássaro** m bird

**passatempos** mpl hobbies
**passe** m season ticket
**passe** go *(when crossing road)* ; walk
**passear** to go for a walk
**passeio** m walk ; pavement
**pasta** f paste
  *pasta dentífrica* toothpaste
**pastéis** mpl pastries
**pastel** m pie ; pastry *(cake)*
  *pastel folhado* puff pastry
**pastelaria** f pastries ; café ; cake shop
**pastilha** f pastille
  *pastilha elástica* chewing gum
  *pastilhas para a garganta* throat lozenges
**pataniscas** fpl salted cod fritters
**patinagem** f skating *(ice)* ; roller-skating
**patinar** to skate
**pátio** m courtyard
**pato** m duck
**pau** m stick
**pé** m foot
  *a pé* on foot
  *de pé* standing up
**peão** m pedestrian
**peça** f part ; play
  *peças e acessórios* spares and accessories
**peça...** ask for...
**pediatra** m/f paediatrician
**pedir** to ask
  *pedir alguma coisa* to ask for something
  *pedir emprestado(a)* to borrow
**peito** m breast ; chest
**peixaria** f fishmonger's
**peixe** m fish
  *peixe congelado* frozen fish
**peixe-espada** m scabbard fish
**pele** f fur ; skin
**película** f film *(for camera)*
**pensão** m guesthouse
  *pensão completa* full board
  *pensão residencial* boarding house
  *meia pensão* half board
**pensar** to think
**penso** m sticking plaster
  *penso higiénico* sanitary towel
**pente** m comb
**Pentecostes** Pentecost
**peões** mpl pedestrians
**pepino** m cucumber
  *pepino de conserva* gherkin
**pequeno(a)** little ; small

**pequeno-almoço** m breakfast
**pêra** f pear
  *pêra abacate* avocado pear
**percebes** mpl edible barnacles
**percurso** m route
**perdão** I beg your pardon ; I'm sorry
**perder** to lose ; to miss (train, etc)
**perdido(a)** lost
  *perdidos e achados* lost and found ;
  lost property
**perdiz** f partridge
**pergunta** f question
  *fazer uma pergunta* to ask a question
**perigo** m danger
  *perigo de incêndio* fire hazard
**perigoso(a)** dangerous
**permitir** to allow
**perna** f leg
**pérola** f pearl
**pertencer:** *pertencer a* to belong to
**perto de** near
**peru** m turkey
**pesado(a)** heavy
**pêsames** mpl condolences
**pesar** to weigh
**pesca** f fishing
**pescada** f hake
**pescadinhas** fpl whiting
**pescar** to fish
**peso** m weight
**pêssego** m peach
**pessoa** f person
**pessoal** adj personal
**pessoal** m staff ; personnel
**petiscos** mpl snacks ; titbits
**petróleo** m oil
**peúgas** fpl socks
**picada** f sting
**picado(a)** chopped ; minced
**picante** spicy
**picar** to sting
  *uma picada de mosquito* a mosquito
  bite
**pilha** f pile ; battery (for torch)
**pílula** f the pill
**pimenta** f pepper
**pimento** m pepper (vegetable)
**pintar** to paint
**pintura** f painting
**pior** worse
**piripiri** m hot chilli dressing
**pisca-pisca** m indicator (on car)

**piscina** f swimming pool
  *piscina aberta* outdoor swimming
  pool
  *piscina para crianças* paddling pool
**piso** m floor ; level ; surface
  *piso escorregadio* slippery surface
**pista** f track ; runway
**planta** f plant ; map
**plataforma** f platform
**plateia** f stalls (in theatre)
**platinados** fpl points (in car)
**pneu** m tyre
  *a pressão dos pneus* tyre pressure
**pó** m dust ; powder
  *pó de talco* talcum powder
**poço** m well
**poder** to be able
**polegar** m thumb
**polícia** f police
**polícia** m policeman ; police officer
  *mulher-polícia* policewoman
**poluição** f pollution
**polvo** m octopus
**pomada** f ointment
  *pomada para o calçado* shoe polish
**pomar** m orchard
**pombo** m pigeon
**ponte** f bridge
**população** f population
**por** by (through)
  *por aqui/por ali* this/that way
  *por hora* per hour
  *por pessoa* per person
**pôr** to put
**porção** f portion
**porco** m pig ; pork
**por favor** please
**pormenores** mpl details
**porque** because
**porquê** why
**porta** f door
  *a porta No. ...* gate number ...
**porta-bagagens** m boot (of car) ;
  luggage rack
**porta-chaves** m key ring
**portagem** f motorway toll
**porta-moedas** m purse
**porteiro** m porter
**porto** m harbour
**Porto :** *o Porto* Oporto
  *o vinho do Porto* Port wine
**português** m Portuguese (language)
**português (portuguesa)** Portuguese
**posologia** f dose (medicine)
**postal** m postcard
**posto** m post ; job
  *posto clínico* first aid post
  *posto de socorros* first aid centre

**pouco(a)** little

**pousada** f state-run hotel ; inn

**povo** m people

**povoação** f small village

**praça** f square (in town) ; market
  *praça de táxis* taxi rank
  *praça de touros* bullring

**praia** f beach ; seaside

**prata** f silver

**prateleira** f shelf

**praticar** to practise

**prato** m dish ; plate ; course of meal
  *prato da casa* speciality of the house
  *prato do dia* today's special

**prazer** m pleasure
  *prazer em conhecê-lo* pleased to meet you

**precipício** m cliff ; precipice

**precisar** to need

**preciso(a): é preciso** it is necessary

**preço** m price

**preencher** to fill in

**preferir** to prefer

**prejuízo** m damage

**prémio** m prize

**prenda** f gift

**preocupado(a)** worried

**preparado(a)** ready

**presente** m gift ; present

**preservativo** m condom

**pressão** f pressure
  *pressão dos pneus* tyre pressure

**presunto** m cured ham

**preto(a)** black

**primavera** f spring (season)

**primeiro(a)** first
  *primeiro andar* first floor
  *de primeira classe* first-class

**primo(a)** m/f cousin

**princípio** m beginning

**prioridade** f priority
  *prioridade à direita* give way to the right

**prisão** f prison
  *ter prisão de ventre* to be constipated

**privado(a)** adj private

**procurar** to look for

**produto** m product ; proceeds
  *produtos alimentares* foodstuffs

**professor(a)** m/f teacher

**profissão** f profession
  *profissão, idade, nome* profession, age and name

**profundidade** f depth

**profundo(a)** deep

**proibido(a)** forbidden
  *proibida a entrada* no entry
  *proibido estacionar* no parking
  *proibido fumar* no smoking
  *proibida a paragem* no stopping
  *proibida a passagem* no access
  *proibido pisar a relva* do not walk on the grass
  *proibido tomar banho* no bathing

**promoção** f special offer ; promotion (at work)

**pronto(a)** ready

**propriedade** f estate (property)

**proprietário(a)** m/f owner

**prospecto** m pamphlet

**prótese dentária** f dental fittings

**provar** to taste ; to try on

**provisório(a)** temporary

**próximo(a)** near ; next

**público** m audience ; public

**pudim** m pudding

**pulmão** m lung

**pulseira** f bracelet ; wrist strap

**pulso** m wrist

**pura lã** f pure wool

**purificador do ar** m air freshener

**puxar** to pull
  *puxe* pull (sign)

# Q

**quadro** m picture ; painting

**qual** which

**qualidade** f quality

**quando** when

**quantidade** f quantity

**quanto(a)** how much
  *quantos(as)?* how many?
  *quanto tempo?* how long? (time)

**quarta-feira** f Wednesday

**quarto** m room ; bedroom
  *quarto com duas camas* twin-bedded room
  *quarto de casal* double room
  *quarto individual* single room

**quarto** fourth ; quarter
  *um quarto de hora* a quarter of an hour

**que** what
  *o que é?* what is it?

**quebra-mar** m pier

**quebrar** to break

**queda** f fall

**queijada** f cheesecake

**queijo** m cheese

**queimadura** f burn
*queimadura do sol* sunburn
**queixa** f complaint
*quero apresentar uma queixa* I want
to make a complaint
**quem** who
**quente** *adj* hot
**querer** to want ; to wish
**quilo(grama) (kg.)** m kilo
**quilómetro** m kilometre
**quinta** f farm
**quinta-feira** f Thursday
**quiosque** m kiosk ; newsstand
**quotidiano(a)** daily

# R

**R.** *see* rua
**rã** f frog
**rabanete** m radish
**rádio** m radio
**radiografia** f X-ray
**raia** f skate *(fish)*
**raiva** f rabies
**raíz** f root
**Ramos (Domingo de Ramos)** Palm
Sunday
**rapariga** f girl
**rapaz** m boy
**rápido** m express *(train)*
**rápido(a)** fast
**raposa** f fox
**raqueta** f racquet ; bat *(for table tennis)*
**rasgar** to tear
**ratazana** f rat
**rato** m mouse
**R/C** *see* rés-do-chão
**real** real ; royal
**reboques** mpl breakdown service
**rebuçado** m boiled sweet
**recado** m message
*dar um recado* to give a message
**receber** to receive
**receita** f recipe
*receita médica* prescription
**recepção** f reception
**recibo** m receipt
**reclamação** f protest ; official complaint
**recolher** to collect
*recolha de bagagem* baggage
reclaim
**recomendar** to recommend
**recompensa** f reward

**reconhecer** to recognize
**recordação** f souvenir
**recordar-se** to remember
**rede** f net
**redução** f reduction ; discount
**reembolsar** to reimburse
**refeição** f meal
**reformado(a)** m/f senior citizen ; retired
**região** f area *(region)*
*região demarcada* official wine-
producing region
**registar** to register
**regulamentos** mpl regulations
**Reino Unido** m United Kingdom
**relógio** m watch ; clock
**relva** f grass
*não pisar a relva* keep off the grass
**remédio** m medicine ; remedy
**remetente** m sender
**renda** f lace ; rent
*rendas de bilros* hand-woven
lacework
**reparação** f repair
**reparar** to fix ; to repair
**repartição** f state department
**repetir** to repeat
**rés-do-chão (R/C)** m ground floor
**reserva de lugar** f seat reservation
**reservado(a)** reserved
**reservar** to book ; to reserve
**residência** f boarding house ; residence
**residir** to live
**respirar** to breathe
**responder** to answer ; to reply
**resposta** f answer
**restaurante** m restaurant
**retalho** m oddment ; remnant
**retrosaria** f haberdashery
**reunião** f meeting
**revelar** to develop *(photos)* ; to reveal
**revisor(a)** m/f ticket collector
**revista** f magazine
**ribeiro** m stream
**rins** mpl kidneys
**rio** m river
**rissol** m rissole
**rochas** fpl rocks
**roda** f wheel
**rolha** f cork
**rolo** m cartridge *(for camera)* ; roll
**rosé** adj rosé *(wine)*
**rosto** m face
**roteiro** m guidebook
**roubar** to steal ; to rob
**roupa** f clothes
*roupa de cama* bedding
*roupa interior* underwear

**roxo(a)** purple
**rua (R.)** f street
**rubéola** f German measles
**ruído** m noise
**ruptura** f break

# S

**S.** *see* São
**sábado** m Saturday
**sabão** m soap
  *sabão em flocos* soapflakes
  *sabão em pó* soap powder
**saber** to know *(fact)*
**sabonete** m toilet soap
**sabor** m flavour ; taste
**saca-rolhas** m corkscrew
**saco** m bag ; handbag
  *saco cama* sleeping bag
  *saco do lixo* bin bag
**safio** m sea eel
**saia** f skirt
**saída** f exit ; way out
  *saídas* departures
**sair** to go out ; to come out
**sal** m salt
**sala** f room
  *sala de chá* tea room ; café
  *sala de embarque* airport lounge
  *sala de espera* waiting room
  *sala de estar* living room ; lounge
  *sala de jantar* dining room
**salada** f salad
**salão** m hall *(for concerts, etc)*
**salário** m wage ; salary
**saldo** m sale
**salgado(a)** salty
**salmão** m salmon
  *salmão fumado* smoked salmon
**salmonete** m red mullet
**salpicão** m spicy sausage
**salsa** f parsley
**salsicha** f sausage
**salsicharia** f delicatessen
**salteado(a)** sautéed
**salvar** to rescue ; to save *(rescue)*
**sandálias** fpl sandals
**sandes** f sandwich
  *sandes de fiambre* ham sandwich
**sanduíche** f sandwich
**sangue** m blood
**sanitários** mpl toilets
**Santíssima Trindade** Holy Trinity
**Santo(a) (Sto./Sta.)** m/f saint
**santo(a)** holy
**santola** f spider crab
**São (S.)** m Saint

**sapataria** f shoe shop
**sapateira** f type of crab
**sapateiro** m shoemaker ; cobbler
**sapato** m shoe
**saquinhos de chá** mpl tea bags
**sarampo** m measles
**sardinha** f sardine
**satisfeito(a)** happy ; satisfied
**saudação** f greeting
**saudável** healthy
**saúde** f health
  *saúde!* cheers!
**se** if ; whether
  *se faz favor (SFF)* please
**sé** f cathedral
**secador** m dryer
**secar** to dry ; to drain *(tank)*
**secção** f department
**seco(a)** dry
**secretária** f desk
**secretário(a)** m/f secretary
**século** m century
**seda** f silk
**sede** f thirst
  *ter sede* to be thirsty
**segredo** m secret
**seguinte** following
**seguir** to follow
  *seguir pela direita* keep to your right
  *seguir pela esquerda* keep to your left
**segunda-feira** f Monday
**segundo** m second *(time)*
**segundo(a)** second
  *segundo andar* second floor
  *de segunda classe* second-class
  *em segunda mão* second-hand
**segurança** f safety
**segurar** to hold
**seguro** m insurance
  *seguro contra terceiros* third party insurance
  *seguro contra todos os riscos* comprehensive insurance
  *seguro de viagem* travel insurance
**seguro(a)** safe ; reliable
**seio** m breast
**selecção** f selection
**selo** m stamp
**selvagem** wild
**sem** without
**semáforos** mpl traffic lights

**semana** f week
  *para a semana* next week
  *na semana passada* last week
  *por semana* weekly (rate, etc)
**semanal** weekly
**sempre** always
**senhor** m sir ; gentleman ; you
  *Senhor* Mr
**senhora** f lady ; madam ; you
  *Senhora* Mrs, Ms
  *a casa de banho das Senhoras* ladies'
  toilet
**senhorio(a)** m/f landlord/lady
**sentar-se** to sit (down)
**sentido** m sense ; meaning
  *sentido único* one-way street
**sentir** to feel
**ser** to be
**serviço** m service ; cover charge
  *serviço de quartos* room service
  *serviço (não) incluído* service (not)
  included
  *serviço permanente* 24-hour service
**servir** to serve
  *pode servir?* can you serve?
**sessão** f session ; performance
**Setembro** m September
**seu (sua)** his ; her ; your
**sexta-feira** f Friday
**SFF** see se faz favor
**significar** to mean
**sim** yes
**simpático(a)** nice ; friendly
**sinal** m signal ; deposit (part payment)
  *sinal de impedido* engaged tone
  *sinal de marcação* dialling tone
  *sinal de trânsito* road sign
**sino** m bell
**sítio** m place ; spot
**situado(a)** situated
**só** only ; alone
**sobre** over ; on top of
  *sobre o mar* overlooking the sea
**sobrecarga** f excess load ; surcharge
**sobremesa** f dessert
**sobressalente** spare
  *a roda sobressalente* spare wheel
**sobretudo** m overcoat (man's)
**sócio** m member ; partner
**socorro** m help ; assistance
  *socorro 115* emergency service 999
**sogro(a)** m/f father-in-law/mother-in-law
**sol** m sun
**solteiro(a)** single (not married)

**solúvel** soluble
**som** m sound
**soma** f amount (sum)
**sombra** f shadow (in sun)
**sono** m sleep
**sopa** f soup
  *sopa à alentejana* garlic, coriander
  and bread soup topped with poached
  egg
**sorte** f luck ; fortune
  *boa sorte* good luck
**sorvete** m sorbet
**sótão** m attic
**soutien** m bra
**sua** see seu
**subida** f rise ; ascent
**subir** to go up
**sudeste** m south-east
**sudoeste** m south-west
**suficiente** enough
**sujo(a)** dirty
**sul** m south
**sumo** m juice
**suor** m sweat
**supermercado** m supermarket
**supositório** m suppository
**surdo(a)** deaf
**surf** m surfing

# T

**tabacaria** f tobacconist's ; newsagent
**tabaco** m tobacco
**tabela** f list ; table
**taberna** f wine bar
**tabuleiro** m tray
**taça** f cup
**tacão** m heel
**talão** m voucher
**talco** m talc
**talheres** mpl cutlery
**talho** m butcher's
**talvez** perhaps
**tamanho** m size
**também** also ; too
**tamboril** m monkfish
**tampa** f lid ; cover ; top ; cap
**tampões** mpl tampons
**tanto(a)** so much
**tão** so
  *isto é tão bonito* this is so beautiful
**tapete** m carpet ; rug
  *tapetes e carpetes* rugs and carpets
**tarde** f afternoon
  *boa tarde* good afternoon

**tarde** adverb late (in the day)
**tarifa** f charge ; rate
  *tarifas de portagem* toll charges
**tarte** f tart
  *tarte de amêndoa* almond tart
**tasca** f tavern ; wine bar ; restaurant
**taxa** f fee ; rate
  *taxa de juro* interest rate
  *taxa normal* peak-time rate
  *taxa reduzida* off-peak rate
**teatro** m theatre
**tecido** m fabric ; tissue ; cloth
**tejadilho** m roof rack
**telecomandado(a)** remote-controlled
**teleférico** m cable car
**telefone** m telephone
**telefonista** f operator
**televisão** f television
**televisor** m television set
**telhado** m roof
**temperatura** f temperature
**tempero** m dressing (for salad) ;
  seasoning
**tempestade** f storm
**tempo** m weather ; time (duration)
  *tempo inteiro* full-time
  *tempo parcial* part-time
**temporada** f season
**temporário(a)** temporary
**tenda** f tent
**ténis** m tennis
**tenro(a)** tender (meat)
**tensão** f tension
  *tensão arterial alta/baixa* high/low
  blood pressure
**tentar** to try
**ter** to have
**terça-feira** f Tuesday
**terceiro(a)** third
  *terceiro andar* third floor
  *para a terceira idade* for the elderly
**termas** fpl spa
**termo** m (vacuum) flask
**termómetro** m thermometer
**terra** f earth ; ground
**terraço** m veranda ; balcony
**terramoto** m earthquake
**terreno** m ground ; land
**tesoura** f scissors
**tesouro** m treasure
**testemunha** f witness
**tímido(a)** shy
**tingir** to dye
**tinta** f ink ; paint
**tinturaria** f dry-cleaner's
**tio(a)** m/f uncle/aunt
**tipo** m sort ; kind

**tira-nódoas** m stain remover
**tirar** to remove ; to take out
**tiro** m shot
**toalha** f towel
**toalhete de rosto** m face cloth ; flannel
  (for washing)
**toalhetes refrescantes** mpl baby wipes
**tocar** to touch ; to ring ; to play
  *tocar piano* to play the piano
**todo(a)** all ; the whole
  *toda a gente* everyone
  *todas as coisas* everything
  *Todos os Santos* All Saints' Day
  *em toda a parte* everywhere
**toldo** f sunshade (on beach)
**tomada** f socket ; power point
**tomar** to take
  *tomar banho* to bathe ; to have a
  bath
  *tomar antes de se deitar* take before
  going to bed
  *tomar em jejum* take on an empty
  stomach
  *tomar... vezes ao dia* take... times a
  day
**tomate** m tomato
**tonelada** f ton
**toranja** f grapefruit
**torcer** to twist ; to turn
**torneio** m tournament
**torneira** f tap
**tornozelo** m ankle
**torrada** f toast
**torre** f tower
**torto(a)** twisted
**tosse** f cough
**tosta** f toasted sandwich
  *tosta de queijo* toasted cheese
  sandwich
**totobola** m football pools
**totoloto** m lottery
**toucinho** m bacon
**tourada** f bullfight
**touro** m bull
**tóxico(a)** poisonous ; toxic
**trabalhar** to work (person)
**trabalho** m work
  *trabalhos na estrada* roadworks
**tradução** f translation
**traduzir** to translate
**tráfego** m traffic
**tranquilo(a)** calm ; quiet
**transferir** to transfer

**trânsito** *m* traffic
  *trânsito condicionado* restricted traffic
  *trânsito proibido* no entry
**transpiração** *f* perspiration ; sweat
**transportar** to transport ; to carry
**transtorno** *m* upset ; inconvenience
**trás:** *para trás* backwards
  *no banco de trás* on the back seat
  *(car)*
  *a parte de trás* the back
**tratamento** *m* treatment
**tratar de** to treat ; to deal with
**travar** to brake
**travessa** *f* lane *(in town)* ; serving dish
**travessia** *f* crossing *(voyage)*
**travões** *mpl* brakes
**trazer** to bring ; to carry
**triângulo** *m* warning triangle
**tribunal** *m* court
**trigo** *m* wheat
**triste** sad
**trocar** to exchange ; to change
**troco** *m* change *(money)*
  *trocos* small change
**trovoada** *f* thunderstorm
**truta** *f* trout
**tu** you *(informal)*
**tubo** *m* exhaust pipe ; tube ; hose
**tudo** everything ; all
**turista** *m/f* tourist

# U

**úlcera** *f* ulcer
**ultimamente** lately ; recently
**último(a)** last ; latest
**ultrapassar** to overtake ; to pass
**um(a)** a ; an ; one
**unha** *f* nail *(on finger, toe)*
**único(a)** single ; unique
**unidade** *f* unit *(hi-fi, etc)* ; unity
**unir** to join
**universidade** *f* university ; college
**urgência** *f* urgency
**urtiga** *f* nettle
**urze** *f* heather
**urso(a)** *m/f* bear
**usado(a)** used *(car, etc)*
**usar** to use ; to wear
**uso** *m* use
  *uso externo* for external use
**útil** useful
**utilização** *f* use

**utilizar** to use
**uva** *f* grape

# V

**vaca** *f* cow
**vacina** *f* vaccination
**vagão** *m* railway carriage ; coach
**vagão-restaurante** *m* buffet car
**vagar** to be vacant
**vagas** *fpl* vacancies
**vale** *m* valley
**valer** to be worth
**validação:** *validação de bilhetes f*
  validate tickets
**válido(a)** valid
  *válido(a) até...* valid until...
**valor** *m* value
**válvula** *f* valve ; tap
**vapor** *m* steam
**varanda** *f* veranda ; balcony
**variado(a)** varied
**varicela** *f* chickenpox
**vários(as)** several
**vazio(a)** empty
**vegetal** *m* vegetable
  *vegetais congelados* frozen
  vegetables
**vegetariano(a)** vegetarian
**veículo** *m* vehicle
  *veículos pesados* heavy goods
  vehicles
**vela** *f* sail ; sailing
**vela** *f* spark plug ; candle
**velho(a)** old
**velocidade** *f* gear ; speed
  *velocidade limitada* speed limit
  in force
**velocímetro** *m* speedometer
**vencimento** *m* wage ; expiry date
**venda** *f* sale *(in general)*
  *venda proibida* not for public sale
  *vendas e reparações* sales and repairs
**vender** to sell
  *vende-se* for sale
**veneno** *m* poison
**vento** *m* wind
**ventoinha** *f* fan *(electric)*
**ver** to see ; to look at
**verão** *m* summer
**verdade** *f* truth
  *não é verdade?* isn't it?
**verdadeiro(a)** true
**verde** green
**verificar** to check
**vermelho(a)** red
**verniz** *m* varnish

**vertigem** f dizziness ; vertigo
**vespa** f wasp
**véspera** f the day before ; the eve
**vestiário** m cloakroom ; changing room
**vestido** m dress
**vestir** to dress ; to wear
  **vestir-se** to get dressed
**vestuário** m clothes
**veterinário(a)** m/f vet
**vez** f time ; turn
  **às vezes** occasionally ; sometimes
  **uma vez** once
  **duas vezes** twice
  **muitas vezes** often
  **é a sua vez** it's your turn
**via** f lane
**via** via
  **via aérea** by air mail
  **via nasal** to be inhaled
  **via oral** orally
**viaduto** m viaduct ; flyover
**viagem** f trip ; journey
  **viagem de negócios** business trip
**viajante** m/f traveller
**viajar** to travel
**vida** f life
**vidros** mpl glassware
**vila** f small town
**vinagre** m vinegar
**vindima** f harvest (of grapes)
**vinho** m wine
  **vinho branco** white wine
  **vinho da casa** house wine
  **vinho de mesa** table wine
  **vinho doce** sweet wine
  **vinho espumante** sparkling wine
  **vinho rosé** rosé wine
  **vinho seco** dry wine
  **vinho tinto** red wine
  **vinho verde** young wine
**vir** to come
**virar** to turn
  **vire à direita** turn right
  **vire à esquerda** turn left
**vírgula** f comma
**visitar** to visit
**vista** f view
  **com linda vista** with a beautiful view
**visto** m visa
**vitela** f veal
**viúvo(a)** m/f widower/widow
**vivenda** f chalet ; villa
**viver** to live
**vivo(a)** alive
**vizinho(a)** m/f neighbour
**você(s)** you
**volante** m steering wheel

**volta** f turn
  **à volta de** about
  **em volta de** around
  **dar uma volta** to go for a short walk/ride
**voltagem** f voltage
**voltar** to return (go/come back)
  **volto já** I'll be back in a minute
**vomitar** to vomit
**voo** m flight
  **voo fretado** charter flight
  **voo normal** scheduled flight
**vos** you ; to you
**vós** you
**vosso(a)** yours
**voz** f voice
**vulcão** m volcano

# W

**WC** m toilet
**wind-surf** m windsurfing

# X

**xadrez** m chess
**xarope** m syrup
  **xarope para a tosse** cough syrup
**xerez** m sherry

# Z

**zero** zero ; nought
**zona** f zone
  **zona azul** permitted parking zone
  **zona de banhos** swimming area
  **zona interdita** no thorough-fare

# HOW PORTUGUESE WORKS

## 18

## NOUNS

*A noun is a word such as car, horse or Mary which is used to refer to a person or thing.*

Portuguese nouns are *masculine* or *feminine*, and their gender is shown by the words for **the** (**o/a**) and **a** (**um/uma**) used before them (the 'article'):

| *masculine* | *feminine* |
|---|---|
| **o/um castelo** the/a castle | **a/uma mesa** the/a table |
| **os castelos** the castles | **as mesas** the tables |
| **(uns) castelos** (some) castles | **(umas) mesas** (some) tables |

It is usually possible to tell whether a noun is *masculine* or *feminine* by its ending: nouns ending in **-o** or **-or** are usually *masculine*, while those ending in **-a**, **-agem**, **-dade** and **-tude** tend to be *feminine*. There are exceptions, however, and it's best to learn the noun and the article together.

## PLURAL

Nouns ending in a vowel form the plural by adding **-s**, while those ending in a consonant usually add **-es**. The exceptions to this are words ending in an **-m** which change to **-ns** in the plural and words ending in **-l** which change to **-is** in the plural: e.g. **hotel – hotéis**.

**NOTE:** When used after the words **a** (to), **de** (of), **em** (in) and **por** (by), the articles (and many other words) contract:

| | |
|---|---|
| **a + as = às** *ash* | to the |
| **de + um = dum** *dooñ* | of a |
| **em + uma = numa** *noo-muh* | to a |
| **por + os = pelos** *pel-oosh* | by the |

## 'This', 'That', 'These', 'Those'

These depend on the gender and number of the noun they represent:

| | | | |
|---|---|---|---|
| **este rapaz** | this boy | **esta rapariga** | this girl |
| **estes rapazes** | these boys | **estas raparigas** | these girls |
| **esse rapaz** | that boy | **essa rapariga** | that girl |
| **esses rapazes** | those boys | **essas raparigas** | those girls |
| **aquele rapaz** | that boy *(over there)* | **aquela rapariga** | that girl *(over there)* |
| **aqueles rapazes** | those boys *(over there)* | **aquelas raparigas** | those girls *(over there)* |

*An **adjective** is a word such as **small**, **pretty** or **practical** that describes a
person or thing, or gives extra information about them.*

Adjectives normally follow the nouns they describe in Portuguese, e.g. **a maçã
verde** the green apple.

Some exceptions which go before the noun are:

> **muito** much, many
> **pouco** little, not much
> **tanto** so much, so many
> **primeiro** first
> **último** last
> **bom** good
> **nenhum** no, not any
> **grande** great, big.

Portuguese adjectives have to reflect the gender of the noun they describe.
To make an adjective feminine, **-o** endings change to **-a**, and **-or** and **-ês** change
to **-ora** and **-esa**. Otherwise they generally have the same form for both
genders. Thus:

| *masculine* | *feminine* |
|---|---|
| **o livro vermelho** | **a saia vermelha** |
| the red book | the red skirt |
| **o homem falador** | **a mulher faladora** |
| the talkative man | the talkative woman |

To make adjectives plural, follow the general rules given for nouns.

### 'My', 'Your', 'His', 'Her'

These words also depend on the gender and number of the following noun
and not on the sex of the 'owner'.

| | *with masc. / with fem.* | *with plural nouns* |
|---|---|---|
| my | **o meu / a minha** | **os meus / as minhas** |
| his/her/its/your | **o seu / a sua** | **os seus / as suas** |
| our | **o nosso / a nossa** | **os nossos / as nossas** |
| their/your | **o seu / a sua** | **os seus / as suas** |

**NOTE:** Since **o seu, a sua**, etc can mean his, her, your, etc, Portuguese will
often replace them with the words for of him, of her, of you, etc ( **dele** , **dela** ,
**de você** , etc) in order to avoid confusion:

| **os livros *dela*** | her books |
|---|---|
| **os livros *de você*** | your books |
| **os livros *deles*** | their books |

## PRONOUNS

## 19

*A **pronoun** is a word that you use to refer to someone or something when you do not need to use a noun, often because the person or thing has been mentioned earlier. Exampales are **it**, **she**, **something** and **him**.*

| SUBJECT | | | OBJECT | | |
|---|---|---|---|---|---|
| I | **eu** | *ay-oo* | me | **me** | *muh* |
| you *(informal)* | **tu** | *too* | you *(informal)* | **te** | *teh* |
| you | **você** | *voh-se* | you | **o/a** | *oo/uh* |
| he | **ele** | *ayl* | him | **o** | *oo* |
| she | **ela** | *eluh* | her | **a** | *uh* |
| it | **ele/ela** | *ayl/eluh* | it | **o/a** | *oo/uh* |
| we | **nós** | *nosh* | us | **nos** | *noosh* |
| you | **vós** | *vosh* | you | **vos** | *voosh* |
| they *(masc.)* | **eles** | *aylush* | them *(masc.)* | **os** | *oosh* |
| they *(fem.)* | **elas** | *elush* | them *(fem.)* | **as** | *ush* |
| you *(informal)* | **vocês** | *voh-sesh* | you *(informal)* | **os/as** | *oosh/ush* |

### NOTES

1. **YOU** The polite form of addressing someone would be with **o Senhor** or **a Senhora** using the **(s)he** form or the verb and the object pronoun **o/a**. The semi-formal **you** is **você** and the informal **you** is **tu** (like French and Spanish).

2. Subject pronouns are normally not used except for emphasis or to avoid confusion:

> ***eu* vou para Lisboa e *ele* vai para Coimbra**
> *I'm going to Lisbon and he's going to Coimbra*

3. Object pronouns are usually placed after the verb and joined with a hyphen:

> **vejo-*o***          I see *him*

However, in sentences beginning with a 'question word' or a 'negative word' the pronoun goes in front of the verb:

> **quando *o* viu?**     when did you see *him*?
> **não *o* vi**          I did not see *him*

Also, in sentences beginning with **that** and **who**, etc, ('subordinate clauses') the pronoun precedes the verb:

> **sei que *o* viu**       I know that you saw *him*
> **o homem que *o* viu**    the man who saw *him*

4. **Me** also = to me and **nos** = to us, but **lhe** = to him/to her/to it/to you *(formal)*, **te** = to you *(informal)* and **lhes** = to them/to you.

5. When two pronouns are used together they are often shortened. The verb will also change spelling if it ends in **-r**, **-s**, **-z** or a nasal sound:

| | | |
|---|---|---|
| **dá-mo** | (= dá + me + o) | he gives me it |
| **dê-lho** | (= dê + lhe + o) | give him it |
| **fá-lo** | (= faz + o) | he does it |
| **dão-nos** | (= dão + os *or* dão + nos) | they give them *or* they give us |

6. The pronoun following a preposition has the same form as the subject pronoun, except for **mim** (me), **si** (you – *formal*), **ti** (you – *informal*).